# the complete *christmas* cookbook

# the complete *christmas* cookbook

INDEX

Published in 1999 by Merehurst Limited
Ferry House, 51-57 Lacy Road, Putney, London SW15 1PR

This edition published 1999 for Index Books Ltd.
Henson Way, Kettering NN16 8PX, United Kingdom

Copyright © Merehurst Limited and Murdoch Books

ISBN 1 85391 851 2

A catalogue record for this book is available from the British Library.

Edited and Designed by Axis Design
Commissioning Editor: Barbara Croxford
Publishing Manager: Fia Fornari
Production Manager: Lucy Byrne
CBO & Publisher: Anne Wilson
Marketing & Sales Director: Kathryn Harvey
International Sales Director: Kevin Lagden

Colour separation by Colourscan
Printed and bound in Spain by Bookprint, S.L., Barcelona

# Contents

# Introduction

*E*ven in this commercial age, Christmas is still a special time of year, when entertaining guests and sharing meals with family and friends play a central role. It is also an immensely busy time of year for the family cook. This comprehensive collection of Christmas recipes will relieve the strain and help you find some time to enjoy the festivities, too. Whether you are planning a buffet for twenty, cooking Christmas lunch for eight, feeding house guests for the entire holiday or preparing a candle-lit dinner for two, you are sure to find exactly the right dishes. Of course, recipes for traditional roasts, Christmas pudding and iced cakes feature, but there are many exciting and innovative ideas for an alternative Christmas, whether vegetarian or simply because you get tired of the sight of turkey — although you will find some clever ways with leftovers.

# Appetisers and Party Food

## Chilli Prawn Skewers

preparation time 25 minutes   total cooking time 10 minutes   makes 30

### INGREDIENTS

30 green king prawns
50 g/2 oz fresh coriander sprigs
2 tablespoons fresh basil leaves
50 g/2 oz butter
1 garlic clove, crushed
2 teaspoons soft brown sugar
2 tablespoons lemon or lime juice
1 tablespoon sweet chilli sauce
pepper to taste

*1* Remove the heads from the prawns. Then peel, leaving the tails intact. Using a sharp knife, slit each prawn down the back and remove the vein.

*2* Finely chop the coriander sprigs and basil leaves.

*3* Heat the butter in a large frying pan or wok. Add the garlic, sugar, juice, coriander, basil and sweet chilli sauce. Mix all together well. Toss the prawns through the mixture, then cook over medium heat for 4–5 minutes, or until the prawns turn a pinkish colour and are cooked through. Sprinkle pepper over the prawn mixture. Thread the prawns onto bamboo skewers or strong cocktail sticks. Serve warm.

## Cook's File

Storage time: Peel and devein the prawns several hours in advance. Cook them just before serving.

Variations: Prawns are also delicious grilled. Thread them onto skewers and grill for 2–3 minutes. Brush the prawns with the butter mixture during cooking. Scallops or oysters can be used instead of prawns, or alternate pieces of fish with prawns on the skewers and add a few bay leaves (bay leaves are for flavouring only; they are too strong to eat). Try substituting herbs such as dill and parsley for the coriander and basil.

# Sweet and Salty Nuts

preparation time 20 minutes

total cooking time 15 minutes

serves 6–8

## INGREDIENTS

250 g/9 oz blanched almonds
250 g/9 oz pecans
50 g/2 oz sugar
1 teaspoon salt
1 teaspoon ground cinnamon
pinch of ground cloves
½ teaspoon curry powder
¼ teaspoon ground cumin
½ teaspoon ground black pepper

1 Preheat the oven to 180°C/350°F/ Gas 4. Place the almonds and pecans on a large baking tray. Bake 5–10 minutes or until golden and crisp. Remove from the oven and allow to cool.

2 Combine the sugar, salt and spices in a small bowl. Mix well.

3 Heat a large frying pan. Add the almonds and pecans. Sprinkle the spice mixture over the nuts. Cook the nuts, stirring constantly, over a medium heat for 5 minutes, or until they turn golden. The sugar will melt and coat the nuts. Shake the frying pan often to ensure even cooking. If the nuts stick together, separate them with a wooden spoon. When the nuts are cooked, remove from the heat. Spread them on a lightly oiled baking tray to cool.

## Cook's File

Storage time: Keep the cooled nuts in tightly sealed jars or containers. They will stay fresh for up to 12 days.

Hint: If using a small frying pan, cook the nuts in batches. Cashews, macadamias or peanuts can be substituted for almonds and pecans.

Step 1

Step 2

Step 3

# Smoked *Salmon* Blini

preparation time 15 minutes

total cooking time 10–15 minutes

makes about 50

## INGREDIENTS

*Blini*
*115 g/4 oz self-raising flour*
*2 eggs, lightly beaten*
*120 ml/4 fl oz milk*
*1 tablespoon soured cream*
*oil or melted butter, for brushing*

*Topping*
*120 ml/4 fl oz soured cream*
*2 tablespoons mayonnaise*
*2 teaspoons lemon juice*
*1 tablespoon finely chopped chives*
*1 tablespoon finely chopped mint*
*130 g/4½ oz sliced smoked salmon*
*strips of lemon peel, to garnish*

*1* Sift the flour into a mixing bowl and make a well in the centre.

*2* Combine the eggs, milk and cream, then add to the well. Gradually incorporate the flour and stir until the batter is smooth and free of lumps. Set aside to stand for 10 minutes.

*3* Heat a large non-stick frying pan and brush lightly with oil or melted butter. Drop teaspoonfuls of the batter into the pan. When bubbles appear on the surface, turn the blini and cook the other side. Remove and set aside. Repeat with the remaining batter.

*4* Combine the soured cream, mayonnaise, lemon juice, chives and mint. Spoon a small amount of the soured cream mixture on top of each blini. Top each with a slice of smoked salmon and garnish with strips of lemon peel. Serve within 1 hour of assembling.

*Step 2*

*Step 3*

*Step 4*

# Sushi Rolls

preparation time 45 minutes

total cooking time 10 minutes

makes about 30

## INGREDIENTS

*200 g/7 oz short-grain white rice*

*250 ml/8 fl oz water*

*2 tablespoons rice vinegar*

*1 tablespoon sugar*

*1 teaspoon salt*

*sheets of nori (see Cook's File)*

*wasabi to taste, optional (see Cook's File)*

*130 g/4½ oz smoked salmon, salmon trout*
*    or fresh sashimi tuna (see Cook's File)*

*1 small cucumber, peeled*

*½ small avocado*

*4 tablespoons chopped stem ginger*

*4 tablespoons soy sauce, to serve*

**1** Rinse the rice in cold water and drain well. Place the rice and water in a medium-size pan. Bring to the boil, reduce the heat and simmer, uncovered, for 4–5 minutes, or until all the water is absorbed. Cover, reduce the heat to very low and cook for a further 4–5 minutes. Remove from the heat and leave to cool.

**2** Combine the rice vinegar, sugar and salt in a small bowl and stir the mixture into the rice. Place 1 sheet of nori on a piece of greaseproof paper on a flat work surface.

**3** Place a quarter of the rice along one end of the nori, leaving a 2 cm/ ¼ inch border around the three sides. Spread a very small amount of wasabi down the centre of the rice.

**4** Slice the fish into very thin strips and cut the cucumber and the avocado flesh into matchsticks. Arrange the fish, cucumber, avocado and chopped ginger over the wasabi.

*Step 1*

*Step 2*

*Step 3*

*Step 4*

*Step 5*

*Step 6*

5 Using the paper as a guide, roll up firmly from the bottom, enclosing the filling in the rice. Press the nori to seal.

6 Using a sharp flat-bladed or an electric carving knife, cut the roll into 2.5 cm/1 inch rounds. Repeat the process with remaining ingredients to make more rolls. Serve the sushi rolls with small shallow bowls of soy sauce, or extra wasabi mixed with soy sauce, for dipping.

## Cook's File

Storage time: Sushi rolls can be made several hours in advance. Store them covered in the refrigerator and slice just before serving.

Notes Nori is an edible seaweed which is sold pressed into dried sheets. It is available from Chinese supermarkets and Asian food stores.

Wasabi is similar to creamed horseradish, but is a pale green colour. As the flavour is much hotter than Western varieties of horseradish, use it very sparingly, adjusting the quantities according to personal taste. Wasabi is available as a paste or in powdered form from most Asian food stores, and many health food shops also stock ingredients for Asian dishes.

Sashimi tuna is available from good fishmongers or fish markets. Make sure that it is extremely fresh. Frozen fish is not suitable for use in this dish.

# Herb Pepper Crisps *with* Blue Cheese Dip

preparation time 20–25 minutes

total cooking time 5 minutes

serves 10–15

## INGREDIENTS

*4 sheets lavash tanoory bread*
*115 g/4 oz butter, melted*
*1 small jar herb pepper seasoning*
*1 tablespoon finely chopped chives*

*Blue Cheese Dip*
*250 g/9 oz blue-veined cheese, chopped*
*50 g/2 oz butter, softened*
*1 tablespoon sweet white wine*
*2 teaspoons chopped mint*
*1 teaspoon chopped rosemary*
*2 teaspoons chopped oregano*
*75 ml/3 fl oz crème fraîche or*
*    soured cream*
*salt and pepper*
*sprig of oregano, to garnish*

*1* Preheat the oven to 180°C/350°F/ Gas 4. Brush each sheet of lavash tanoory bread with melted butter. Sprinkle with herb pepper seasoning and chives.

*2* Cut each sheet into 20 squares, then each piece in half to make triangles. Place on baking trays and bake for 5 minutes, or until crisp. Remove and cool.

*3* Beat together the cheese and butter with an electric mixer until smooth and creamy. Add the wine, mint, rosemary and oregano and mix well. Fold in the crème fraîche or soured cream. Season to taste. Spoon into serving dishes, garnish with oregano and serve with the crisps.

## Cook's File
Storage time: Herb pepper crisps may be stored in an airtight container for up to 2 weeks.

*Step 1*

*Step 2*

*Step 3*

# Prune and Bacon Skewers

preparation time 35 minutes

total cooking time 5 minutes

makes about 60

## INGREDIENTS

20 rashers bacon, rinds removed
115 g/4 oz cream cheese
1 tablespoon mayonnaise
1 tablespoon German or French mustard
1 tablespoon finely chopped chives
750 g/1 lb 10 oz stoned prunes
chives, to garnish

1 Cut the bacon into 5 cm/2 inch lengths. Beat the cream cheese with an electric mixer until soft and creamy. Add the mayonnaise, mustard and chopped chives and beat until all the ingredients are thoroughly combined.

2 Spoon the cream cheese mixture into a piping bag and pipe a little into the centre of each stoned prune.

3 Roll each prune in a strip of bacon and carefully secure the end of the bacon with a small bamboo skewer or cocktail stick. Grill under a moderately hot grill for 3–5 minutes, turning frequently, until the bacon is crisp and browned. Serve either hot or cold, garnished with chives.

## Cook's File

Storage time: Prune and bacon skewers can be assembled up to a day in advance. Store in the refrigerator, covered, until needed. Cook the skewers just before serving, if serving hot. If serving as a cold hors d'oeuvre, cook in advance, cool and then chill in the refrigerator for several hours.

Hint: Soften the cream cheese by bringing it to room temperature. Low-fat cream cheese can be used if preferred.

Step 1

Step 2

Step 3

# *Herbed* Chicken *Drumsticks*

preparation time 15 minutes

total cooking time 45 minutes

makes 12 drumsticks

## INGREDIENTS

12 small chicken drumsticks
115 g/4 oz butter
1 onion, grated
½ teaspoon grated lemon rind
2 tablespoons finely chopped parsley
1 tablespoon finely chopped mint
1 tablespoon finely chopped coriander
½ teaspoon hot pepper sauce
1 tablespoon lemon juice
1 tablespoon clear honey
2 teaspoons soy sauce
sprigs of parsley, to garnish

*1* Preheat the oven to 180°C/350°F/ Gas 4. Wash the drumsticks and pat dry on kitchen paper. Loosen the skin around each drumstick with your finger to form a pocket for the herb mixture.

*2* Beat together the butter, onion and lemon rind with an electric mixer until just combined. Add the herbs and pepper sauce and stir until just combined.

*3* Divide the mixture into 12 portions. Place one portion of herb mixture under the skin of each drumstick. Hold the skin over the filling, and press gently to distribute the herb mixture.

*4* Arrange the drumsticks in a single layer over the base of a shallow ovenproof dish. Combine the lemon juice, honey and soy sauce in a small bowl. Brush the mixture over the drumsticks. Bake for 20 minutes, basting occasionally with the lemon and honey mixture. Turn the drumsticks over, baste again and bake for a further 25 minutes. Serve warm or cold, garnished with parsley.

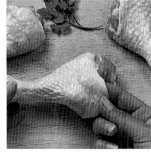

*Step 1*

*Step 3*

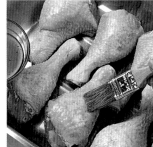

*Step 4*

# Spicy Tortilla Triangles

preparation time 20 minutes

total cooking time 5 minutes

makes 24

## INGREDIENTS

*2 x 23 cm/9 inch flour tortillas*

*4–5 tablespoons vegetable oil*

*1 onion, finely chopped*

*2 garlic cloves, crushed*

*2 small red chillies, finely chopped*

*425 g/15 oz can pinto beans, drained and roughly mashed*

*250 ml/8 fl oz ready-made chunky salsa*

*2 tablespoons chopped coriander*

*75 g/3 oz Cheddar cheese, grated*

*sprigs of coriander, to garnish*

1 Cut the tortillas into quarters. Cut each quarter into 3 triangles. Heat 2 tablespoons of the oil in a frying pan. Add a few triangles and cook for 30 seconds on each side, or until crisp and golden brown. Remove and drain on kitchen paper. Repeat with the remaining triangles, adding extra oil as necessary.

2 Heat 1 tablespoon of the remaining oil in a medium-size pan. Add the onion, garlic and chilli and cook over a medium heat, stirring, for 3 minutes, or until softened. Stir in the beans, salsa and coriander. Remove from the heat and cool.

3 Spread the bean mixture on the triangles and sprinkle with cheese. Cook under a preheated grill for 1 minute or until the cheese has melted. Garnish with coriander and serve immediately.

## Cook's File

Storage time: The tortilla triangles can be made a day ahead; store in an airtight container. The topping can be made a day ahead and stored in the refrigerator.

*Step 1*

*Step 2*

*Step 3*

# Cheese, Basil and Pine Nut Triangles

preparation time 30 minutes

total cooking time 15 minutes

makes 28

## INGREDIENTS

115 g/4 oz feta cheese
115 g/4 oz ricotta cheese
2 tablespoons chopped basil
25 g/1 oz pine nuts, toasted
1 egg, lightly beaten
salt and pepper
14 sheets filo pastry, thawed if frozen
115 g/4 oz butter, melted

*1* Combine the cheeses, basil, pine nuts and egg in a medium-size bowl. Season with salt and pepper to taste. Preheat the oven to 200°C/400°F/ Gas 6.

*2* Place a sheet of filo pastry on a work surface and brush all over with melted butter. Top with another sheet of pastry and brush with butter. Cut the pastry lengthways into four strips.

*3* Place 1 tablespoon of the cheese mixture on the end of each strip. Fold the pastry over and up to enclose the filling and form a triangle. Brush the triangles with butter and place on a baking tray. Repeat with the remaining filo pastry and filling. Bake the triangles for 15 minutes, or until golden brown. Serve hot.

## Cook's File

Storage time: The triangles can be assembled several hours ahead; cook just before serving. Cooked triangles can be frozen in a single layer on a baking tray until firm, then transferred to an airtight container.

Hint: Handle filo pastry quickly and carefully because it becomes brittle when exposed to air. Cover spare sheets with a damp tea towel while assembling the triangles.

Step 1

Step 2

Step 3

# Crab Cakes *with* Avocado Dip

preparation time 30 minutes

total cooking time 4 minutes per batch

makes about 30

## INGREDIENTS

500 g/1¼ lb crab meat
115 g/4 oz fresh breadcrumbs
120 ml/4 fl oz mayonnaise
4 spring onions, chopped
4 tablespoons chopped coriander
2 tablespoons lemon juice
1 teaspoon grated lemon rind
1 teaspoon sambal oelek
2 eggs, lightly beaten
oil, for shallow frying

*Avocado Dip*
1 small ripe avocado
1 garlic clove, crushed
5 tablespoons plain yogurt
4 tablespoons water
strips of red pepper, to garnish

*1* Preheat the oven to 180°C/350°F/ Gas 4. Combine the crab meat, breadcrumbs, mayonnaise, spring onions, coriander, lemon juice, lemon rind, sambal oelek and eggs in a large bowl.

*2* Heat 1 tablespoon of the oil in a frying pan. Drop spoonfuls of the mixture, about 2 cm/¾ inch apart, into the pan. Cook over a medium heat for about 2 minutes, or until undersides are golden. Turn and cook for 2 minutes more. Remove from the pan, drain on kitchen paper and keep warm. Repeat with the remaining mixture, adding more oil.

*3* To make the dip, place the avocado, garlic, yogurt and water in a food processor or blender. Using pulse action, process for 10 seconds, or until smooth and creamy. Garnish with red pepper strips and serve with the crab cakes.

*Step 1*

*Step 2*

*Step 3*

# Sweet *Chilli* *Wings*

preparation time 30 minutes, plus marinating

total cooking time 90–105 minutes

serves 10

## INGREDIENTS

2 kg/4½ lb chicken wings
2 garlic cloves, crushed
¼ teaspoon salt
1 teaspoon black pepper
1 tablespoon oil
4 tablespoons sweet chilli sauce
2 tablespoons clear honey
1 tablespoon white vinegar
4 tablespoons soy sauce
2 teaspoons grated fresh root ginger
1 tablespoon soft brown sugar
fresh red chillies and lemon slices,
    to garnish

*1* Trim the fat and sinew from the chicken and cut each wing into 3 sections, discarding the tips. (Freeze them and use for making stock.)

*2* Combine the remaining ingredients in a large bowl and mix well. Add the chicken and stir until coated. Cover and refrigerate for several hours or overnight.

*3* Preheat the oven to 180°C/350°F/ Gas 4. Drain the chicken and reserve the marinade. Place the chicken on a rack over a roasting tin or in a deep ovenproof dish. Bake, brushing frequently with the reserved marinade, for 1½ hours, or until crisp and cooked through. Serve hot, garnished with chillies and lemon slices.

## Cook's File

Storage time: Cook the chicken up to 2 days in advance. Store, covered with clear film, in the refrigerator. Reheat in a preheated oven at 180°C/350°F/ Gas 4 for 10–15 minutes, or until heated through.

*Step 1*

*Step 2*

*Step 3*

# Parmesan and Pesto Toasts

preparation time 15 minutes, plus freezing

total cooking time 5 minutes

makes about 40

## INGREDIENTS

3 small baguettes or large hot dog rolls

16 large sun-dried tomatoes, cut into
thin strips

150 g/5 oz Parmesan cheese, thinly shaved

Pesto

50 g/2 oz basil leaves

2 tablespoons chopped chives

5 tablespoons pine nuts

2–3 garlic cloves

4 tablespoons extra virgin olive oil

*1* Freeze the baguette or rolls until firm. Cut the frozen bread or rolls into very thin slices using a serrated knife or an electric carving knife. Toast the bread slices under a hot grill until they are golden brown on both sides.

*2* To make pesto, place the basil leaves, chives, pine nuts, garlic and olive oil in a food processor and process for 20–30 seconds, or until smooth and all the ingredients are fully incorporated.

*3* Spread the pesto mixture evenly over the slices of toast. Top with strips of tomato and shavings of Parmesan cheese.

## Cook's File

Storage time: The bread slices can be toasted up to one week in advance. Store in an airtight container. Assemble just before serving.

Hint: Although extra virgin olive oil is expensive, its flavour is superb. It is worth buying for making pesto and salad dressings, but not for cooking.

# Olive and Rosemary Palmiers

preparation time 20 minutes

total cooking time 15 minutes

makes 30

## INGREDIENTS

*melted butter, for brushing*
*50 g/2 oz chopped, stoned black olives*
*25 g/1 oz grated Parmesan cheese*
*1 tablespoon chopped rosemary*
*4 slices salami, chopped*
*2 tablespoons vegetable oil*
*2 teaspoons Dijon mustard*
*2 sheets ready-rolled puff pastry*
*olives and sprigs of rosemary, to garnish*

*1* Preheat the oven to 200°C/400°F/ Gas 6. Brush two baking trays with melted butter. Combine the olives, cheese, rosemary, salami, oil and mustard in a blender or food processor. Process for 30 seconds, or until mixture forms a paste.

*2* Place a sheet of pastry on a work surface and spread evenly with half the olive paste. Fold two opposite sides over to meet, edge to edge, in the centre. Fold once again, then fold in half to give 8 layers of pastry.

*3* Cut into 1 cm/½ inch slices and place, cut side up, on the prepared trays, allowing room for spreading. Open the slices out slightly at the folded end to give a V shape. Repeat with the remaining pastry and olive paste. Bake for 15 minutes or until golden brown. Serve garnished with olives and rosemary sprigs.

## Cook's File

Storage time: Uncooked or cooked palmiers can be prepared in advance, covered and refrigerated. Bake just before serving, or bake in advance and reheat in a preheated oven at 180°C/350°F/Gas 4 for 5 minutes.

# Wontons with Honey Chilli Dip

preparation time 40 minutes

total cooking time 10–15 minutes

makes 48

## INGREDIENTS

250 g/9 oz lean pork

115 g/4 oz raw prawns, peeled

50 g/2 oz canned bamboo shoots, drained
    and rinsed

3 spring onions, chopped

1 cm/½ inch piece fresh root
    ginger, peeled

25 g/1 oz chopped unsalted peanuts

½ teaspoon sugar

1 tablespoon chopped coriander

salt and freshly ground white pepper

48 wonton wrappers

oil, for deep-frying

sprigs of coriander, to garnish


Honey Chilli Dip

4 tablespoons clear honey

4 tablespoons sweet chilli sauce

1 teaspoon chopped fresh root ginger

1 teaspoon rice vinegar

1 Trim any excess fat from the pork and cut the flesh into cubes. Place the pork, prawns, bamboo shoots, spring onions and ginger in a food processor. Process for 20–30 seconds, or until the mixture is smooth.

2 Transfer the mixture to a medium-size bowl. Add the peanuts, sugar and coriander, season to taste with salt and pepper and mix well. Place 1 teaspoon of the mixture in the centre of each wrapper. Brush the edges with a little water. Bring the edges together to form pouches and press gently to seal.

3 Heat the oil in a deep, heavy-based pan to 180°C/350°F, or until a cube of bread browns in 30 seconds. Lower the wontons into the oil and cook in batches over a medium heat for about 1 minute, or until golden, crisp and cooked through. Remove with a slotted spoon and drain thoroughly on kitchen paper.

4 To make the honey chilli dip, combine the honey, sweet chilli sauce, root ginger and rice vinegar in a small bowl and mix well. Garnish the wontons with coriander and serve with the dip.

*Step 2*

# Fruity Meat Balls

preparation time 20 minutes, plus 1 hour chilling

total cooking time 15 minutes

makes about 64

## INGREDIENTS

500 g/1¼ lb minced beef
1 medium onion, grated
4 tablespoons fruit chutney
1 tablespoon Worcestershire sauce
8 tablespoons dried breadcrumbs
1 egg, lightly beaten
½ teaspoon garlic salt
¼ teaspoon pepper
120 ml/4 fl oz vegetable oil
1 tablespoon chopped parsley

Fruity Cream
175 g/6 oz fruit chutney
120 ml/4 fl oz soured cream
1 tablespoon chopped fresh chives

*1* First make the fruity cream. Combine all the ingredients in a small bowl and mix well. Chill in the refrigerator for 1 hour, or until required.

*2* Put the beef, onion, chutney, Worcestershire sauce, breadcrumbs, egg, garlic salt and pepper in a medium-size bowl and mix until thoroughly combined. Taking 2 teaspoons of the mixture at time, form it into balls by rolling between the palms of the hands.

*3* Heat the oil in a medium-size, heavy-based pan. Add the meat balls and cook, in batches, over a medium heat for 5 minutes, or until golden brown and cooked through. Remove from the pan with a slotted spoon and drain on kitchen paper. If serving the meat balls hot, keep warm while you cook the remaining meat balls. Transfer the meat balls to a serving dish, garnish with parsley and serve hot or cold with the fruity cream.

## Cook's File

It can be difficult to divide the mixture evenly to get the right number of uniformly sized meatballs. An easy way is to place the mixture on a clean surface. Use your hands to flatten it to about 2.5 cm/1 inch thick and shape it roughly into a square. With a knife, mark the square into 8 strips crossways and then 8 strips lengthways — this will give you 64 small squares. Then just pick up 1 square at a time and roll the meatball into shape.

# Prawn  Toasts

preparation time 20 minutes

total cooking time 10–15 minutes

makes 48

## INGREDIENTS

350 g/12 oz raw prawns, peeled
and deveined

1 garlic clove

75 g/3 oz canned water chestnuts or
bamboo shoots, drained and rinsed

1 tablespoon chopped coriander

2 cm/¼ inch piece fresh root ginger

2 eggs, separated

¼ teaspoon freshly ground white pepper

¼ teaspoon salt

12 slices white bread

225 g/8 oz sesame seeds

vegetable oil, for deep-frying

strips of spring onion, to garnish

chilli sauce or sweet-and-sour sauce,
to serve

*1* Put the prawns, garlic, water chestnuts or bamboo shoots, coriander, ginger, egg whites, pepper and salt in a food processor. Process for 20–30 seconds, or until the mixture is smooth. Using a 5 cm/2 inch round cutter, cut circles from the bread slices.

*2* Brush the top of each bread circle with lightly beaten egg yolk, then spread each evenly with the prawn mixture. Sprinkle with sesame seeds.

*3* Heat the oil in a deep heavy-based pan until moderately hot. Deep-fry the toasts, in small batches, with the coated side down, for 10–15 seconds, or until golden and crisp and both sides are cooked. Remove from the oil with tongs or a slotted spoon. Drain well on kitchen paper. Serve hot, garnished with strips of spring onions and with chilli sauce or sweet-and-sour sauce.

# Antipasti

Enticing to the eye, emanating a mouthwatering scent and captivating the palate, these seductive appetisers assault the senses, whether eaten on their own or as a tempting introduction to a meal.

## Marinated Roasted Peppers

Grill 1 large red pepper, 1 large yellow pepper, 1 large green pepper and, if available, 1 large purple pepper, until the skin blisters and blackens. Cover the peppers with a tea towel to cool slightly before peeling. Cut the peppers into thick strips and place in a bowl, add 2 crushed garlic cloves, 2 tablespoons of balsamic vinegar, 2 tablespoons of shredded fresh basil and 60 ml/2 fl oz of olive oil. Cover and refrigerate for 3 hours. Return to room temperature before serving. Serve on toasted bruschetta or focaccia. Serves 4–6.

## Sweet and Sour Onions

Carefully peel 3 medium (500 g/1¼ lb) red onions, keeping the ends intact so that the layers stay together. Cut into eighths and place in a non-stick baking dish. Combine 2 tablespoons each of wholegrain mustard, honey, red wine vinegar and oil. Brush this mixture over the onions, cover the dish and bake in a preheated oven at 220°C/425°F/Gas 7 for 20 minutes. Uncover and bake for another 15–20 minutes, or until soft and caramelised. Serves 4–6.

## Char-grilled Spring Onions and Asparagus

Cut 300 g/11 oz of asparagus and 12 spring onions into 13 cm/ 5 inch lengths. Brush the spring onions and asparagus lightly with macadamia nut oil and cook on a preheated char-grill or barbecue for 3 minutes, or until the vegetables are tender. Pour some balsamic vinegar over the top, sprinkle with pepper and then top with shavings of Parmesan cheese. Serves 4–6.

# Golden Deep-fried Goat's Cheese Slices

Cut 225 g/8 oz of goat's cheese into 5 mm/¼ inch thick slices. Dust lightly with seasoned flour. Dip the slices into 2 lightly beaten eggs and gently toss to coat in a mixture of 75g/3 oz of fresh breadcrumbs, 40 g/1½ oz of grated pecorino cheese and 1 teaspoon of sweet paprika. Refrigerate for 1 hour. Deep-fry the crumbed goat's cheese in batches in hot oil for 2 minutes, or until the crust is crisp and golden. Serve with your favourite relish or a sweet dipping sauce. It is best to use the small logs of goat's cheese for this recipe. Serves 4.

# Mushrooms in Lime and Chilli

Brush 250 g/9 oz of button mushrooms with oil; cook under a preheated grill, or on a barbecue grill, until tender. Combine 1 teaspoon chilli flakes, 1 tablespoon shredded lime rind, 1 crushed garlic clove, 1 tablespoon chopped fresh coriander, 1 teaspoon soft brown sugar, 2 tablespoons of lime juice and 60ml/2 fl oz of olive oil in a bowl. Toss the mushrooms in the lime and chilli mixture and refrigerate for 1 hour before serving. Serves 2–4.

*CLOCKWISE, FROM TOP LEFT*
*Golden Deep-fried Goat's Cheese Slices; Marinated Roasted Peppers; Sweet and Sour Onions; Char-grilled Spring Onions and Asparagus; Mushrooms in Lime and Chilli*

# Mushroom *Croûtes*

preparation time 40 minutes

total cooking time 20 minutes

makes 48

## INGREDIENTS

*8 slices white bread*

*75 g/3 oz butter, melted*

*1 tablespoon olive oil*

*1 garlic clove, crushed*

*½ small onion, finely chopped*

*375 g/13 oz small button mushrooms,*
  *thinly sliced*

*salt and pepper*

*1 tablespoon dry sherry*

*2 teaspoons cornflour*

*75 ml/3 fl oz soured cream*

*1 tablespoon finely chopped parsley*

*1 teaspoon finely chopped thyme*

*25 g/1 oz freshly grated Parmesan cheese*

*sprigs of basil, to garnish*

**1** Preheat the oven to 180°C/350°F/
Gas 4. Line a baking tray with foil.
Cut the crusts from the bread. Brush both
sides of the bread with the melted butter.
Cut each slice in half vertically, then cut
each half into three horizontally. Place the
bread croûtes on the prepared baking tray
and bake 5–10 minutes, or until they are
golden and crisp.

**2** Heat the oil in a large frying pan.
Add the garlic and onion and cook,
stirring constantly, over a low heat, until
the onion is soft and translucent. Add the
mushrooms and cook over a medium heat
for 5 minutes, or until tender. Season to
taste with salt and pepper.

**3** Pour in the sherry. Mix the cornflour
and soured cream to a smooth paste,
add to the mushroom mixture and stir
until the mixture boils and thickens.
Remove from the heat and stir in the
parsley and thyme. Set aside to cool.

**4** Spread the mushroom mixture on to
each croûte. Top with the grated
Parmesan cheese. Place on a baking tray
and return the croûtes to the oven. Bake
for 5 minutes, or until the croûtes are
heated through. Transfer to a warm
serving dish, garnish with sprigs of basil
and serve immediately.

## Cook's File

Storage time: Make the bread croûtes up to
4 days in advance and store in an airtight
container. Make the mushroom topping and
assemble just before serving.

Variation: Purée the mushroom mixture, spoon
into small dishes and chill. Serve as a pâté with
the bread croûtes.

Hint: If mushrooms need to be cleaned, simply
wipe with a damp cloth. Washing them dilutes
the flavour as they absorb water easily.

*Step 1*

*Step 2*

*Step 3*

*Step 4*

# Chicken Satay *with* Peanut Sauce

preparation time 40 minutes, plus marinating

total cooking time 10 minutes

makes 30

## INGREDIENTS

750 g/1 lb 10 oz chicken breast fillet
1 tablespoon Thai fish sauce
2 teaspoons ground coriander
2 tablespoons chopped coriander roots
    and stems
1 teaspoon black pepper
2 garlic cloves, crushed
lime wedges and sprigs of coriander,
    to garnish

Peanut Sauce
1 tablespoon peanut oil
1 medium onion, finely chopped
2–3 garlic cloves, crushed
1 teaspoon ground cumin
½ teaspoon ground coriander
½ teaspoon ground turmeric
115 g/4 oz crunchy peanut butter
1 tablespoon sweet chilli sauce
40 g/1½ oz creamed coconut

*1* Cut the chicken into thin diagonal strips and thread on to skewers. Place in one layer in a shallow, non-metallic dish. Combine the fish sauce, coriander, pepper and garlic and spread over the chicken skewers. Cover with clear film and marinate in the refrigerator overnight.

*2* To make the peanut sauce, heat the oil in a pan. Fry the onion over a medium heat for 2 minutes. Add the garlic and spices and cook, stirring, for 1 minute. Stir in the peanut butter, chilli sauce and coconut. Stir over a low heat until hot.

*3* Cook the skewers under a preheated grill for 3–5 minutes, turning once, until cooked through. Garnish with lime wedges and coriander. Serve with the sauce.

## Cook's File

Storage time: The chicken skewers can be prepared a day ahead. Cook just before serving. Make the sauce several hours ahead; reheat gently and add a little water if the sauce seems to be too thick.

Hint: To prevent the bamboo skewers from burning, soak them in cold water for 20 minutes before threading on the chicken.

*Step 1*

# Prawn Cocktail

preparation time 20 minutes

total cooking time Nil

serves 4–6

## INGREDIENTS

24 medium-size cooked prawns
lettuce leaves and buttered brown bread,
  to serve
lemon wedges, to garnish

Cocktail Sauce
250 ml/8 fl oz thick mayonnaise
2 tablespoons tomato sauce
2 tablespoons double cream
dash of Tabasco sauce
1 teaspoon lemon juice
1 teaspoon Worcestershire sauce

1 First, make the sauce. Combine the mayonnaise, tomato sauce, cream, Tabasco sauce, lemon juice and Worcestershire sauce in a large bowl and mix thoroughly. Cover with clear film and chill in the refrigerator until required.

2 Peel and devein the prawns with the tip of a sharp knife, but leave the tails intact on 6–8 prawns and reserve these for the garnish. Remove and discard the tails from the remaining prawns and add them to the cocktail sauce. Mix gently until thoroughly coated.

3 Arrange the lettuce leaves in the base of 4–6 individual serving dishes or bowls. Divide the prawn mixture equally between the dishes. Garnish with the reserved prawns and lemon wedges and serve with buttered brown bread.

## Cook's File

Note: The cocktail sauce may be prepared several hours ahead and stored, covered, in the refrigerator until required. The lettuce may be shredded for easier eating, but small whole leaves look more attractive.

# Butterfly Prawns with Tartare Sauce

preparation time 30 minutes, plus chilling

total cooking time 10 minutes

serves 4–6

## INGREDIENTS

24 raw king prawns, peeled, tails intact
4 eggs
2 tablespoons soy sauce
cornflour, for coating
dry breadcrumbs, for coating
oil, for deep-frying
pak choi and lemon wedges, to garnish

Tartare Sauce
250 ml/8 fl oz mayonnaise
1 tablespoon grated onion
1 tablespoon capers, chopped
1 tablespoon gherkins, finely chopped
1 tablespoon lemon juice
1 tablespoon finely chopped parsley
dash of Tabasco sauce

1 To butterfly the prawns, slit them open down the back, remove the vein with the point of a sharp knife and flatten the bodies gently with the palm of your hand.

2 Beat together the eggs and soy sauce in a small bowl until thoroughly combined. Put the cornflour and dried breadcrumbs into separate shallow bowls. Dip the prawns, one by one, first in cornflour, then in the egg and soy sauce mixture and, finally, in dried breadcrumbs. Spread them out on a plate and chill in the refrigerator to firm up.

3 Heat the oil in a deep pan to 180°C/350°F, or until a cube of bread browns in 30 seconds. Deep-fry the prawns, in batches if necessary, until lightly golden. Drain well on kitchen paper and set aside to cool, but do not chill.

4 To make tartare sauce, combine the mayonnaise, onion, capers, gherkins, lemon juice and parsley in a medium-size bowl and mix thoroughly. Stir in Tabasco sauce to taste, cover with clear film and chill in the refrigerator until required.

5 Arrange the deep-fried butterfly prawns, together with 2–3 leaves of pak choi on 4–6 individual serving plates. Garnish with lemon wedges and serve with the tartare sauce.

# Peppery Pecans and Noodles

preparation time 5 minutes

total cooking time 30 minutes

serves 4

## INGREDIENTS

*115 g/4 oz shelled pecan nuts*
*50 g/2 oz fried egg noodles*
*50 g/2 oz butter*
*2 teaspoons soy sauce*
*½ teaspoon hot pepper sauce*
*¼ teaspoon ground coriander*

*1* Preheat the oven to 160°C/325°F/ Gas 3. Line a 33 x 28 cm/13 x 11 inch baking tray with foil. Combine the pecan nuts and egg noodles in a medium-size mixing bowl. Melt the butter in a small saucepan, pour it over the nuts and noodles and stir well. Spread the mixture over the base of the prepared baking tray and bake, stirring frequently, for about 30 minutes, or until golden.

*2* Combine the soy sauce, hot pepper sauce and coriander in a small bowl. Pour the mixture over the nuts and noodles and mix thoroughly. Spread out on kitchen paper to cool. Store in an airtight container until required.

## Cook's File

Note: This recipe is also suitable for frying. Melt the butter in a large, heavy-based saucepan or a preheated wok. Add the pecan nuts and egg noodles and fry, stirring and tossing briskly, for 5 minutes, until the nuts are golden brown and coated all over with butter. Remove from the heat, add the soy sauce, hot pepper sauce and coriander and mix thoroughly. Spread out on kitchen paper to cool completely before storing.

# Tex Mex Cheese Crisps

preparation time 20 minutes, plus 20 minutes chilling

total cooking time 12 minutes

makes 80

## INGREDIENTS

melted butter, for brushing
225 g/8 oz plain flour
1 teaspoon chilli powder
1 teaspoon garlic salt
½ teaspoon paprika
200 g/7 oz butter, diced
1 egg, lightly beaten
200 g/7 oz Cheddar cheese, grated

*1* Preheat the oven to 220°C/425°F/ Gas 7. Brush two 33 x 28 cm/13 x 11 inch baking trays with melted butter.

*2* Sift the flour, chilli powder, garlic salt and paprika into a food processor and add the butter. Process for 30 seconds, or until the mixture is fine and crumbly.

*3* Add the egg and cheese to the food processor and process for 10 seconds, or until all the ingredients are just combined. Turn the dough on to a lightly floured surface. Knead for 1 minute, or until smooth. Shape the dough into a ball, cover with clear film and chill in the refrigerator for 20 minutes.

*4* Roll out the dough to a thickness of 3 mm/⅛ inch on a lightly floured surface. Cut out shapes using a 6 cm/ 2½ inch star-shaped biscuit cutter. Re-roll the trimmings and cut out more shapes. Place the crisps on the prepared baking trays, allowing room for them to spread.

*5* Bake for 12 minutes, or until crisp. Leave the cheese crisps on the baking trays for 2 minutes, then transfer them to wire racks to cool completely.

# Marinated Baby Mushrooms

preparation time 15 minutes, plus 1 hour marinating

total cooking time Nil

serves 6–8

## INGREDIENTS

*500 g/1¼ lb button mushrooms, halved*
*120 ml/4 fl oz extra virgin olive oil*
*120 ml/4 fl oz white wine vinegar*
*3 garlic cloves, chopped*
*2 tablespoons chopped parsley*
*2 teaspoons chopped fresh chilli*
*1 teaspoon caster sugar*
*salt and pepper*

1 Wipe the mushrooms with a damp cloth and trim the stalks to the level of the caps. Place the mushrooms in a large bowl. Combine the olive oil, vinegar, garlic, parsley, chilli and sugar in a screwtop jar and season to taste with salt and pepper. Shake vigorously until the ingredients are thoroughly combined and the marinade has emulsified.

2 Pour the marinade over the mushrooms and toss thoroughly to combine. Cover with clear film and leave in the refrigerator to marinate for at least 1 hour. Turn the mushrooms occasionally as they marinate to ensure that they are evenly coated.

3 Remove the mushrooms from the refrigerator 30 minutes before serving. Serve at room temperature with other marinated vegetables as an antipasto platter, if desired.

## Cook's File

Note: Mushrooms can be marinated for up to 2 days, depending on the flavour required.

# Chicken Liver *and* Grand Marnier Pâté

preparation time 20 minutes, plus soaking and refrigeration

total cooking time 10 minutes   serves 8

## INGREDIENTS

750 g/1 lb 10 oz chicken livers, trimmed
250 ml/8 fl oz milk
200 g/7 oz butter, softened
65g/2½ oz finely chopped spring onions
1 tablespoon Grand Marnier
1 tablespoon frozen orange juice
concentrate, thawed
salt and pepper
½ orange, very thinly sliced

*Jellied Layer*
1 tablespoon frozen orange juice
concentrate, thawed
1 tablespoon Grand Marnier
300 ml/11 fl oz canned chicken
consommé, undiluted
2½ teaspoons gelatine

1 Place the livers in a large bowl, add the milk and stir to combine. Cover and refrigerate for 1 hour. Drain the milk from the livers. Rinse well in cold water, drain and pat dry with paper towels.

2 Melt a third of the butter in a frying pan, add the spring onions and cook for 2–3 minutes, until tender but not brown. Add the livers and cook, stirring, over a medium heat for 4–5 minutes, until just cooked. Remove from heat and cool a little.

3 Place the contents of the pan in a food processor and process until very smooth. Chop the remaining butter, and add to the food processor with the Grand Marnier and orange concentrate. Process until creamy and season. Place the pâté in a 1.25 litre/2 pint serving dish, cover the surface of the pâté with clear film and refrigerate for 1½ hours, or until firm.

4 To make the jellied layer, whisk together the orange juice concentrate, Grand Marnier and 120 ml/4 fl oz of the consommé, and sprinkle on the gelatine in an even layer. Leave until the gelatine is spongy — do not stir. Heat the remaining consommé, remove from the heat and add the gelatine mixture to the pan. Stir to dissolve the gelatine and leave to cool and thicken to the consistency of uncooked egg white.

5 Press the orange slices lightly into the surface of the pâté and spoon the thickened jelly over the top. Refrigerate until set. Serve at room temperature with toast or crackers.

# Dips and Spreads

## Aubergine Dip

Halve 2 small aubergines lengthways, sprinkle with salt; stand for 15–20 minutes. Rinse and pat dry with kitchen paper. Bake in the oven at 180°C/ 350°F/Gas 4 for 20 minutes or until soft. Peel away the skin and discard. Place the flesh in a food processor with 3–4 crushed garlic cloves, 2 tablespoons lemon juice, 2 tablespoons tahini, 1 tablespoon olive oil and salt and pepper to taste. Process for 20–30 seconds. Sprinkle paprika on top.

## Best-Ever Guacamole

Combine in a medium bowl 1 large ripe mashed avocado, 2 tablespoons sour cream, 1 tablespoon mayonnaise, 4–5 teaspoons lemon juice, 1 small finely chopped red onion, 1 teaspoon each of ground cumin and coriander, 1 clove crushed garlic, 1 finely chopped tomato, 1 tablespoon chopped chives, salt and pepper, and some chilli powder or Tabasco sauce to taste. Mix well to combine and serve with corn chips, crackers or crudités.

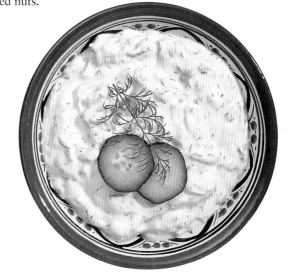

## Cheesy Nut Log

Place in food processor: 130 g/4½ oz chopped Camembert cheese, 25 g/1 oz grated Cheddar cheese, 50 g/2 oz softened cream cheese, 1 tablespoon chopped fresh chives, 3–4 teaspoons white wine or dry sherry, 1 garlic clove, crushed (optional), salt and pepper to taste. Process for 10–20 seconds only. Shape the mixture into a log or a flat round. Roll in finely crushed nuts. Serve with water crackers or savoury wafers.

## Minted Cucumber Dip

Finely grate 1 cucumber; squeeze out any excess moisture. Combine in a bowl with 2 crushed garlic cloves, 250 ml/8 fl oz plain yogurt, 1 teaspoon each fresh chopped dill and mint, and salt and pepper. Mix well and serve.

# Creamy Herb Dip

Beat 150 g/5 oz cream cheese until light and creamy. Add 2 tablespoons each of soured cream and whole egg mayonnaise, 2 tablespoons chopped chives, 1 tablespoon each chopped parsley, lemon thyme and basil, and salt and pepper to taste. Beat until smooth and serve.

# Smoked Trout Pâté

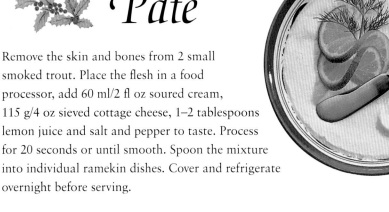

Remove the skin and bones from 2 small smoked trout. Place the flesh in a food processor, add 60 ml/2 fl oz soured cream, 115 g/4 oz sieved cottage cheese, 1–2 tablespoons lemon juice and salt and pepper to taste. Process for 20 seconds or until smooth. Spoon the mixture into individual ramekin dishes. Cover and refrigerate overnight before serving.

# Tomato and Olive Dip

Heat 1 tablespoon olive oil and 20 g/¾ oz butter in a medium pan. Add 1 small finely chopped onion, 1 crushed garlic clove, 2 teaspoons Italian dried mixed herbs, 1 teaspoon cracked pepper and 1 teaspoon ground cumin. Cook over a medium heat for 2 minutes. Stir in one 425 g/15 oz can of chopped tomatoes, 2 tablespoons tomato paste, 60 ml/2 fl oz red wine and 115 g/4 oz tomato purée. Bring to the boil, reduce heat; simmer for 5–10 minutes or until sauce has thickened and reduced by half. Stir in 50 g/2 oz chopped black or green olives. Serve warm.

# Hummus

Place in food processor: one 425 g/15 oz can drained chickpeas, 2–3 tablespoons each lemon juice and olive oil, 2 crushed garlic cloves, and salt and pepper to taste. Process for 20–30 seconds or until smooth. Add 25g/1 oz tahini paste to the mixture, if desired. Serve.

# Cheese Crab Puffs

preparation time 12 minutes

total cooking time 15 minutes

makes 60

## INGREDIENTS

*50 g/2 oz butter, diced*
*120 ml/4 fl oz water*
*115 g/4 oz plain flour, sifted*
*3 eggs, lightly beaten*
*165 g/5½ oz can crab meat, well drained*
*50 g/2 oz Cheddar cheese, grated*
*2 tablespoons snipped chives*
*½ teaspoon sweet paprika*
*oil, for deep-frying*
*chilli sprigs, to garnish (optional)*
*plum sauce, to serve*

*1* Put the butter and water in a medium-size pan. Stir over a low heat for 3 minutes, or until the butter has melted. Bring to the boil. Remove the pan from the heat and add the flour all at once. Using a wooden spoon, beat the mixture until it is smooth. Return the pan to the heat and cook, stirring constantly, for 5 minutes, or until the mixture thickens and comes away from the side and base of the pan. Remove from the heat and set aside to cool slightly.

*2* Transfer the mixture to a small mixing bowl. Gradually add the eggs, beating constantly with an electric mixer until the mixture is glossy. Add the crab meat, grated cheese, chives and paprika and mix well.

*3* Heat the oil in a medium pan. Lower a heaped teaspoon of the mixture at a time into the hot oil. Cook the puffs in batches, turning constantly, until they are well puffed up and golden brown. Remove the puffs with a slotted spoon and drain on kitchen paper. Garnish the crab puffs with fresh chilli sprigs, if desired, and serve with plum sauce.

*Step 1*

*Step 2*

*Step 3*

# Dill Blini with Creamy Egg Topping

preparation time 12 minutes

total cooking time 8 minutes

makes 30

## INGREDIENTS

50 g/2 oz self-raising flour
1 tablespoon finely chopped
   blanched almonds
5 teaspoons finely chopped dill
1 egg, lightly beaten
75 ml/3 fl oz milk
20 g/¼ oz butter, melted

Creamy Egg Topping
2 hard-boiled eggs, finely chopped
2 tablespoons soured cream
1 tablespoon tomato purée
1 tablespoon finely chopped red pepper
1 teaspoon red wine vinegar
salt and pepper

*1* Sift the flour into a bowl. Stir in the almonds and 1 teaspoon of the dill and make a well in the centre. Mix the egg and milk together and pour into the well. Beat with a wooden spoon until the liquid is incorporated and a smooth batter forms.

*2* Brush the base of a 23 cm/9 inch frying pan with melted butter. Drop teaspoons of the mixture, a few at a time, on to the base of the pan, spaced apart.

*3* Cook over a medium heat for about 1 minute, or until the undersides are golden and crisp. Turn the blini over and cook the other side. Remove from the pan and repeat with the remaining mixture.

*4* To make the topping, mix together the eggs, cream, tomato purée, red pepper and vinegar in a small bowl and season to taste. Arrange the blini on a serving platter and top each with the egg mixture. Sprinkle with the remaining dill.

# Traditional Roasts

## Beef with Blue Cheese in Pastry

preparation time 45 minutes    total cooking time 40 minutes    serves 8

### INGREDIENTS

*1 bunch spinach or 500 g/1¼lb*
*frozen spinach, thawed*
*50 g/2 oz butter or margarine*
*1.5 kg/3 lb 5oz piece topside, trimmed*
*2 sheets frozen puff pastry, thawed*
*200 g/7 oz blue vein cheese, softened*
*extra puff pastry to decorate (optional)*
*1 egg, lightly beaten*

*1* Preheat the oven to 200°C/400°F/ Gas 6. To prepare fresh spinach: remove the stalks by cutting along both sides of each stalk through the centre of the leaf. Wash the leaves well. If using frozen spinach, squeeze out excess water.

*2* Drop fresh spinach into boiling water. Cook for 30 seconds or until the leaves are just softened. Drain. Refresh in cold water. Pat dry with kitchen paper. Set aside.

*3* Heat the butter in a large pan. Add the meat. Brown on all sides to seal in juices. Cool. Retain the pan juices.

*4* Place the pastry on a flat surface. Overlap edges by 1 cm/½ inch. Press together well. Arrange the spinach over the pastry leaving a 5 cm/2 inch border.

*5* Spread or crumble the cheese over the spinach. Place the beef in the centre of the pastry. Fold in the narrow ends. Fold the remaining pastry over to enclose the beef. Turn the seam to the underside. Decorate with extra pastry if desired. Brush with egg.

*6* Place the beef on a lightly greased baking tray. Bake in the oven for 25–30 minutes, or until the pastry is golden. Let stand, covered with foil, for 10 minutes before slicing.

## Cook's File

Pieces of meat are often 'seared' before roasting by browning quickly in hot butter or oil to seal in juices and to give a tender result.

# Stuffed Turkey *with* Sour Cherry Sauce

preparation time 20 minutes

total cooking time 2 hours 55 minutes

serves 8–10

## INGREDIENTS

4 kg/8¼ lb self-basting oven-ready turkey

50 g/2 oz butter

1 large onion, finely chopped

225 g/8 oz can water chestnuts, drained,
    rinsed and chopped

2 tablespoons chopped blanched almonds

1 medium apple, peeled and chopped

2 spring onions, chopped

salt and pepper

2 tablespoons chopped flat leaf parsley

1 egg

225 g/8 oz cooked long-grain rice

475 ml/16 fl oz water

Sour Cherry Sauce

675 g/1½ lb jar stoned morello cherries

4 tablespoons redcurrant jelly

2 teaspoons balsamic vinegar

salt and pepper

50 g/2 oz cornflour

5 tablespoons water

*1* Preheat the oven to 180°C/350°F/ Gas 4. Rinse the turkey and pat dry. Tuck the wing tips to the underside and place the turkey, breast side up, on a rack in a deep roasting tin.

*2* Melt the butter in a medium-size saucepan. Add the onion and stir over a low heat for 5 minutes. Add the chestnuts and almonds and cook, stirring occasionally, for 5 minutes. Add the apple and spring onions and stir until heated through. Remove from the heat, season to taste and stir in the parsley, egg and rice. Spoon the mixture into the turkey cavity and secure with string or a skewer. Pack the remaining mixture in the neck cavity and secure. Add the water to the tin.

*3* Roast the turkey for 2 hours, basting occasionally with the juices in the tin. Prick the turkey all over with a fork and roast for a further 30 minutes. Remove from the oven and let stand for 15 minutes. Strain and reserve the cooking juices.

*4* Meanwhile, make the sauce: drain the cherry juice into a medium-size heavy-based pan and reserve the cherries.

Add the jelly, vinegar and 475 ml/16 fl oz of the reserved cooking juices. Cook over a medium heat, stirring, for 10 minutes, or until slightly reduced. Add the cherries and boil for 2 minutes. Season. Blend the cornflour with the water to a smooth paste and add to the pan. Stir over a medium heat until the sauce boils and thickens. Remove the trussing and carve the turkey. Serve with the stuffing and sauce.

# Roast Chicken *with* Breadcrumb Stuffing

preparation time 25 minutes

total cooking time 1½ hours

serves 6

## INGREDIENTS

3 rashers bacon, finely chopped

6 slices wholemeal bread, crusts removed

3 spring onions, chopped

2 tablespoons chopped pecan nuts

2 teaspoons currants

4 tablespoons finely chopped parsley

1 egg, lightly beaten

4 tablespoons milk

salt and pepper

1.4 kg/3 lb oven-ready chicken

40 g/1½ oz butter, melted

1 tablespoon vegetable oil

1 tablespoon soy sauce

350 ml/12 fl oz water

1 garlic clove, crushed

1 tablespoon plain flour

1 Preheat the oven to 200°C/400°F/ Gas 6. Dry-fry the bacon in a small pan over a high heat for 5 minutes, or until crisp. Cut the bread into 1 cm/½ inch cubes and place in a large mixing bowl. Add the bacon, spring onions, nuts, currants and parsley. Mix together the egg and milk, add to the bowl, season and mix well.

2 Wipe the chicken and pat dry with kitchen paper. Spoon the stuffing into the cavity and close the cavity with a skewer. Tie the wings and drumsticks securely in place with string. Rub the chicken all over with salt and pepper.

3 Place the trussed chicken on a roasting rack in a deep roasting tin. Mix together the butter, oil and soy sauce and brush this mixture over the chicken. Pour any remaining butter mixture and half the water into the roasting tin and add the garlic.

4 Roast the chicken, basting occasionally with the cooking juices, for 1¼ hours, or until browned and the juices run clear when the thigh is pierced with a skewer or a sharp knife. Transfer the chicken to a serving dish, cover loosely with foil and let stand in a warm place for 5 minutes before carving.

5 Meanwhile, make the gravy. Set the roasting tin on a low heat. Stir in the flour to a smooth paste and simmer for 5 minutes, or until the mixture browns. Add the remaining water and stir until the mixture thickens. (Add extra water if necessary.) Season to taste, strain into a jug and serve with the chicken and stuffing.

# Roast Turkey *with* Cashew Nut Stuffing

preparation time 50 minutes

total cooking time 2–2½ hours

serves 6–8

## INGREDIENTS

*3 kg/6 lb 10 oz oven-ready turkey*
*50 g/2 oz butter*
*1 large onion, chopped*
*900 g/2 lb cooked brown rice*
*450 g/1 lb chopped dried apricots*
*115 g/4 oz unsalted cashew nuts*
*8 tablespoons finely chopped parsley*
*5 tablespoons finely chopped mint*
*2 tablespoons lemon juice*
*120 ml/4 fl oz chicken stock*
*2 tablespoons vegetable oil*

*Wine Gravy*
*25 g/1 oz plain flour*
*350 ml/12 fl oz chicken stock*
*120 ml/4 fl oz white wine*

*1* Preheat the oven to 180°C/350°F/ Gas 4. Wash the turkey well, pat dry with kitchen paper and set aside.

*2* Melt the butter in a large pan. Add the onion and cook, stirring, until golden. Remove from the heat and stir in the rice, apricots, cashew nuts, parsley, mint and lemon juice.

*3* Spoon the stuffing loosely into the cavity of the turkey and secure with a skewer. Tuck the wings under the turkey and tie the legs together. Place the turkey on a rack in a roasting tin. Roast for 2– 2½ hours, basting frequently with a mixture of the chicken stock and oil. Cover the breast and legs with foil after 1 hour so that the skin does not darken too much. Remove from the oven and allow to stand for 20 minutes before carving. Keep warm.

*4* Meanwhile, make the wine gravy. Drain off all but 2 tablespoons of the cooking juices from the roasting tin. Place the tin over a low heat. Stir in the flour, scraping the base of the tin to incorporate all the sediment. Cook, stirring constantly, over a medium heat until well browned, taking care not to burn. Mix together the stock and wine and gradually stir into the flour mixture. Heat, stirring constantly, until gravy boils and thickens. Pour into a jug and serve with the turkey and stuffing.

# Roast Chicken *with* Tarragon and Bacon

preparation time 30 minutes

total cooking time 1½ hours

serves 4

## INGREDIENTS

1.5 kg/3 lb 5 oz oven-ready chicken

2 large sprigs of fresh tarragon or
   rosemary, plus extra to garnish

15g/½ oz butter, melted

3 rashers bacon, rind removed

1 tablespoon vegetable oil

120 ml/4 fl oz chicken stock

2 teaspoons chopped tarragon

salt and pepper

*1* Preheat the oven to 180°C/350°F/ Gas 4. Rinse the chicken well and pat thoroughly dry with kitchen paper. Place the sprigs of tarragon or rosemary in the cavity of the prepared chicken. Pour the melted butter into the cavity.

*2* Cut the bacon rashers in half lengthways and arrange the strips criss-cross over the chicken breast. Secure the bacon in several places with small skewers or cocktail sticks.

*3* Place the chicken, breast side up, on a rack in a roasting tin and brush all over with the oil. Roast, basting frequently with the chicken stock, for about 1½ hours. Cover the chicken with foil if necessary to prevent the bacon from over-browning. Remove the chicken from the oven and allow to stand for 15 minutes before carving. Keep warm.

*4* Meanwhile, reheat the cooking juices over a medium heat and stir in the chopped tarragon. Season with salt and pepper to taste. Place the chicken on a carving dish or serving platter, garnish with tarragon sprigs and serve with the tarragon gravy.

# Roast Quails *with* Bacon and Rosemary

preparation time 40 minutes   total cooking time 25 minutes   serves 4

## INGREDIENTS

*8 quails*
*1 medium onion, chopped*
*3 rashers bacon, chopped*
*1 tablespoon rosemary leaves*
*25 g/1 oz butter, melted*
*120 ml/4 fl oz ruby port*
*4 tablespoons water*
*120 ml/4 fl oz single cream*
*1 teaspoon cornflour*

*1* Preheat the oven to 180°C/350°F/ Gas 4. Thoroughly rinse and dry the quails. Tie the legs and wings of each bird close to its body with string.

*2* Spread the chopped onion, bacon and rosemary over the base of a roasting tin and place the quails on top. Brush each quail with melted butter. Mix together the port and water in a measuring jug and pour 120 ml/4 fl oz of the mixture over the quails.

*3* Roast for about 25 minutes, until cooked through. Remove the quails from the oven and allow to stand for 10 minutes before serving. Keep warm.

*4* Carefully strain any juices from the roasting tin into a small pan, add the remaining port and water mixture and bring to the boil. Reduce the heat. Stir the cream and cornflour to a smooth paste, then gradually stir the mixture into the pan. Cook, stirring, until slightly thickened. Serve the quails with sauce.

## Cook's File

Hint: When eating quail it is quite correct to use your fingers after eating the flesh from the breast with a knife and fork. Provide guests with finger bowls filled with warm water. Add lemon slices or fragrant flowerheads for a special touch.

Hint: Trussing keeps the bird in compact shape, ensures even browning and cooking and makes handling the bird easier.

# Roast Duck *with* Mandarin Sauce

preparation time 30 minutes

total cooking time 1 hour 50 minutes

serves 8

## INGREDIENTS

*3 x 1.6 kg/3½ lb oven-ready ducks*
*50 g/2 oz butter, melted*

*Stuffing*
*75g/3 oz butter*
*12 spring onions, chopped*
*3 garlic cloves, crushed*
*1 tablespoon grated fresh root ginger*
*4 tablespoons chopped coriander*
*450 g/1 lb fresh white breadcrumbs*
*2 eggs, lightly beaten*

*Mandarin Sauce*
*300 g/11 oz can mandarin segments*
*2 tablespoons cornflour*
*1 litre/1¼ pints chicken stock*
*120 ml/4 fl oz orange juice*
*2 tablespoons lemon juice*
*1 tablespoon clear honey*
*1 tablespoon soy sauce*
*2 teaspoons grated fresh root ginger*
*1 tablespoon sugar*

**1** Preheat the oven to 180°C/350°F/ Gas 4. Rinse the ducks and pat dry with kitchen paper.

**2** To make the stuffing, melt the butter in a medium pan. Add the spring onions, garlic and ginger and stir-fry for 3 minutes, until soft. Stir in the coriander, breadcrumbs and eggs. Remove the pan from the heat. Spoon the stuffing into the ducks, dividing it equally between them.

**3** Tie the wings and drumsticks securely in place. Place the ducks on a roasting rack over a shallow roasting tin and brush with the butter. Roast, basting occasionally with the juices, for 1 hour.

**4** Meanwhile, make the mandarin sauce Put the mandarin segments and their juice into a blender or food processor and process until smooth. Put the cornflour in small pan, add a little stock and stir until smooth. Add the remaining stock, orange and lemon juice, honey, soy sauce, ginger, sugar and mandarin purée. Stir over a medium heat until boiling and thickened.

**5** Remove the ducks from the oven and drain the roasting tin. Put the ducks in the tin and pour over the mandarin

sauce. Roast for a further 40 minutes. Insert a skewer into the thigh and, if the juices runs clear, the duck is ready. Strain the sauce and serve with the ducks.

## Cook's File

To prepare ducks for cooking, remove the fat sac at the base of the tail, rinse in cold water and dry with kitchen paper. Prick the duck all over with a fine metal skewer. For roasting, skewer the neck skin to the back, tie the legs to the tail and turn the wing tips underneath.

# Duck with Orange Sauce

preparation time 40 minutes

total cooking time 1 hour

serves 4

## INGREDIENTS

*1.2 kg/2 lb 10 oz duckling*
*strips of orange rind and bay leaves,*
*    to garnish*

*Stuffing*
*450 g/1 lb cooked rice*
*50 g/2 oz pine nuts*
*65 g/2½ oz sultanas*
*4 shallots, chopped*
*juice and rind of 1 orange*
*1 garlic clove, crushed*
*pepper*

*Sauce*
*2 tablespoons plain flour*
*250 ml/8 fl oz white wine*
*120 ml/4 fl oz orange juice*
*pepper*
*2 oranges, segmented*

*1* Preheat the oven to 180°C/350°F/ Gas 4. Remove all loose fat from the duckling. Wash and dry thoroughly with kitchen paper. Set aside.

*2* To prepare the stuffing, mix together the rice, pine nuts, sultanas, shallots, orange juice and rind and garlic until thoroughly combined. Season to taste with pepper. Press the stuffing into the cavity of the prepared duckling. Secure the edges of the cavity with a skewer.

*3* Place the duckling on a rack in a roasting tin. Roast for about 1 hour, then remove from the tin and keep warm.

*4* To prepare the sauce, drain off all but 2 tablespoons of the cooking juices from the tin. Set over a low heat and stir in the flour. Cook 1 minute. Remove from the heat and stir in the wine and orange juice.

*5* Return the roasting tin to the heat. Cook, stirring constantly, until the sauce boils and thickens. Simmer for 3 minutes. Season to taste with pepper and gently stir in the orange segments.

*6* Garnish the duckling with orange rind and bay leaves and serve with the orange sauce.

## Cook's File

Hint: If desired, rub a little salt into the skin of the duck for added crispness.

## How to Carve a Duck

Follow these simple step-by-step instructions to cut and serve roast duck with skill and ease. You will need sharp poultry shears or kitchen scissors.

*1* Rest the bird for about 15 minutes after roasting. Starting at the tail opening, cut with poultry shears through the breast and up to the neck.

*2* Turn the bird over and cut with the shears along one side of the backbone and then separate the bird into halves.

*3* Follow the natural line between the breast and thigh and cut crossways into quarters. (Use this method to carve small game birds also.)

*Step 1*                    *Step 2*                    *Step 3*

# Roast

*Goose*

preparation time 40 minutes

total cooking time 2¾ hours

serves 6

## INGREDIENTS

*3 kg/6 lb 10 oz oven-ready goose*
*25 g/1 oz butter*
*1 onion, finely chopped*
*2 apples, peeled, cored and chopped*
*350 g/12 oz chopped, stoned prunes*
*75 g/3 oz small cubes of bread*
*2 teaspoons grated lemon rind*
*25 g/1 oz parsley, chopped*
*2 tablespoons plain flour*
*2 tablespoons brandy*
*350 ml/12 fl oz chicken stock*

*To Garnish*
*sprigs of watercress*
*orange slices*
*orange rind*

*1* Preheat the oven to 200°C/400°F/ Gas 6. Remove all loose fat from the goose. Using a fine skewer, prick the skin across the breast. Set aside.

*2* Melt the butter in a pan. Fry the onion, stirring, until golden. Stir in the apples, prunes, bread, lemon rind and parsley. Spoon the stuffing loosely into the cavity of the goose, then secure with a skewer. Tie the legs together.

*3* Sprinkle half the flour over the goose. Place it on a rack in a roasting tin and roast for 15 minutes. Discard the fat from the tin. Prick the skin and cover with foil. Reduce the oven temperature to 180°C/350°F/Gas 4 and roast for a further 2 hours, basting occasionally. Discard the fat from the tin frequently. Remove the foil and roast a further 15 minutes, or until the goose is golden. Remove from the oven and let stand for 15 minutes before carving.

*4* Drain all but 2 teaspoons of fat from the roasting tin and set it over a low heat. Add the remaining flour and stir well to incorporate all the sediment. Cook, stirring constantly, over a medium heat until well browned, taking care not to burn. Gradually stir in the brandy and stock. Heat, stirring constantly, until the gravy is boiling and thickened. Serve the goose, garnished with watercress sprigs, orange slices and orange rind and hand the gravy separately.

## Cook's File

Note: Geese usually weigh 3–5 kg/ 6 lb 10 oz–11 lb, making goose a meal for at least six people; one serving is approximately 500 g/1¼ lb. Choose a young bird in the mid-weight range and, if possible, a hen.

Hint: Scattering flour over the top of the bird will coat the skin in dark, crusty speckles. Alternatively, increase the heat of the oven for a few minutes, then splash the bird with a few drops of cold water to leave the skin crisp.

# Roast Beef with Yorkshire Pudding

preparation time 15 minutes

total cooking time 1½–2 hours

serves 6

## INGREDIENTS

2 kg/4½ lb piece of sirloin on the bone
½ teaspoon dry mustard
½ teaspoon pepper
salt
50 g/2 oz dripping or 50 ml/2 fl oz
    vegetable oil

Yorkshire Puddings
115 g/4 oz plain flour
pinch of salt
1 egg, lightly beaten
4 tablespoons water
120 ml/4 fl oz milk
25 g/1 oz dripping or butter, melted

*1* Preheat the oven to 180°C/350°F/ Gas 4. Trim the meat and score the fat. Mix together the mustard, pepper and salt to taste and rub all over the meat. Heat the dripping or oil in a frying pan. Add the meat, fat side down, and seal quickly. Brown on all sides.

*2* Place the meat on a rack in a roasting tin, fat side up. Roast the beef according to taste, following the times indicated below. Allow the meat to stand for 15 minutes before carving.

*3* Preheat oven to 220°C/425°F/Gas 7. To make Yorkshire puddings, sift the flour and salt into a bowl. Mix together the egg and water, add to the bowl and mix to a paste. Heat the milk and add to the mixture, beating until smooth. Set aside. Add dripping or butter to each cup of a 12-cup Yorkshire pudding tin. Heat in the oven for 5 minutes. Remove from the oven and spoon the batter into the cups. Bake for 10–15 minutes, or until puffed.

## Cook's File

Use the following times as a guide to roasting beef, according to how rare or well done you like it. Times given are per 500 g/1¼ lb of beef.

Rare: 20–25 minutes (60°C/140°F internal temperature on a meat thermometer)

Medium: 25–30 minutes (70°C/160°F internal temperature)

Well done: 30–35 minutes (75°C/170°F internal temperature)

If using a meat thermometer, insert it in the thickest part of the meat away from fat or bone.

# Preparing the Roast

 ## Beef

A piece of meat, such as a whole fillet of beef, needs almost no preparation. Remove any outside fat or sinew. Brush the meat with a little oil and season with salt and pepper to taste. Tie the meat, at regular intervals, securely with string, so that it retains its shape as it cooks. Do not be afraid to undercook beef slightly, as it will cook a little longer as it stands. After removing it from the oven, cover the meat with foil to keep warm and allow it to stand for 10 minutes or so. (This will settle the juices into the meat, so very little of them will be lost when the meat is sliced.) When ready to serve, remove the string and slice the meat with a sharp carving knife.

Beef is not regarded as traditional at Christmas, although spiced beef used to be a regular Christmas dish in many English farmhouses. However, with the addition of a béarnaise sauce, some roasted root vegetables and a choice of steamed green vegetables, beef makes a very elegant Christmas meal, especially if there are only a small number of guests.

*Tie the meat securely with trussing or kitchen string at regular intervals.*

 ## Turkey

Traditionally, turkey always has at least one stuffing. On page 66 of this book are a number of different styles of stuffing for the body cavity and neck-end stuffing. Neck-end stuffing, while obviously a little extra effort, is a delicious touch that adds to the enjoyment of what can often be a somewhat dry and uninteresting meat.

To stuff the neck of a turkey, turn the bird breast side down and push the stuffing into the neck cavity. Turn the bird over, loosen the skin around the neck and squeeze the stuffing under the skin, pressing gently to distribute the mixture evenly. Fold the neck flap under the body and secure with a skewer or stitch together with trussing thread.

To stuff the body cavity, remove the neck and any giblets. (Reserve these for stock, if you like.) Trim any fat or overhanging skin flaps. Rinse the cavity under cold water and pat dry with kitchen paper. Spoon the stuffing into the cavity but do not fill it to capacity. The stuffing will expand during cooking and may ooze out if there is too much. (A slice of bread can be placed over the stuffing to act as a plug.) Tie the turkey legs together securely with string and tuck the wings under the body to help retain the shape during cooking.

Christmas turkey is traditionally served hot with cranberry sauce, gravy and roast potatoes. However, it can also be served at room temperature with cranberry sauce and various salads. Turkey does not taste so good when it has been refrigerated — it becomes dry and can be rather tasteless.

*Turn turkey breast side down and push stuffing into the neck cavity.*

*Tying up the drumsticks will help the bird to retain its shape.*

# Carving Turkey

To settle the juices and moisten the flesh, always allow a roast turkey to stand for 10–15 minutes before carving. (Cover with foil to retain the heat, if desired.) Make sure that the carving knife and fork are very sharp. Make clean, single cuts wherever possible. Use the carving fork to steady the bird on the carving tray or board. Cut into the turkey where the ball joint of the drumstick meets the body and loosen the meat.

Tilt the bird to see the angle of separation between the breast and the thigh. Starting at the top, cut down through the skin and meat to the hip joint. Continue cutting through the hip socket until the thigh and leg section can be loosened and completely removed from the body. Place that section on the carving board. Cut the meat around the top of the wing until the wing can also be separated from the body.

On the carving board, separate the thigh from the leg (drumstick) by cutting through the joint. Cut the meat from the thigh into long, thin slices. Serve the legs whole or sliced, according to size and preference. Carve the breast, starting at the top of the breast where the bone is and carving at an angle into even slices.

Repeat for the other side of the bird. The wishbone can be removed by snipping the sinews on either side. Serve a piece of leg with a piece of breast and a portion of the stuffing. If turkey has a neck-end stuffing, slice it with the breast meat.

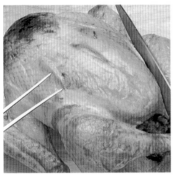
*Steadying the bird with a fork, cut into ball joint of leg.*

*Remove thigh and drumstick. Loosen the meat around wing.*

*Cut through the joint to separate the thigh and drumstick.*

*Carve the breast at a slight angle for thin, even slices.*

# Carving Ham

Many people are daunted by the prospect of carving ham on the bone. Use a clean tea towel or napkin to grasp the bone firmly while you carve. Use a ham knife — a long, round-tipped, thin bladed knife — or the sharpest knife in the kitchen. Sharpen with a steel beforehand. Hold the leg firmly and slice down into the meat about 10 cm/4 inches from the knuckle. Make another cut at an angle to the first and remove a wedge of ham. Cut several thin slices right down to the bone. To release the slices, run the knife along the bone.

*Starting from the knuckle end, slice down firmly into the meat.*

*Remove the first wedge of ham by making another cut at an angle.*

*Run the knife along the bone to detach the slices of ham.*

# Beef Fillet *with* Peppercorn Sauce

preparation time 12 minutes

total cooking time 30 minutes

serves 6–8

## INGREDIENTS

1.5 kg/3 lb 5 oz piece whole beef fillet
2 tablespoons olive oil
1 teaspoon dry mustard
½ teaspoon sugar
250 ml/8 fl oz chicken stock

Peppercorn Sauce
120 ml/4 fl oz double cream
5 tablespoons dry white wine
2 tablespoons bottled green peppercorns,
  rinsed and drained well

*1* Preheat the oven to 240°C/475°F/ Gas 9. Trim the meat and tie securely with string at regular intervals to retain its shape. Combine 1 tablespoon of the oil with the mustard and sugar in a small bowl. Rub the beef all over with this mixture.

*2* Heat the remaining oil in a roasting tin over a high heat. Add the beef and brown all over for about 5 minutes. Remove from the heat, add half the stock to the tin and transfer to the oven.

*3* Roast the beef for 20 minutes, basting occasionally with the cooking juices. Remove the tin from the oven and transfer the beef to a carving dish. Reserve the cooking juices. Cover the beef with foil and let stand in a warm place 10 minutes. Remove the string before slicing.

*4* To make the sauce, put 475 ml/ 16 fl oz of the reserved juices in a small pan, add the remaining stock and bring to the boil. Add the cream, wine and peppercorns. Boil uncovered over a high heat 3 minutes, stirring constantly, until slightly thickened. Serve with the beef.

*Step 1*

*Step 2*

*Step 3*

*Step 4*

# Standing Rib Roast *with* Pâté

preparation time 30 minutes

total cooking time 1¾ hours

serves 8

## INGREDIENTS

*1 rasher rindless bacon, chopped*
*1 small onion, finely chopped*
*115 g/4 oz mushrooms, finely chopped*
*115 g/4 oz ready-made peppercorn pâté*
*30 g/1¼ oz dry breadcrumbs*
*2 tablespoons chopped parsley*
*¼ teaspoon dried mixed herbs*
*1 egg, lightly beaten*
*pepper*
*3 kg/6 lb 10 oz standing rib of beef (see Cook's File)*
*gravy and vegetables, to serve*

**1** Preheat the oven to 220°C/425°F/ Gas 7. Place the bacon in a dry frying pan. Heat gently until it is just beginning to soften. Add the onion and mushrooms and cook, stirring constantly, for about 3 minutes until the onion is soft and translucent. Transfer to a bowl. Mix in the pâté, breadcrumbs, parsley, mixed herbs and egg and season to taste with pepper.

**2** Cut a slit in the meat between the rib bones and the outer layer of fat at the narrow end. Remove any excess fat.

**3** Fill the cavity with stuffing. Replace the flap and secure with a skewer.

**4** Place the meat in a roasting tin, fat side up (the bones form a natural rack). Roast for 15 minutes, then reduce the oven temperature to 180°C/350°F/ Gas 4. Continue to roast for a further 1½ hours, or until done to taste.

**5** Remove the meat from the oven, cover with foil and leave to stand for 15 minutes before carving. Serve hot with gravy and vegetables of your choice.

## Cook's File

Hint: Ask your butcher to help prepare your roast by sawing through the upper spinal bones, so that they will be easy to remove before carving.

Note: You can calculate the cooking time at 20 minutes per 500 g/1¼ lb This will produce a roast which is well done on the outside and rare on the inside.

Note: Make gravy from the cooking juices, diluted with a little red wine or stock.

# Rack of Veal *with* Herb Crust

preparation time 30 minutes

total cooking time 1–1½ hours

serves 6

## INGREDIENTS

1.5 kg/3 lb 5 oz rack of veal (6 cutlets)
50 g/2 oz fresh breadcrumbs
30 g/1¼ oz dry breadcrumbs
1 tablespoon finely chopped parsley
1 tablespoon finely chopped basil
2 egg whites, lightly beaten
2 garlic cloves, crushed
1 tablespoon vegetable oil
25 g/1 oz butter, melted

*Lemon Sauce*
4 tablespoons dry white wine
4 tablespoons water
2 tablespoons lemon juice
1 teaspoon sugar
90 g/3½ oz butter, diced
2 teaspoons finely chopped parsley

*1* Preheat the oven to 160°C/325°F/ Gas 3. Trim any excess fat from the veal. Combine the fresh and dry breadcrumbs, parsley and basil. Mix together the egg whites, garlic, oil and butter, add to the breadcrumb mixture and mix well. Add a little water if the mixture is too dry.

*2* Press the mixture firmly over the fatty side of the rack of veal. Place the veal, crust side up, in a roasting tin. Roast for 1–1½ hours.

*3* Remove the veal from the oven, cover with foil and let stand in a warm place for 10–15 minutes before slicing. Drain off all except 2 tablespoons of the cooking juices in the roasting tin.

*4* To prepare the lemon sauce, set the roasting tin over a medium heat. Add the white wine, water, lemon juice and sugar. Bring to the boil, stirring constantly, then reduce the heat to low. Simmer the sauce, uncovered, until reduced to about 120 ml/4 fl oz.

*5* Whisk in the butter, one piece at a time, making sure that each piece is fully incorporated before adding the next. Stir in the parsley. Pour a little lemon sauce over each veal cutlet to serve.

# Roast Lamb *with* Orange *and* Rosemary Stuffing

preparation time 50 minutes   total cooking time 1½ hours   serves 6

## INGREDIENTS

2 kg/4½ lb leg of lamb, boned
50 g/2 oz fresh breadcrumbs
2 tablespoons finely chopped rosemary
2 tablespoons coarsely chopped
    pecan nuts
4 tablespoons orange marmalade
3 teaspoons grated orange rind
2 tablespoons orange juice
120 ml/4 fl oz dry white wine

*1* Preheat the oven to 220°C/425°F/ Gas 7. Trim the excess fat from the lamb and open out to a flat surface. Mix together the breadcrumbs, rosemary and pecans. Mix together 1 tablespoon of the marmalade, 2 teaspoons of the grated orange rind and the orange juice and add to the breadcrumb mixture. Mix lightly, adding extra orange juice if necessary.

*2* Spread the stuffing over the lamb, roll up and tie securely at intervals with string. Place the lamb in a roasting tin and brush with 1 tablespoon of the remaining marmalade. Roast for 10–15 minutes, then reduce the temperature to 180°C/350°F/ Gas 4 and continue roasting for about 1–1½ hours, until tender and cooked according to taste. Cover the lamb with foil if it is browning too quickly. Remove from the oven, cover and leave to stand for 10–15 minutes before carving.

*3* Set the roasting tin over a low heat. Stir in the wine, incorporating any sediment. Bring to the boil, lower the heat and simmer until reduced to a thin sauce. Stir in the remaining marmalade and rind.

*4* Remove the string and slice the lamb thinly. Spoon the sauce over to serve.

## Cook's File

Note: Ask your butcher to bone the leg for you.

# Roast Leg of Lamb *with* Redcurrant Sauce

preparation time 30 minutes

total cooking time 2 hours

serves 6

## INGREDIENTS

*2 leeks, sliced*
*4 tablespoons sultanas*
*4 tablespoons ready-made stuffing mix*
*2 tablespoons pine nuts*
*1 tablespoon tomato ketchup*
*1 egg, beaten*
*2 kg/4½ lb leg of lamb, boned*
*pepper*
*4 tablespoons water*
*120 ml/4 fl oz chicken stock*
*1 tablespoon brandy*
*1 tablespoon redcurrant jelly*
*1 tablespoon cornflour*
*vegetables, to serve*

*1* Preheat the oven to 180°C/350°F/ Gas 4. Mix together the leeks, sultanas, stuffing mix, pine nuts, tomato ketchup and egg. Push the mixture into the opening in the leg of lamb and secure with skewers and string if necessary.

*2* Slash the fat on the top side of the leg with a sharp knife in a criss-cross pattern. Rub with pepper. Place the lamb, fat side up, on a rack in a roasting tin. Roast for 40 minutes.

*3* Pour the water into the roasting tin and return to the oven for a further 1½ hours, until the meat is cooked to taste.

*4* Remove the lamb from the oven, cover with foil and let stand for 15 minutes before carving. Strain the cooking juices and return them to the tin. Add the stock, brandy and redcurrant jelly.

*5* Blend the cornflour with a little of the liquid to form a smooth paste.

Stir the mixture into the sauce. Heat, stirring constantly, until the sauce boils and thickens. Reduce the heat to low and simmer for 3 minutes. Serve the lamb with the sauce and vegetables of your choice.

## Cook's File

Hint: There is a variety of packet stuffings on the market. You can vary the flavour by adding other ingredients, such as fresh herbs, spices and citrus rind.

# Rack of Lamb
## *with* Chive Crust

preparation time 30 minutes

total cooking time 1 hour

serves 4

**INGREDIENTS**

2 teaspoons chopped chives

2 teaspoons chopped mint

1 garlic clove, crushed

30 g/1¼ oz dry breadcrumbs

1 tablespoon lemon juice

1 teaspoon lemon rind

2 racks of lamb, each with
    6 cutlets, trimmed

50 g/2 oz butter or margarine, melted

Sauce

4 tablespoons white wine

4 tablespoons water

1 teaspoon brown sugar

1 tablespoon lemon juice

115 g/4 oz butter, diced

1 tablespoon mint jelly

*1* Preheat the oven to 180°C/350°F/ Gas 4. Mix together the herbs, garlic, breadcrumbs and lemon juice and rind in a small bowl. A little water may be required if the mixture is too dry. Press the mixture firmly over the fatty side of the racks of lamb. Drizzle melted butter over the crust.

*2* Place the lamb racks, crust side up, in a roasting tin and roast for 45 minutes–1 hour. Remove the lamb from the oven, cover with foil and let stand for 15 minutes before carving. Drain off all except 2 tablespoons of the cooking juices in the tin.

*3* To prepare the sauce, set the roasting tin over a medium heat and stir the wine and water into the cooking juices, incorporating the sediment from the base of the tin. Bring to the boil, stirring constantly, and boil until reduced by half.

*4* Stir in sugar and lemon juice. Whisk in the butter one piece at a time.

Blend in the mint jelly and heat until melted. Serve the lamb with the sauce.

# Crown Roast of Lamb *with* Rosemary Stuffing

preparation time 20 minutes  total cooking time 45 minutes  serves 6

## INGREDIENTS

1 crown roast of lamb (minimum
     12 cutlets)
15 g/½ oz butter, plus extra for greasing
2 onions, chopped
1 green eating or cooking apple, peeled
     and chopped
115 g/4 oz fresh breadcrumbs
2 tablespoons chopped rosemary
1 tablespoon chopped parsley
4 tablespoons unsweetened apple juice
2 eggs, separated
sprigs of rosemary, to garnish
vegetables, to serve

*1* Preheat the oven to 220°C/425°F/
Gas 7. Trim the meat and set aside.

*2* Melt the butter in a medium-size pan.
Add the onion and apple and fry
until soft. Remove from the heat and stir in
the breadcrumbs and herbs. Whisk
together the apple juice and egg yolks and
stir into the breadcrumb mixture.

*3* Place the egg whites in a small, dry
mixing bowl and beat with an electric
mixer until soft peaks form. Fold lightly
into the stuffing mixture.

*4* Place the lamb in a roasting tin. Place
a sheet of lightly greased foil
underneath the roast to hold the stuffing.
Spoon the stuffing into the cavity. Roast the
lamb for 45 minutes, or until cooked to
taste. Transfer the roast to a serving dish,
garnish with rosemary and serve with
vegetables of your choice. Cut between the
cutlets with a sharp knife to separate them.

## Cook's File

Note: Order the crown roast in advance and ask your butcher to shape and tie it with string. Wrap foil around the ends of the cutlet bones to prevent them from burning – discard before serving.

# Roast Leg of Pork

preparation time 30 minutes

total cooking time 3½ hours

serves 6–8

## INGREDIENTS

4 kg/8¾ lb leg of pork
cooking salt
sprigs of basil, to garnish

Apple Sauce
500 g/1¼ lb green eating or cooking
  apples, peeled, cored and quartered
120 ml/4 fl oz water
1 tablespoon caster sugar
50 g/2 oz butter, diced

Gravy
1 tablespoon brandy or Calvados
2 tablespoons plain flour
475 ml/16 fl oz chicken stock

*1* Preheat the oven to 240°C/475°F/ Gas 9. Score the pork rind with a sharp knife and rub with cooking salt. Put the pork, rind side up, on a rack in a large roasting tin. Add a little water to the tin. Roast for 30 minutes, or until the skin begins to crackle and bubble. Reduce the oven temperature to 180°C/350°F/Gas 4 and roast for a further 2 hours 40 minutes, until cooked through. Baste the meat occasionally with cooking juices. Remove from the oven, cover with foil and let stand for 10 minutes before carving.

*2* To make the apple sauce, put the apples and water in a small pan. Cover and simmer for 10 minutes until very soft. Remove the pan from the heat and stir in the sugar and butter. The sauce may be pushed through a fine sieve if a smoother texture is desired.

*3* To make the gravy, discard all but 2 tablespoons of the cooking juices and set the roasting tin over a medium heat. Stir in the brandy or Calvados, incorporating the sediment from the base of the tin. Cook for 1 minute. Remove from the heat and stir in the flour. Return the tin to the heat and cook, stirring constantly, for 2 minutes. Gradually stir in the chicken stock. Cook, stirring occasionally, until thickened. Garnish the pork with basil and serve with the gravy.

*Step 1*

*Step 2*

# Boned Pork Loin *with* Maple Glaze

preparation time 30 minutes

total cooking time 2 hours

serves 8

## INGREDIENTS

2 kg/4½ lb boned pork loin, skin removed

50 g/2 oz butter

2 tablespoons finely chopped chives

2 teaspoons ground coriander

½ teaspoon pepper

5 tablespoons maple syrup

150 g/5 oz brown sugar

1 tablespoon wholegrain mustard

sprigs of basil, to garnish

vegetables, to serve

*1* Preheat the oven to 180°/350°F/Gas 4. Remove excess fat from the pork, leaving just enough to keep it moist during cooking. Open the loin out, spread with half the butter and sprinkle with the chives. Roll up and secure with string. Mix the coriander and pepper and sprinkle evenly over the pork.

*2* Melt the remaining butter and mix it with the maple syrup, brown sugar and mustard. Place the pork on a rack in a roasting tin. Brush with 1 tablespoon of the maple syrup mixture. Pour a little water into the roasting tin.

*3* Roast the pork for 1½–2 hours, basting frequently with the maple glaze and adding more water to the roasting tin to prevent the cooking juices and glaze from burning. When cooked, remove the pork from the oven, cover with foil and let stand for 15 minutes before carving. Keep warm.

*4* Brush the pork loin with the remaining glaze, slice, garnish with basil sprigs and serve with the vegetables of your choice.

## Cook's File

To make crackling to serve with the pork, rub the skin generously with lemon juice, score with a sharp knife and grill under a preheated hot grill until really crispy.

# Spicy Leg of Pork

preparation time 30 minutes

total cooking time 1½ hours

serves 6

## INGREDIENTS

1.5 kg/3 lb 5 oz leg of pork, skin removed
2 teaspoons ground cumin
2 teaspoons ground cardamom
2 teaspoons ground ginger
3 large onions, sliced
1 tablespoon oil
120 ml/4 fl oz water
2 tablespoons brown sugar
sprigs of bay leaves, to garnish
vegetables, to serve

1 Preheat the oven to 180°C/350°F/ Gas 4. Trim any excess fat from the pork and score at regular intervals. Mix together the cumin, cardamom and ginger and rub evenly over the pork.

2 Arrange the onions over the base of a roasting tin, put the pork on top and pour the oil over the pork. Pour the water into the base of the roasting tin. Cover with foil and roast for 1¼ hours.

3 Remove the foil, sprinkle the pork with the brown sugar and roast for a further 15–20 minutes, or until golden. Remove the pork from the oven, cover with foil and let rest for 15 minutes before carving. Keep warm. Garnish the pork with sprigs of bay leaves and serve with vegetables or salad of your choice.

## Cook's File

When testing roast meat for 'doneness' with a meat thermometer, insert the thermometer in the thickest part of meat well away from fat or bone, as these can cause inaccurate temperature readings. To determine 'doneness', calculate the weight and refer to the thermometer guidelines for accurate results.

# Roast Pork Loin *with* Mango Chutney

preparation time 20 minutes

total cooking time 1½ hours

serves 6–8

## INGREDIENTS

1.5 kg/3 lb 5 oz boned and rolled loin
    of pork
1 tablespoon brown sugar
1 teaspoon dry mustard
1 teaspoon chicken stock granules
1 tablespoon lemon juice
2 teaspoons soy sauce

Mango Chutney
4 tablespoons olive oil
2 onions, sliced
1 teaspoon brown mustard seeds
1 large mango, peeled, stoned
    and chopped
2 tablespoons coarsely chopped roasted
    salted cashew nuts
1 tablespoon brown vinegar
2 tablespoons orange juice
2 teaspoons currants
1 tablespoon chopped coriander

*1* Preheat the oven to 220°C/425°F/ Gas 7. Score the pork rind in a criss-cross pattern. Mix together the sugar, mustard, stock granules, juice and soy sauce. Rub the mixture all over the pork.

*2* Place the loin on a rack, scored side up, in a shallow roasting tin and roast for 1¼ hours. Remove from the oven and let stand, uncovered, for 10 minutes. Remove the string before slicing.

*3* To make the mango chutney, heat the oil in a medium-size pan. Add the onions and cook over a medium heat for 10 minutes, stirring occasionally.

*4* Stir in the mustard seeds, chopped mango, nuts, vinegar, juice and currants, Simmer, uncovered, over a low heat for 5 minutes, stirring. Remove from the heat and add the coriander.

*5* Use a sharp serrated knife to cut through the crackling and pork. (Alternatively, remove the crackling and cut into pieces with kitchen scissors.) Serve the pork and crackling with mango chutney.

## Cook's File

Note: Use the cooking juices to make your favourite gravy, if preferred.

Hint: If the crackling does not reach the required crispness, remove it from the cooked pork using a sharp knife. Roast in a hot oven for up to 15 minutes. Remove from the oven and let stand for 5 minutes before serving.

# Orange-glazed Ham

preparation time 10 minutes, plus 1 hour standing

total cooking time 3¾ hours

serves 20

## INGREDIENTS

*7 kg/15½ lb leg of ham*
*1 large orange*
*475 ml/16 fl oz water*
*about 60 cloves*
*275 g/10 oz brown sugar*
*1 tablespoon dry mustard*
*250 ml/8 fl oz golden syrup*
*1 teaspoon yellow mustard seeds*

*Mustard Cream*
*2 tablespoons French mustard*
*120 ml/4 fl oz soured cream*
*120 ml/4 fl oz double cream*

*Step 1*            *Step 2*            *Step 3*

*1* Preheat the oven to 180°C/350°F/ Gas 4. Remove the rind from the ham by running a thumb around the edge, under it. Begin pulling from the widest edge. When the rind has been removed to within 10 cm/4 inches of the shank end, cut through it around the shank. Using a sharp knife, remove the excess fat. Squeeze the orange juice and reserve. Peel the rind into long, thin strips. Place the ham on a roasting rack in a deep roasting tin. Add the water, orange rind and 6 cloves to the tin. Cover the ham and roasting tin securely with foil and cook for 2 hours.

*2* Remove the roasting tin from the oven. Drain the meat and reserve 250 ml/8 fl oz of the cooking juices. With a sharp knife, score across the fat with deep cuts crossways and then diagonally to form a diamond pattern. Mix together the sugar, mustard and golden syrup to a thick paste. Spread half the paste thickly over the ham. Return to the oven, increase the temperature to 220°C/425°F/Gas 7 and cook, uncovered, for 30 minutes.

*3* Mix together the reserved orange juice, the mustard seeds and remaining brown sugar paste to make a glaze. Remove the ham from the oven and brush with a little of the glaze. Press a clove into each diamond. Return the ham to the oven and roast, uncovered, for 1 further hour, brushing with the glaze every 10 minutes.

*4* Place the reserved cooking juices and any remaining orange glaze in a small pan over a low heat and stir until the mixture comes to the boil. Continue to boil, without stirring, for 3 minutes. Remove the pan from the heat and set aside.

*5* To make the mustard cream, place the French mustard, soured cream and cream in a bowl and stir well to combine thoroughly. Cover and set aside for 1 hour. Slice the ham and serve warm or cold with the glaze and mustard cream.

# Stuffings and Sauces

## Pistachio
 Stuffing

Heat 1 tablespoon of oil in a small pan and cook 3 finely chopped spring onions and 1 teaspoon grated fresh root ginger for 2 minutes. Add 3 chopped rashers of bacon and cook for a further 3–4 minutes. Transfer to a bowl to cool. When cool, add 175 g/ 6 oz pork and veal mince, 50 g/2 oz fresh breadcrumbs, 3 tablespoons marmalade, 4 tablespoons chopped parsley, 1 beaten egg and 50 g/2 oz shelled pistachio nuts; season with salt and pepper to taste. Mix well.

## Citrus
 Stuffing

Heat 1 tablespoon of oil in a small pan. Add 1 finely chopped large onion and cook until softened. Set aside to cool. In a bowl, mix together 200 g/7 oz sausagemeat, 115 g/4 oz fresh white breadcrumbs, 2 crushed garlic cloves, 2 teaspoons each grated lemon and orange rind, and 50 g/2 oz finely chopped pecans. Season with salt and pepper to taste and mix well.

## Rice
Stuffing

Lightly toast 25 g/1 oz flaked almonds in a dry pan until golden, then set aside. Melt 50 g/2 oz butter in a small pan. Add 1 finely chopped onion and cook until softened. Mix together the almonds and onion in a bowl with 1 grated apple, 5 tablespoons drained and chopped water chestnuts, 2 tablespoons chopped parsley, 1 beaten egg and 225 g/8 oz cooked rice. Season to taste with salt and pepper and mix well.

## Pork and Veal Neck Stuffing

Combine 200 g/7 oz pork and veal mince, 1 finely chopped onion, 50 g/2 oz fresh breadcrumbs, 2 teaspoons finely grated lemon rind and 1 teaspoon dried mixed herbs in a bowl. Loosen the skin of the turkey breast and fill the neck cavity with the stuffing. Press the skin to flatten the stuffing evenly over the breast, fold the neck skin and secure with a skewer. Note: This is a traditional stuffing, known as forcemeat, which flavours and moistens the breast of the turkey. When carving, slice through forcemeat as well as the breast and serve both stuffing and meat as a single item, if desired.

# Classic  *Gravy*

Transfer the cooked turkey to a platter and strain the juices from the roasting tin into a small jug. Pour the fat from the surface of the juices into a small pan. Add 25 g/1 oz plain flour and stir until smooth. Cook over a medium heat for 3–4 minutes, until lightly golden. Remove the pan from the heat. Gradually add the remaining pan juices and 250 ml/8 fl oz chicken stock, stirring until thoroughly combined. Return to the heat and cook, stirring constantly, until thickened.

*LEFT TO RIGHT  Turkey with Rice Stuffing; Turkey with Pork and Veal Neck Stuffing; Turkey with Citrus Stuffing; Orange Cranberry Sauce; Classic Gravy; Bread Sauce; Roast Turkey with Pistachio Stuffing*

# Bread  *Sauce*

Peel a medium onion and stud with 4 whole cloves. Place in a pan with 750 ml/1¼ pints milk and 2 bay leaves. Bring to the boil, remove from the heat and cover. Leave for 30 minutes for the flavours to infuse. Remove and discard the onion and bay leaves. Add 150 g/5 oz fresh white breadcrumbs and bring to the boil, stirring constantly. Lower the heat and simmer for 3–4 minutes. Stir in 25 g/1 oz butter and season with salt and white pepper to taste. Alternatively, place the studded onion, milk and bay leaves in a small pan and simmer for 20 minutes. Strain and then stir in breadcrumbs and butter. Serve immediately. Hint: Bread sauce is a traditional accompaniment to roast turkey, goose or chicken. Freshly grated nutmeg and ground cloves also add flavour to this traditional favourite.

# Orange Cranberry *Sauce*

Mix together 250 ml/8 fl oz white wine, 250 ml/8 fl oz chicken stock and 250 ml/8 fl oz cranberry sauce in a medium-size pan. Add 2 wide strips of orange rind from which the white pith has been completely removed. Stir until the cranberry sauce has dissolved. Bring to the boil, reduce the heat slightly and simmer for 5 minutes. Stir 1 tablespoon of cornflour with a little water to make a smooth paste. Add the paste to the pan and stir until the mixture boils and thickens, then simmer for a further 2 minutes. Remove the orange rind and discard.

# Cumberland Sauce

preparation time 15 minutes

total cooking time 10 minutes

makes about 475 ml/16 fl oz

## INGREDIENTS

1 orange
1 lemon
250 ml/8 fl oz redcurrant jelly
2 tablespoons French mustard
4 tablespoons port
pepper

1 Remove the rind from the orange and lemon and cut into fine strips. Cover with water, simmer over a low heat for 5 minutes then drain and reserve the rind.

2 Mix together the juice from the orange and lemon, the redcurrant jelly and mustard in a small pan. Heat gently, stirring until the redcurrant jelly has melted. Add the port and simmer for 3 minutes.

3 Season with pepper to taste and add the orange and lemon rind to serve.

# Walnut and Ham Stuffing

preparation time 10 minutes

total cooking time Nil

makes about 400 g/14 oz

## INGREDIENTS

175 g/6 oz ham, finely diced
50 g/2 oz walnuts, finely chopped
50 g/2 oz mushrooms, finely chopped
115 g/4 oz fresh breadcrumbs
4 tablespoons chopped parsley
1 egg, lightly beaten

1 Place all ingredients together in a large bowl and combine thoroughly.

## Cook's File

Hint: If making in advance, place the stuffing in a freezer container or plastic bag. Seal and freeze until required. To use, thaw completely. Place in the cavity of the prepared bird and seal the cavity with a skewer.

# Apple Sauce

preparation time: 20 minutes

total cooking time: 30 minutes

makes about 475 ml/16 fl oz

## INGREDIENTS

4 large green dessert apples, peeled
and cored
25 g/1 oz butter
4 tablespoons sugar
2 teaspoons grated lemon rind
4 tablespoons water

1 Place the apples, butter, sugar, lemon rind and water in a heavy-based pan. Cook over a low heat, stirring frequently, until the apples are soft and pulpy. Serve the sauce warm with roast pork, roast duck or roast goose.

## Cook's File

Hint: Apple sauce may be made up to 3 days in advance and stored, covered, in the refrigerator.

# Apricot and Herb Stuffing

preparation time: 10 minutes

total cooking time Nil

makes about 675 g/1½ lb

## INGREDIENTS

225 g/8 oz chopped dried apricots

115 g/4 oz sultanas

1 onion, chopped

1 celery stick, finely chopped

175 g/6 oz fresh breadcrumbs

1 tablespoon finely chopped parsley

¼ teaspoon dried sage

¼ teaspoon dried rosemary

¼ teaspoon dried thyme

1 egg, beaten

*1* Place all ingredients together in a large bowl and combine thorougly.

## Cook's File

Hint: If making in advance, place the stuffing in a freezer container or plastic bag. Seal and freeze until required. To use, thaw completely. Place in the cavity of the prepared bird and seal the cavity with a skewer.

---

# Sage and Onion Stuffing

preparation time 20 minutes

total cooking time 10 minutes

makes about 450 g/1 lb

## INGREDIENTS

25 g/1 oz butter

1 large onion, finely chopped

2 rashers bacon, chopped

1 tablespoon chopped sage

2 teaspoons grated lemon rind

175 g/6 oz dry breadcrumbs

1 egg, lightly beaten

*1* Heat the butter in a pan. Add the onion and bacon and cook, stirring constantly, until soft.

*2* Mix together the onion and bacon mixture, the sage, lemon rind, breadcrumbs and egg.

## Cook's File

Hint: If making in advance, place the stuffing in a freezer container or plastic bag. Seal and freeze until required. To use, thaw completely. Place in the cavity of the prepared bird and seal the cavity with a skewer.

---

# Mint Sauce

preparation time 10 minutes

total cooking time 10 minutes

makes about 475 ml/16 fl oz

## INGREDIENTS

4 tablespoons water

4 tablespoons sugar

5 tablespoons vinegar

4 tablespoons finely chopped mint

*1* Put the water and sugar in a small saucepan. Bring to the boil, stirring until the sugar is dissolved. Add the vinegar and bring back to the boil. Remove from the heat and stir in the mint. Cool. Stir before serving with roast lamb.

## Cook's File

Hint: Chop the mint just before adding it to the vinegar to prevent discoloration.

# Yorkshire

## Puddings

preparation time 15 minutes, plus 1 hour standing

total cooking time 25 minutes

serves 8

### INGREDIENTS

*115 g/4 oz plain flour*
*pinch of salt*
*1–2 eggs*
*250 ml/8 fl oz milk*
*1 tablespoon water*
*3 tablespoons lard or beef dripping,*
    *melted*

*Step 1*

*1* Sift the flour and the salt together into a large bowl. Make a well in the centre and add the eggs. Using a wooden spoon, gradually beat in sufficient milk to make a stiff but smooth batter, making sure there are no lumps. Gradually beat in the remaining milk. Strain into a jug. Cover with clear film and refrigerate for 1 hour. Stir in the water.

*2* Preheat the oven to 200°C/400°F/ Gas 6. Spoon ¼ teaspoon of the fat into the base of each of 12 deep metal Yorkshire pudding tins. Place the tins in the hot oven for 3–5 minutes to heat the fat.

*3* Carefully fill each Yorkshire pudding tin two-thirds full with batter. Increase the oven temperature to 220°C/425°F/Gas 7.

*4* Bake the puddings for 15–20 minutes, or until risen, golden and crisp. Carefully remove the puddings from the tins, transfer to a warm serving dish and serve at once.

## Cook's File

Hint: Traditionally, Yorkshire pudding is baked in one large dish and served with plenty of gravy before the main course of roast beef, roast potatoes and vegetables to take the edge off the appetite. To do this, bake the batter in a 23 x 18 cm/9 x 7 inch deep roasting tin or ovenproof dish.

Hint: For a lighter batter, use skimmed milk or a mixture of 150 ml/5 fl oz milk and 5 tablespoons iced water.

Variation: 1 tablespoon of chopped fresh herbs or dried thyme to taste could be added to the batter for herbed Yorkshire puddings.

# Game

## Chips

preparation time 20 minutes, plus 1 hour standing

total cooking time 15 minutes

serves 4

### INGREDIENTS

*500 g/1¼ lb old potatoes*
*vegetable oil, for deep-frying*

*1* Peel and slice the potatoes very thinly, using a mandolin or very sharp knife. Put the slices in a bowl, cover with cold water and set aside for 1 hour. Drain and dry thoroughly on kitchen paper.

*2* Heat the oil for deep-frying in a heavy-based pan or deep-fryer to 180°C/350°F or until a cube of bread browns in 30 seconds. Fry the potatoes in small batches until light golden brown. Remove from the pan or deep-fryer and drain well on kitchen paper.

*3* To serve, reheat the oil and fry the potatoes again until they are crisp. Drain and serve immediately with roast game, turkey or goose.

# *Vegetarian*

## *Christmas*

## *Spanish*

## *Pizza*

preparation time 30 minutes, plus standing   total cooking time 35 minutes serves 4–6

### INGREDIENTS

*Base*
*melted butter or oil, for brushing*
*7 g/¼ oz sachet dried yeast*
*1 teaspoon caster sugar*
*275 g/10 oz plain flour*
*250 ml/8 fl oz warm water*

*Topping*
*10 spinach leaves, shredded*
*1 tablespoon olive oil*
*2 garlic cloves, crushed*
*2 onions, chopped*
*400 g/14 oz can tomatoes, drained*
  *and crushed*
*¼ teaspoon black pepper*
*12 stoned black olives, chopped*

*1* Brush a 30 x 25 cm/12 x 10 inch Swiss roll tin with melted butter or oil.

*2* To make the base, mix together the yeast, sugar and flour in a large bowl. Gradually add the warm water and blend until smooth. Turn out and knead the dough on a lightly floured surface until smooth and elastic.

*3* Place in a lightly oiled bowl, cover with a tea towel and leave to rise in a warm place for 15 minutes, or until it has almost doubled in bulk.

*4* To make the topping, put the spinach in a large pan, cover and cook on a low heat for 3 minutes. Drain and cool. Squeeze out the excess moisture with your hands and set aside.

*5* Heat the oil in a pan. Add the garlic and onions and cook over a low heat for 5–6 minutes. Add the tomatoes and pepper and simmer gently for 5 minutes.

*6* Preheat the oven to 220°C/425°F/ Gas 7. Knock back the dough, remove from the bowl and knead on a lightly floured board for 2–3 minutes. Roll out the dough and place it in the tin. Spread with spinach, top with the tomato mixture and sprinkle the olives on top.

*7* Bake for 25–30 minutes. Cut into small squares and serve hot or cold.

## Cook's File

Hint: After it has been mixed and kneaded for the first time, yeast dough is set aside in a warm place to rise. When it has doubled in bulk, it is knocked back. To do this, gently punch the centre of the dough with your fist to deflate it. Then fold the edges of the dough into the centre. Turn out on to a floured board and knead lightly again for 2–3 minutes. Some recipes, usually for breads, require a second proving. The dough should be shaped into a ball, placed in a greased container, covered and set aside in a warm place.

# Sour Cream

## Tomato Pizza

preparation time 30 minutes, plus 1½ hours
standing time

total cooking time 40 minutes

serves 4

**INGREDIENTS**

*Base*
*1 teaspoon dried yeast*
*1 teaspoon caster sugar*
*150 ml/5 fl oz warm water*
*225 g/8 oz plain flour*
*pinch of salt*
*120 ml/4 fl oz olive oil*

*Topping*
*120 ml/4 fl oz soured cream*
*90 g/3½ oz ricotta cheese*

*2 tablespoons chopped herbs, such as*
*basil, lemon thyme and sage*
*2 tablespoons vegetable oil*
*2 medium onions, thinly sliced*
*5 ripe tomatoes, sliced*
*2 garlic cloves, thinly sliced*
*40 g/1½ oz marinated olives*
*10 sprigs of fresh lemon thyme*
*pepper*

*1* To make the base, put the yeast, sugar and warm water into a bowl and mix to dissolve the sugar. Set aside in a warm, draught-free place for 5 minutes, or until the mixture is foamy.

*2* Put the flour and salt into a food processor, then, with the motor running, add the oil and the yeast mixture and process to form a rough dough. Turn out on to a lightly floured surface and knead until smooth. Place in a lightly oiled bowl, cover and set aside in a warm place for 1½ hours, or until doubled in bulk.

*3* Knock back the dough and remove from the bowl. Knead and roll out to a 30 cm/12 inch circle, or four 14 cm/

# Santa Fe

## Pizzetta

preparation time 15 minutes

total cooking time 15 minutes

serves 6

**INGREDIENTS**

*6 ready-made small pizza bases*
*175 ml/6 fl oz ready-made spicy*
*tomato salsa*
*4 spring onions, sliced*
*1 red pepper, seeded and sliced*
*400 g/14 oz can red kidney beans, drained*
*and rinsed*
*2 tablespoons chopped basil*
*75 g/3 oz mozzarella cheese, grated*
*25g/1 oz Cheddar cheese, grated*
*115 g/4 oz corn chips*
*120 ml/4 fl oz soured cream*
*6 sprigs of dill, to garnish*

*Guacamole*
*1 garlic clove, crushed*
*1 small red onion, finely chopped*
*1 large avocado, stoned, peeled*
*and roughly mashed*
*1 teaspoon lemon juice*
*1 tablespoon ready-made tomato salsa*
*2 tablespoons soured cream*

*1* Preheat the oven to 200°C/400°F/ Gas 6. Place the pizza bases on a large baking tray. Spread them evenly with the spicy tomato salsa.

*2* Top with the sliced spring onions, sliced red pepper, kidney beans and chopped basil.

*3* Sprinkle with the grated mozzarella and Cheddar cheese. Bake for about 15 minutes, or until the pizza bases are crisp and the cheese is golden brown.

5½ inch circles, and place on a non-stick baking tray. Use your finger to push up the edge slightly to make a rim. Preheat the oven to 200°C/400°F/Gas 6.

4 Mix together the cream, cheese and herbs and spread evenly over the pizza base, leaving a 1 cm/½ inch border.

5 Heat the oil in a frying pan. Add the onions and cook, stirring occasionally, for 10 minutes, or until they have caramelized. Cool slightly, then spoon the onions over the ricotta mixture. Top with the sliced tomatoes, garlic, olives and lemon thyme and season to taste with pepper. Bake for 15–30 minutes, depending on the size, until crisp and golden.

4 Meanwhile, make the guacamole. Place the garlic, onion, avocado, lemon juice, salsa and soured cream in a bowl and stir to combine.

5 Top each pizzetta with corn chips, soured cream and guacamole, garnish with a sprig of dill and serve immediately.

## Cook's File

Note: Do not make the guacamole in advance, as it will discolour, turning grey.

# Aubergine and Tomato Bake

preparation time 20 minutes

total cooking time 1¼ hours

serves 6

## INGREDIENTS

*2 large aubergines*

*salt*

*4 tablespoons olive oil*

*2 large onions, chopped*

*1 teaspoon ground cumin*

*250 ml/8 fl oz good-quality white wine*

*2 x 400 g/14 oz cans tomatoes, drained
    and crushed*

*2 garlic cloves, crushed*

*2 fresh red chillies, seeded and
    finely chopped*

*75 g/3 oz currants*

*3 tablespoons chopped coriander*

*sprigs of tarragon, to garnish*

*ribbon pasta, such as tagliatelle,
    to serve*

*1* Preheat the oven to 220°C/425°F/ Gas 7. Cut the aubergines into 2 cm/ ¼ inch thick slices. Place them on a tray and sprinkle generously with salt. Set aside for 20 minutes.

*2* Meanwhile, heat 2 tablespoons of the oil in a large pan. Add the onions and cook over a medium heat for 5 minutes, or until softened. Add the cumin and cook, stirring, for 1 minute. Add the wine and bring to the boil. Reduce the heat and simmer for 10 minutes, or until the mixture has reduced by three-quarters.

*3* Add the tomatoes, bring to the boil, then simmer for 10 minutes. Add the garlic, chillies and currants and simmer for 5 minutes. Remove the pan from the heat.

*4* Rinse the aubergine slices well and squeeze them dry using kitchen paper. Heat the remaining oil in a large frying pan. Fry the aubergine slices over a medium heat for 3–4 minutes. Drain on kitchen paper.

*5* Layer the aubergine slices and tomato mixture in a large ovenproof dish, sprinkling coriander between each layer. Finish with a layer of aubergine. Bake for 30 minutes. Garnish with sprigs of tarragon and serve with ribbon pasta.

## Cook's File

Hint: When buying aubergines look for firm, glossy fruit that are neither wrinkled nor patchy and feel heavy and solid.

# Mange tout with Red Pepper

preparation time 15–20 minutes

total cooking time 7 minutes

serves 4

### INGREDIENTS

1 large onion
175 g/6 oz mange tout
1 tablespoon vegetable oil
1 tablespoon grated fresh root ginger
1 red pepper, seeded and cut into strips
1 small garlic clove, crushed
1 tablespoon oyster sauce (optional)
1 teaspoon sugar
pinch of salt
1 tablespoon water

*1* Cut the onion in half and slice thinly into rings. Top and tail the mange tout and string if necessary.

*2* Heat the oil in a frying pan or preheated wok. Add the onion, ginger and red pepper and stir-fry over a high heat for 4–5 minutes, or until the vegetables are just tender. Add the garlic and mange tout and stir-fry for 2 minutes, or until the mange tout become bright green and are tender, but still crisp.

*3* Add the oyster sauce, sugar, salt and water to the pan or wok and mix well. Serve immediately.

## Cook's File

Hint: A vegetarian version of oyster sauce is available from health food shops and some supermarkets. Otherwise, you could substitute dark soy sauce. Remember, however, that soy sauce is very salty, so take care when seasoning the stir-fry.

# Thai Coconut Vegetables

preparation time 15–20 minutes

total cooking time 15 minutes

serves 4–6

### INGREDIENTS

1 tablespoon vegetable oil
2 small onions, cut into wedges
1 teaspoon ground cumin
150 g/5 oz cauliflower florets
1 medium red pepper, seeded and chopped
2 celery sticks, sliced diagonally
175 g/6 oz grated pumpkin
250 ml/8 fl oz coconut milk
250 ml/8 fl oz vegetable stock
1 tablespoon sweet chilli sauce
150 g/5 oz green beans, trimmed and cut in half
1 tablespoon finely chopped coriander
steamed rice, to serve

*1* Heat the oil in a frying pan or preheated wok. Add the onion and cumin and stir-fry over a medium heat for 2 minutes, or until the onion is golden.

*2* Add the cauliflower and stir-fry over a high heat for 2 minutes. Add the red pepper, celery and pumpkin and stir-fry over a high heat for 2 minutes, or until the vegetables have begun to soften.

*3* Add the coconut milk, stock and chilli sauce and bring to the boil. Reduce the heat and cook for 8 minutes, or until the vegetables are almost tender. Add the green beans to the pan or wok together with the coriander, and cook for a further 2 minutes, or until the beans are just tender. Serve with steamed rice.

# Layered Potato and Apple Bake

preparation time 30 minutes

total cooking time 45 minutes

serves 6

## INGREDIENTS

*melted butter or vegetable oil, for brushing*
*2 large potatoes*
*3 medium green eating apples*
*1 medium onion*
*50 g/2 oz Cheddar cheese, finely grated*
*250 ml/8 fl oz double cream*
*¼ teaspoon ground nutmeg*
*pepper*
*mixed salad leaves, to serve*

1 Preheat the oven to 180°C/350°F/ Gas 4. Brush a large, shallow ovenproof dish with melted butter or oil. Peel the potatoes and cut into thin slices. Peel, core and quarter the apples, then cut the quarters into thin slices. Slice the onion into very fine rings.

2 Arrange the sliced potatoes, apples and onion in layers in the prepared dish, finishing with a layer of potatoes.

Sprinkle evenly with the grated Cheddar cheese. Pour the cream over the top, covering the surface as evenly as possible.

3 Sprinkle with nutmeg, and pepper to taste. Bake for 45 minutes, or until the top is golden brown. Remove the dish from the oven and allow to stand for 5 minutes before serving. Serve with strongly-flavoured mixed salad leaves or as a side dish.

# Spicy Chickpea and Vegetable Casserole

preparation time 25 minutes, plus overnight soaking   total cooking time 1½ hours    serves 4

## INGREDIENTS

*350 g/12 oz dried chickpeas*
*2 tablespoons vegetable oil*
*1 large onion, chopped*
*1 garlic clove, crushed*
*1 tablespoon ground cumin*
*½ teaspoon chilli powder*
*½ teaspoon ground allspice*
*400 g/14 oz can tomatoes, drained*
  *and crushed*
*350 ml/12 fl oz vegetable stock*
*300 g/11 oz pumpkin, cut into large cubes*
*150 g/5 oz green beans, trimmed*
*200 g/7 oz winter squash,*
  *quartered and peeled*
*2 tablespoons tomato purée*
*1 teaspoon dried oregano*

1 Place the chickpeas in a large bowl, cover with cold water and set aside to soak overnight.

2 Heat the oil in a large pan. Add the onion and garlic and stir-fry for 2 minutes, or until tender. Add the cumin, chilli powder and allspice and stir-fry for 1 minute. Drain the chickpeas and add them to the pan, together with the tomatoes and stock. Bring to the boil, reduce the heat, cover and simmer, stirring occasionally, for 1 hour.

3 Add the pumpkin, green beans, squash, tomato purée and oregano to the pan and stir well to combine. Cover and simmer for a further 15 minutes. Remove the lid from the pan and simmer for a further 10 minutes to reduce and thicken the sauce slightly.

## Cook's File

Note: With the exception of soya beans, chickpeas require more soaking than any other pulse. A quick way to soak them is to place them in a large pan and cover with cold water. Bring to the boil; remove from the heat and set aside to soak for 2 hours before draining and adding them to the casserole.

Hint: If you are really in a hurry, substitute canned chickpeas for the dried. Use two 425 g/15 oz cans and drain and rinse thoroughly before use. You could also use canned pumpkin, but this does not have such a delicious flavour as fresh.

Variation: A variety of winter squashes is available from most supermarkets. However, if you prefer you could substitute courgettes (which do not require peeling).

# Filo Risotto Pie

preparation time 45 minutes

total cooking time 1¾ hours

serves 8

## INGREDIENTS

2 large red peppers
250 ml/8 fl oz white wine
1 litre/1¼ pints vegetable stock
2 tablespoons vegetable oil
1 garlic clove, crushed
1 leek, sliced
1 fennel bulb, thinly sliced
400 g/14 oz arborio or other
    risotto rice
50 g/2 oz freshly grated Parmesan cheese
salt and pepper
10 sheets filo pastry
4 tablespoons olive oil
500 g/1¼ lb spinach, blanched
225 g/8 oz feta cheese, sliced
1 tablespoon sesame seeds

1 Cut the peppers in half lengthways. Remove the seeds and membrane and then cut into large, flattish pieces. Grill until the skin blackens and blisters. Place on a chopping board, cover with a tea towel and allow to cool. Peel the peppers and cut the flesh into smaller pieces.

2 Put the wine and vegetable stock in a large pan. Bring to the boil and then reduce the heat.

3 Heat the oil and garlic in a large heavy-based pan. Add the leek and fennel and cook over a medium heat, stirring frequently, for 5 minutes, or until lightly browned. Add the rice and cook, stirring constantly, for 3 minutes or until the rice is translucent and all the grains are coated with oil.

4 Add 250 ml/8 fl oz of the hot stock mixture to the rice and cook, stirring constantly, until all the liquid is absorbed. Continue adding the hot stock mixture 120 ml/4 fl oz at a time, stirring constantly, until all the stock mixture has been used and the rice is tender. This will take about 40 minutes. Make sure the stock mixture stays hot, as the risotto will become soggy if it isn't. Remove the pan from the heat, stir in the Parmesan cheese and season to taste with salt and pepper. Set aside until cooled slightly.

# Mediterranean Lentil Salad

preparation time 10 minutes, plus 4 hours marinating

total cooking time 20–25 minutes

serves 6–8

## INGREDIENTS

1 large red pepper
1 large yellow pepper
225 g/8 oz red lentils
1 red onion, finely chopped
1 cucumber, chopped

Dressing
5 tablespoons olive oil
2 tablespoons lemon juice
1 teaspoon ground cumin
2 garlic cloves, crushed
salt and pepper

1 Cut the peppers in half lengthways. Remove the seeds and membrane and then cut into large, flattish pieces. Grill until the skin blackens and blisters. Place on a chopping board, cover with a tea towel and allow to cool. Peel the peppers and cut the flesh into 5 mm/¼ inch strips.

2 Rinse the lentils well under cold running water. Place in a saucepan, cover with boiling water and simmer for 10–20 minutes, or until tender. Do not add salt or the lentils will become tough, and do not overcook or they will become mushy. Drain well.

3 Place the peppers, lentils, onion and cucumber in a serving bowl and toss well to combine.

4 Make the dressing. Place the olive oil, lemon juice, cumin and garlic in a small bowl, season to taste with salt and pepper and whisk thoroughly to combine.

5 Pour the dressing over the salad and toss gently to mix thoroughly. Cover the salad with clear film and set aside in the refrigerator for 4 hours to allow the flavours to mingle. Allow the salad to return to room temperature before serving.

5 Preheat the oven to 190°C/375°F/ Gas 5. Brush each sheet of filo with olive oil and fold in half lengthways. Arrange like overlapping spokes of a wheel in a 23 cm/9 inch springform tin, with one end of pastry hanging over the side.

6 Spoon half the risotto mixture evenly over the pastry base and top with half the red peppers, half the spinach and half the feta cheese slices. Repeat the layers with the remaining ingredients.

7 Fold the pastry over the filling, brush lightly with oil and sprinkle with sesame seeds. Bake for 50 minutes, or until crisp and golden and heated through.

## Cook's File

Note: There are several types of lentils, which differ in size and colour. Red lentils are easily available, but can quickly cook down to a smooth purée. Yellow lentils are not suitable for salads, as they invariably cook to a smooth purée. Puy lentils, a tiny, grey-green French variety, have the best flavour and retain their shape when cooked, so they are ideal for salads. However, they may be difficult to find. Larger flat green lentils and brown lentils, although not quite so flavoursome, are more widely available and they also retain their shape well when cooked.

Variation: If you have plenty of time, this dish could also be made with *ful medames*, small, brown Egyptian broad beans. These require soaking in cold water for at least 5 hours, preferably overnight, and then simmering for about 3 hours, until tender.

# Vegetable Couscous

preparation time 40 minutes

total cooking time 30 minutes

serves 4–6

## INGREDIENTS

3 tablespoons olive oil

2 small onions, thinly sliced

1 teaspoon ground turmeric

½ teaspoon chilli powder

2 teaspoons grated fresh root ginger

1 cinnamon stick

2 medium carrots, thickly sliced

2 medium parsnips, thickly sliced

350 ml/12 fl oz vegetable stock

275 g/10 oz pumpkin, cut into
    small cubes

225 g/8 oz cauliflower, cut into
    small florets

2 medium courgettes, cut into thick slices

425 g/15 oz can chickpeas, drained

pinch of saffron threads

2 tablespoons chopped coriander

2 tablespoons chopped flat-leaf parsley

225 g/8 oz instant couscous

250 ml/8 fl oz boiling water

25 g/1 oz butter

1 Heat 2 tablespoons of the oil in a large pan. Add the onions and cook over a medium heat, stirring occasionally, for 3 minutes, or until softened. Add the turmeric, chilli powder and ginger and cook, stirring, for a further minute.

2 Stir in the cinnamon, carrots, parsnips and stock. Cover and bring to the boil. Reduce the heat and simmer for 5 minutes, or until the vegetables are almost tender.

3 Add the pumpkin, cauliflower and courgettes and simmer for a further 10 minutes. Stir in the chickpeas, saffron, coriander and parsley and simmer, uncovered, for 5 minutes. Remove the cinnamon stick.

4 Place the couscous in a bowl and add the boiling water. Allow to stand for 2 minutes, then add the remaining oil and the butter and fluff with a fork. Place a bed of couscous on each serving plate and top with the vegetables.

## Cook's File

Hint: The vegetables may be cooked up to a day in advance and refrigerated. The couscous, available from supermarkets or delicatessens, is best prepared just before serving.

Note: Couscous is made from semolina grain and semolina flour, rolled into tiny pellets. It is a staple in North African cooking and is traditionally steamed over a pot of stew in a *couscousière*. The couscous seen most commonly is an 'instant' variety, which needs only to be combined with boiling water and left to stand for a couple of minutes. Butter and oil are then forked through the grains. The name couscous also refers to the whole dish of a stew served over couscous grains.

# Vegetarian Rice Noodles

preparation time 20 minutes, plus soaking

total cooking time 10 minutes

serves 4–6

## INGREDIENTS

8 dried Chinese mushrooms

225 g/8 oz dried rice noodles

2 tablespoons vegetable oil

3 garlic cloves, chopped

4 cm/1½ inch piece fresh root
    ginger, grated

115 g/4 oz fried tofu, cut into 2.5 cm/
    1 inch cubes

1 medium carrot, cut into fine shreds

115 g/4 oz green beans, cut into 3 cm/
    1¼ inch lengths

½ red pepper, seeded and cut into
    fine strips

2 tablespoons dark soy sauce

1 tablespoon fish sauce (optional)

2 teaspoons brown sugar

115 g/4 oz beansprouts

75 g/3 oz finely shredded cabbage

50 g/2 oz beansprouts, to garnish

Thai sweet chilli sauce, to serve

*1* Soak the mushrooms in hot water for 20 minutes; drain and slice. Put the noodles in a bowl, cover with boiling water and soak them for 1–4 minutes, until soft. Drain well.

*2* Heat a wok or large heavy-based frying pan. Add the oil, and when hot, add the garlic, ginger and tofu. Stir-fry for 1 minute. Add the carrot, beans, red pepper and mushrooms and stir-fry for 2 minutes.

*3* Add the sauces and sugar, toss well, cover and steam for 1 minute. Add the noodles, beansprouts and cabbage, then toss, cover and steam for 30 seconds.

*4* Arrange the noodles on a serving platter, garnish with beansprouts and serve immediately with chilli sauce.

## Cook's File

Note: The most common type of beansprouts are mung beans, but many other beans and seeds may be sprouted – soya and aduki beans, chickpeas, lentils, alfalfa, poppy and sunflower seeds. Grow them in a special sprouter or in a jar covered with a piece of muslin. Water and drain each day.

# Fettuccine with Creamy Mushroom and Bean Sauce

preparation time 20 minutes   total cooking time 20 minutes   serves 4

## INGREDIENTS

115 g/4 oz pine nuts

250 g/9 oz dried fettuccine

225 g/8 oz green beans, trimmed

2 tablespoons vegetable oil

1 onion, chopped

2 garlic cloves, crushed

225 g/8 oz mushrooms, thinly sliced

120 ml/4 fl oz white wine

300 ml/11 fl oz single cream

120 ml/4 fl oz vegetable stock

1 egg

3 tablespoons chopped basil

40 g/1½ oz sun-dried tomatoes, cut into
    thin strips

salt and pepper

50 g/2 oz Parmesan cheese, shaved,
    to garnish

1 Place the pine nuts in a small pan. Stir over a medium heat until golden. Set aside. Cook the fettuccine in a large pan of lightly salted boiling water for 8–10 minutes, until just tender. Drain well and keep warm.

2 Cut the beans into long thin strips. Heat the oil in a large heavy-based frying pan. Add the onion and garlic and cook over medium heat for 3 minutes, or until softened. Add the mushrooms and cook, stirring, for 1 minute. Add the wine, cream and stock. Bring to the boil, reduce the heat and simmer for 10 minutes.

3 Lightly beat the egg in a small bowl. Stirring constantly, add a little cooking liquid. Pour the mixture slowly into the pan, stirring constantly for 30 seconds. Keep the heat very low – if the mixture boils, it will curdle. Add the beans, basil, pine nuts and tomatoes and stir until heated through. Season to taste with salt and pepper. Divide the pasta among warmed serving plates and spoon the sauce over the top. Garnish with shavings of Parmesan cheese.

## Cook's File

Note: There are dozens of varieties of green beans to choose from. Whatever the type, the beans should be crisp and bright. Avoid buying any limp or overly mature beans with tough-looking pods: the beans should literally snap when bent. Most beans need topping and tailing and some types need stringing.

# Carrot Pesto Bake

preparation time 45 minutes, plus 30 minutes standing

total cooking time 55 minutes

serves 4

## INGREDIENTS

*vegetable oil, for brushing*
*50 g/2 oz butter*
*50 g/2 oz plain flour*
*750 ml/1¼ pints milk*
*150 ml/5 fl oz crème fraîche*
*1 teaspoon crushed black peppercorns*
*175 g/6 oz Cheddar cheese, grated*
*4 eggs, lightly beaten*
*2 tablespoons ready-made pesto*
*675 g/1¼ lb carrots, grated*
*225 g/8 oz no-precook lasagne sheets*
*sprig of bay leaves, to garnish*
*green salad, to serve*

*1* Brush a 30 x 20 cm/12 x 8 inch ovenproof dish with oil. Melt the butter in a large pan. Add the flour and stir over a low heat until the mixture is lightly golden and bubbling. Mix together the milk, crème fraîche and peppercorns and gradually add to the pan, stirring between each addition until the mixture is smooth. Stir constantly over a medium heat for 5 minutes, or until the mixture boils and thickens. Boil for a further minute, then remove from heat. Stir in 115 g/4 oz of the cheese and let cool slightly. Gradually add the beaten eggs, stirring constantly.

*2* Pour a third of the sauce into another bowl to make the topping and set aside. Add the pesto and grated carrot to the remaining sauce, stirring to combine.

*3* Preheat the oven to 150°C/300°F/ Gas 2. Beginning with one-third of the carrot mixture, make alternate layers of carrot mixture and lasagne in the prepared dish. Use three layers of each, finishing with lasagne sheets. Spread the reserved sauce evenly over the top. Sprinkle with the remaining grated cheese. Set aside for 15 minutes before cooking to allow the pasta to soften. Bake for about 40 minutes, or until the sauce has set and the top is golden brown.

*4* Remove the lasagne from the oven, cover and let stand for 15 minutes — this will ensure that it will slice cleanly and easily. Garnish with bay leaves and serve with a crisp green salad.

## Cook's File

Note: Pesto Genovese is the classic basil pesto and is a simple combination of basil leaves, pine nuts, freshly grated Parmesan cheese, garlic cloves, extra virgin olive oil and salt and pepper. All pestos are highly flavoured and should be used sparingly to complement, rather than overwhelm, the foods they accompany. In Italian the word pesto means 'pounded', the traditional method of making pesto being to grind the ingredients in a mortar with a pestle.

# Potato Pizza *with* Onions and Goat's Cheese

preparation time 40 minutes, plus standing    total cooking time 55 minutes    serves 4

## INGREDIENTS

*Base*
*120 ml/4 fl oz warm milk*
*50 g/2 oz fresh yeast, crumbled, or*
*    2 x 7 g/¼oz sachets dried yeast*
*½ teaspoon sugar*
*salt and pepper*
*165 g/5½ oz mashed potato*
*115 g/4 oz plain flour*
*2 tablespoons chopped parsley*

*Topping*
*2 tablespoons olive oil*
*1 kg/2¼ lb red onions, thinly sliced*
*200 g/7 oz roasted red pepper, cut*
*    into strips (see page 80)*
*75 g/3 oz black olives*
*50 g/2 oz goat's cheese, cut into*
*    small pieces*
*crushed black peppercorns*

*1* Mix together the warm milk, yeast, sugar and a pinch of salt in a small bowl. Cover the bowl with clear film and set aside in a warm place for about 10 minutes, or until frothy.

*2* Put the potato, flour, parsley and yeast mixture in a large bowl and season to taste with salt and pepper. Stir well until thoroughly mixed and a soft dough forms. Turn out on to a lightly floured work surface and knead for 10 minutes, or until the dough is smooth and elastic and springs back when pressed gently.

*3* Shape the dough into a ball and transfer it to a large, clean, lightly greased bowl. Cover with clear film and set aside in a warm place for 1–1½ hours, or until the dough has doubled in bulk.

*4* To make the topping, heat the oil in a heavy-based pan over a low heat. Cook the onions, covered, stirring occasionally, for 20–30 minutes, or until golden and glossy. Remove from the heat.

*5* Preheat the oven to 220°C/425°F/ Gas 7. Turn the dough out on to a floured surface, gently knock back and knead for a further 2 minutes. Generously oil a pizza tray or 2 small baking trays. Put the dough on the tray and press out to fit. Top the dough with the caramelized onions, red pepper, olives and goat's cheese and sprinkle with peppercorns. Bake for 20–25 minutes and serve immediately.

## Cook's File

Hint: The caramelized onions can be prepared a day in advance. Be careful to cook them over a low heat so that they become sweet and delicious. If they burn, they will be bitter.

Note: Yeast dough may be made up to the stage where it is left to double in size (this is called 'proving') well in advance. Place the dough in a lightly oiled bowl, cover with clear film and refrigerate for up to 8 hours. The dough will still rise, it just happens much more slowly at the cooler temperature. Never leave dough to rise in a very hot environment, thinking it will happen more quickly. The yeast will develop a sour taste or may even be killed.

# Borlotti Bean Moussaka

preparation time 45 minutes, plus overnight soaking

total cooking time 2¼–2½ hours

serves 6

## INGREDIENTS

*225 g/8 oz dried borlotti beans*
*2 large aubergines, sliced*
*salt*
*5 tablespoons olive oil*
*1 garlic clove, crushed*
*1 onion, chopped*
*115 g/4 oz button mushrooms, sliced*
*2 x 400 g/14 oz cans tomatoes, chopped*
*250 ml/8 fl oz red wine*
*1 tablespoon tomato purée*
*1 tablespoon chopped oregano*

*Topping*
*250 ml/8 fl oz natural yogurt*
*4 eggs, lightly beaten*
*475 ml/16 fl oz milk*
*¼ teaspoon ground paprika*
*50 g/2 oz freshly grated Parmesan cheese*
*25 g/1 oz fresh breadcrumbs*

*1* Put the borlotti beans in a bowl, cover with cold water and set aside to soak overnight. Rinse and drain well.

*2* Place the beans in a large heavy-based pan, cover with water and bring to the boil. Reduce the heat and simmer for 1½ hours, or until tender. Drain well.

*3* Meanwhile, sprinkle the aubergine slices with salt and set aside for 30 minutes. Rinse well and pat dry with kitchen paper. Brush the aubergine slices with a little of the oil and cook under a preheated grill for 3 minutes on each side or until golden. Drain on kitchen paper.

*4* Preheat the oven to 200°C/400°F/Gas 6. Heat the remaining oil in a large heavy-based pan. Add the garlic and onion and cook over a medium heat, stirring frequently, for about 3 minutes, or until the onion is golden. Add the sliced mushrooms and cook for 3 minutes, or until browned.

*5* Stir in the tomatoes, together with their juice, the wine, tomato purée and chopped oregano and bring to the boil. Reduce the heat to low and simmer for about 40 minutes, or until the sauce has thickened.

*6* To assemble the moussaka, spoon the borlotti beans into a large, ovenproof dish and top with the tomato sauce and aubergine slices.

*7* To make the topping, whisk together the yogurt, eggs, milk and paprika. Pour the mixture over the aubergines and set aside for 10 minutes. Combine the Parmesan and breadcrumbs in a bowl. Sprinkle the mixture over the moussaka. Bake for 45–60 minutes, or until heated through and the top is golden.

## Cook's File

Note: Borlotti beans are brown with speckled red markings and are also known as Roman beans. They have a distinctive chestnut flavour and a creamy texture. Fresh borlotti beans have a long, burgundy speckled pod and can be purchased in spring and summer.

# Vegetable Tart with Salsa Verde

preparation time 30 minutes, plus 30 minutes chilling

total cooking time 40 minutes

serves 6

## INGREDIENTS

*Pastry*
225 g/8 oz plain flour
½ teaspoon salt
115 g/4 oz butter, chilled and diced
4 tablespoons single cream
1–2 tablespoons iced water

*Salsa Verde*
1 garlic clove
40 g/1½ oz flat-leaf parsley
5 tablespoons extra virgin olive oil
15 g/½ oz chopped dill
2 tablespoons Dijon mustard
1 tablespoon red wine vinegar
1 tablespoon baby capers, drained

*Filling*
1 large Desirée potato (about 250 g/9 oz),
    chopped into 2 cm/¾ inch cubes
1 tablespoon olive oil
2 garlic cloves, crushed
1 red pepper, seeded and chopped into
    3 cm/1¼ inch squares
1 red onion, sliced into rings
2 courgettes, sliced
2 tablespoons chopped dill
1 tablespoon chopped thyme
1 tablespoon baby capers, drained
150 g/5 oz marinated artichoke
    hearts, drained
salt and pepper
25 g/1 oz baby spinach leaves

1 First, make the pastry. Sift the flour and the salt into a large bowl. Add the diced butter and rub in with the fingertips until the mixture resembles fine breadcrumbs. Add the cream and water and mix with a flat-bladed knife until the mixture just comes together in small beads. Gather the dough into a ball and turn out on to a lightly floured work surface. Gently flatten into a disc, cover with clear film, and chill in the refrigerator for 30 minutes.

2 Preheat the oven to 200°C/400°F/ Gas 6. Lightly grease a 27 cm/ 10½ inch shallow fluted flan tin with a removable base.

3 Roll out the dough between 2 sheets of greaseproof paper large enough to line the flan tin. Remove the paper and carefully lift the pastry into the flan tin, pressing it gently into the fluted sides. Trim any excess pastry. Line the pastry with crumpled greaseproof paper or foil and fill with baking beans or rice.

4 Place the flan tin on a baking tray and bake for 15–20 minutes. Remove the paper and beans or rice. Reduce the oven temperature to 180°C/350°F/Gas 4 and bake for a further 20 minutes, or until the pastry case is dry and golden.

5 Meanwhile, make the salsa verde. Put the garlic, parsley, olive oil, dill, mustard, red wine vinegar and baby capers in a food processor and process until almost smooth.

6 Boil, steam or microwave the potato until just tender, but do not overcook. Drain if necessary. Heat the oil in a large frying pan and add the garlic, pepper and onion. Cook over a medium-high heat for 3 minutes, stirring frequently. Add the courgettes, dill, thyme and capers and cook for a further 3 minutes, stirring frequently. Add the potato and artichoke hearts, reduce the heat to low and cook for a further 3–4 minutes, or until the potato and artichokes are heated through. Season to taste with salt and pepper.

7 To assemble the tart, spread about 4 tablespoons of the salsa verde over the base of the pastry case. Spoon the vegetable mixture into the case and drizzle with half the remaining salsa verde. Pile the baby spinach leaves in the centre and drizzle with the remaining salsa verde. Serve immediately.

## Cook's File

Note: Baking blind is cooking the pastry case without any filling. Line the flan tin with the pastry and prick the base all over with a fork. Lay a circle of greaseproof paper or foil over the base of the flan case. Add enough dried beans or special ceramic or metal baking beads to cover the base in a fairly thick layer. The purpose of these weights is to prevent the pastry case from rising too much and becoming distorted. The baking beads, whether real or man-made, can be stored and re-used for baking blind. However, dried beans cannot be cooked and eaten after baking.

Hint: To trim excess pastry when lining a flan tin, gently press the excess pastry over the rim of the tin, then roll across it with a rolling pin. The edges of the tin will cut off the excess pastry, which can then be easily removed.

Step 1

Step 3

Step 5

# Festive Vegetables and Salads

## Grilled Vegetables with Garlic Mayonnaise

preparation time 30 minutes   total cooking time 15 minutes   serves 8

### INGREDIENTS

*2 medium aubergines, cut into thin slices*
*salt*
*2 medium red peppers*
*4 small leeks, halved lengthways*
*4 small courgettes, halved lengthways*
*8 large flat mushrooms*

*Dressing*
*1 tablespoon balsamic vinegar*
*2 tablespoons Dijon mustard*
*2 teaspoons dried oregano leaves*
*250 ml/8 fl oz olive oil*

*Garlic Mayonnaise*
*2 egg yolks*
*1 tablespoon lemon juice*
*2 cloves garlic, crushed*
*250 ml/8 fl oz olive oil*
*1 tablespoon chopped chives*
*1 tablespoon chopped parsley*
*1 tablespoon water*

*1* Sprinkle the aubergine slices with salt and allow to stand for 30 minutes. Rinse under cold water, then pat dry with kitchen paper. Cut the peppers into eighths.

*2* Place the aubergines, leeks, peppers and courgettes in a single layer on a flat grill pan and brush with dressing. Cook under a preheated grill on high for 5 minutes, brushing occasionally with dressing. Add the mushrooms, cap side up, to the grill pan and brush with dressing. Continue to cook the vegetables for 10 minutes or until tender, turning the mushrooms only once. Brush the vegetables several times with dressing during cooking.

*3* To make the garlic mayonnaise, place the egg yolks, lemon juice and garlic in a food processor bowl or blender and blend for 5 seconds until combined. With the motor running, add the oil slowly in a thin, steady stream until all the oil is added and the mayonnaise is thick and creamy. Add the chives, parsley and water, and blend for 3 seconds until combined.

### Cook's File

Storage time: The mayonnaise can be made several days ahead; store in the refrigerator. Cook the vegetables just before serving.

Hint: Do not worry if the dressing separates; simply brush on as required.

# Braised

## Celery

preparation time 15 minutes

total cooking time 40 minutes

serves 6

## INGREDIENTS

*25 g/1 oz butter, plus extra for greasing*

*1 celery head*

*475 ml/16 fl oz chicken stock*

*2 teaspoons finely grated lemon rind*

*4 tablespoons lemon juice*

*4 tablespoons single cream*

*2 egg yolks*

*1 tablespoon cornflour*

*4 tablespoons chopped parsley*

*½ teaspoon ground mace*

*salt and freshly ground white pepper*

*1* Lightly brush a 1.5 litre/2½ pint shallow ovenproof dish with melted butter. Preheat the oven to 180°C/350°F/ Gas 4. Trim the celery and cut it into 5 cm/2 inch lengths. Melt the butter in a large pan over a medium heat. Add the celery and toss to coat evenly. Cover and cook for 2 minutes.

*2* Add the stock, lemon rind and juice. Lower the heat, cover and simmer for 10 minutes. Remove the celery with a slotted spoon and place in the prepared dish. Reserve 475 ml/16 fl oz of the cooking liquid.

*3* Blend the cream, egg yolks and cornflour together. Whisk in the reserved cooking liquid and pour into a medium-size pan. Cook over a medium heat until the mixture boils and thickens. Add the parsley and mace and season to taste with salt and pepper.

*4* Pour the sauce evenly over the celery and cook in the oven for about 15–20 minutes, or until the celery is tender. Serve immediately.

*Step 1*

*Step 2*

*Step 4*

# Sautéed Rosemary Potatoes

preparation time 15–20 minutes

total cooking time 35 minutes

serves 4–6

## INGREDIENTS

*675 g/1¼ lb baby new potatoes*
*25 g/1 oz butter*
*2 tablespoons olive oil*
*pepper*
*2 garlic cloves, crushed*
*1 tablespoon finely chopped rosemary*
*1 teaspoon coarse sea salt*
*½ teaspoon crushed black peppercorns*

*1* Wash the potatoes and pat dry with kitchen paper. Cut the potatoes in half and lightly boil or steam them until just tender. Drain and let cool slightly.

*2* Heat the butter and oil in a large heavy-based frying pan. When the mixture is foaming, add the potatoes and season with pepper. Cook over a medium heat for 5–10 minutes, or until golden and crisp, tossing regularly to ensure that the potatoes are evenly coloured.

*3* Stir in the garlic, rosemary and sea salt. Cook for 1 minute, or until well coated. Add the crushed pepper and mix well. Serve hot or warm.

## Cook's File

Variation: Finely chopped thyme or parsley or a mixture of both would work extremely well in this recipe instead of the rosemary. You could also use rock salt as a substitute for the coarse sea salt.

# Seasonal Vegetables

There are numerous delicious vegetable accompaniments to any of our roast meats. Choose two or three of your favourites at their fresh seasonal best to enhance and supplement your roast.

## Broccoli with Almonds

Cut 500 g/1¼ lb broccoli into small florets. Heat 2 teaspoons of oil and 20 g/¾ oz butter in a large frying pan, add 1 crushed garlic clove and 20 g/¾ oz flaked almonds. Cook for 1–2 minutes, or until the almonds are golden. Remove and set aside. Add the broccoli to the pan and toss, cooking for 3–5 minutes or until the broccoli is just tender. Return the almonds to the pan and stir to combine. Serve hot. Serves 4–6.

## Honey-roasted Pumpkin

Preheat the oven to 200°C/400°F/Gas 6. Bring a large pan of water to the boil. Add 1 kg/2¼ lb peeled butternut pumpkin, cut into 2.5 cm/ 1 inch chunks, and 2 tablespoons of honey. Boil for 3–5 minutes, or until just tender. Drain well. Place in a baking dish and drizzle with 1 tablespoon oil and 1 tablespoon honey. Toss to coat. Bake for 30–40 minutes, or until cooked through. Sprinkle with 2 teaspoons toasted sesame seeds and serve. Serves 6–8.

## Celeriac and Tarragon Purée

Bring 500 ml/18 fl oz vegetable stock, 500 ml/18 fl oz water and the juice of 1 lemon to the boil. Add 3 peeled and chopped medium celeriacs, and cook for 10–15 minutes, or until tender. Drain and place in a food processor with 40 g/1½ oz butter and 1 tablespoon cream. Season and process until smooth. Add 1 tablespoon finely chopped fresh tarragon and process for a further 10 seconds. If it is too thick, add a little water. Serves 6.

*LEFT TO RIGHT Celeriac and Tarragon Purée; Vichy Carrots; Broccoli with Almonds; Honey-roasted Pumpkin; Duchess Potatoes; Brussels Sprouts and Chestnuts*

# Duchess Potatoes

Preheat the oven to 180°C/350°F/Gas 4. Quarter 1 kg/2¼ lb floury potatoes and steam or boil until just tender. Drain well, return to the pan and mash. Beat together 2 eggs, 80 ml/3 fl oz cream and ¼ teaspoon grated nutmeg. Season to taste with salt and black pepper. Add to the potato and mash until smooth and thick, but not too stiff. Allow to cool slightly. Put the potato in a piping bag with a 2 cm/¾ inch star nozzle. Pipe in swirls, not too close together, on to two greased baking trays. Brush with an egg yolk. Bake for 15–20 minutes, or until golden. Serves 6–8.

# Brussels Sprouts and Chestnuts

Make slits in the skins of 500 g/1¼ lb chestnuts and put them in a pan. Cover with cold water and place over high heat. Bring to the boil, then reduce the heat and simmer for 10 minutes; drain and leave until cool enough to handle. Peel off the skins. Trim 1 kg/ 2¼ lb of Brussels sprouts and cut a cross in the bottom of each. Bring a pan of water to the boil, add the sprouts and cook at a fast simmer for 5–8 minutes, or until just tender. Melt 25 g/1 oz of butter in a large frying pan and add the chestnuts. Cook until they begin to brown then add the sprouts, tossing together. Season well with salt, pepper and nutmeg. Serves 6–8.

# Vichy Carrots

Trim and peel 1 kg/2¼ lb carrots and cut into batons. Bring a pan of water to the boil and cook the carrots for 3–5 minutes, or until tender. Drain well. Melt 40 g/1½ oz butter in the pan and add 2 teaspoons of sugar. Return the carrots to the pan and toss together until the carrots start to colour a little. Add 2 teaspoons of lemon juice and 2 teaspoons of chopped fresh parsley and toss together. Serves 6.

# Honeyed Baby Turnips with Lemon Thyme

preparation time 10 minutes

total cooking time 10 minutes

serves 4

## INGREDIENTS

*500 g/1¼ lb baby turnips*

*40 g/1½ oz butter*

*4 tablespoons clear honey*

*1 tablespoon lemon juice*

*½ teaspoon grated lemon rind*

*1 tablespoon lemon thyme leaves*

*1* Rinse and lightly scrub the turnips under cold running water and trim the tips and stalks. Cook in boiling water for 1 minute. Drain, rinse under cold water and drain again.

*2* Heat the butter in a medium-size pan. Add the honey and bring to the boil, then add the lemon juice and rind. Continue to boil over a high heat for 3 minutes. Add the turnips to the pan. Cook over high heat for 3 minutes, or until the turnips are almost tender and well glazed (test with a skewer).

*3* Add the lemon thyme. Remove the pan from the heat and toss until the turnips are well coated with the honey mixture. Serve warm.

## Cook's File

Note: If you can find French turnips, also known as navets, use these instead as they have a much more delicate flavour than winter turnips. They are small and relatively flat with attractive purple and white skins. Really fresh, unblemished navets do not require peeling, which makes for a colourful dish.

# Sugar Snap Peas *and* Carrots in Lime Butter

preparation time 10 minutes    total cooking time 10 minutes    serves 4

## INGREDIENTS

*115 g/4 oz carrots*

*115 g/4 oz sugar snap peas*

*40 g/1½ oz butter*

*2 garlic cloves, crushed*

*1 tablespoon lime juice*

*½ teaspoon brown sugar*

*rind of 1 lime, cut into strips, to garnish*

*1* Cut the carrots into thin diagonal slices. Wash and, if necessary, string the sugar snap peas. Melt the butter in a large heavy-based frying pan. Add the garlic and cook over a low heat, stirring constantly, for 1 minute. Add the lime juice and sugar. Cook over a low heat, stirring constantly until the sugar has dissolved.

*2* Add the peas and carrots and cook over a medium heat for 2–3 minutes, or until the vegetables are tender but still crisp. Serve hot, garnished with lime rind.

## Cook's File

Variation: For Peppered Peas and Garlic, heat 1 tablespoon vegetable oil in a heavy-based frying pan. Add 2 crushed garlic cloves and 1 teaspoon crushed black peppercorns. Stir in 225 g/8 oz frozen green peas and ½ teaspoon sugar. Cook over a medium heat for 2–3 minutes, or until the peas are tender. Drizzle with balsamic vinegar and serve hot.

For Sautéed Peas and Spring Onions, heat 25 g/1 oz butter in a heavy-based frying pan. Add 225 g/8 oz frozen green peas, 1 crushed garlic clove and 2 finely sliced spring onions. Stir over a medium heat for 2–3 minutes, or until the peas and onions are just tender. Serve hot.

For Sweet Coriander Peas, heat 25 g/1 oz butter in a pan. Add 1½ teaspoons lemon juice, ½ teaspoon sugar and 225 g/8 oz frozen green peas. Cook over a medium heat for 2–3 minutes, or until just tender. Add 2 tablespoons finely chopped coriander leaves and toss well.

Note: To make the garnish, peel the lime rind into long strips with a vegetable peeler. Remove the pith and cut the rind into thin strips with a sharp knife.

# Potato

## Salad

preparation time 15 minutes

total cooking time 25 minutes

serves 8

## INGREDIENTS

8 large waxy potatoes, diced into 2 cm/
  ¼ inch cubes
4 tablespoons mayonnaise
40 g/1½ oz coriander leaves
2 tablespoons olive oil
1 teaspoon lemon juice
salt and pepper
1 teaspoon olive oil
6 small spring onions, very thinly sliced
1 tablespoon balsamic vinegar
4 tomatoes, seeded and finely chopped
300 g/11 oz bacon, rind removed and
  thinly sliced
1 hard-boiled egg
50 g/2 oz mangetout sprouts

1 Boil or microwave the potato until just tender – do not overcook. Refresh under cold water, drain and place in a large bowl.

2 Combine the mayonnaise, coriander leaves, olive oil and lemon juice in a blender or food processor and process until smooth. Season to taste.

3 Heat the oil in a frying pan. Add the spring onions and balsamic vinegar and stir. Cook over a low heat for about 3 minutes; cool and add to the mayonnaise mixture, together with the chopped tomatoes. Pour over the potato and toss to coat. Cover with clear film and refrigerate until ready to serve.

4 Fry the bacon until very crisp and then drain on kitchen paper. Grate or finely chop the hard-boiled egg. Add the bacon, egg and mangetout sprouts to the salad, toss and serve.

*Step 3*

*Step 4*

# Orange Poppy Seed Vegetables

preparation time 20 minutes

total cooking time 50–60 minutes

serves 6–8

## INGREDIENTS

500 g/1¼ lb new potatoes, halved
6 parsnips, quartered lengthways
500 g/1¼ lb sweet potatoes, diced
350 g/12 oz baby carrots, with tops
6 pickling onions, halved
5 tablespoons vegetable oil
2 tablespoons poppy seeds
200 g/7 oz Brie, thinly sliced

Orange Dressing
120 ml/4 fl oz orange juice
2 garlic cloves, crushed
1 tablespoon Dijon mustard
1 teaspoon white wine vinegar
1 teaspoon sesame oil

1 Preheat the oven to 200°C/400°F/ Gas 6. Put the potatoes, parsnips, sweet potatoes, carrots, onions and oil in a large, deep ovenproof dish. Toss all the vegetables well to coat with the oil. Bake, tossing every 15 minutes, for 50–60 minutes, or until the vegetables are crisp and tender. Remove from the oven and sprinkle with the poppy seeds.

2 Meanwhile, make the orange dressing. Whisk together the orange juice, garlic, mustard, vinegar and sesame oil in a small bowl to combine.

3 Pour the dressing over the warm vegetables and toss to coat. Transfer to a large serving bowl, top with the Brie and serve immediately, while still warm.

Step 1.

Step 2

# Cabbage and Cauliflower

Cabbage, so often overcooked, has not always been kindly looked upon. One of the most nutritious vegetables, it can be delicious if imaginatively prepared. Cauliflower has also suffered by being buried under thick white sauce. Here are some tasty alternatives.

## Quick Coleslaw

Finely shred ½ a small green cabbage. Combine with 2 grated carrots, 1 finely chopped celery stick, 1 finely chopped onion, 1 finely chopped small green or red pepper and 120 ml/4 fl oz prepared coleslaw dressing in a large bowl. Toss well to combine. Add mixed freshly chopped herbs if desired. Chill well before serving. Serves 4–6.

## Sweet Red Cabbage with Caraway Seeds

Finely shred ½ a small red cabbage. Heat 25 g/1 oz butter, 1 teaspoon of caraway seeds, 1 teaspoon of balsamic vinegar and 1 teaspoon of soft brown sugar in a pan. Add the cabbage; cook, stirring, for 2–3 minutes or until just tender. Serve hot. Serves 4–6.

## Cabbage and Potato Cakes

Combine 115 g/4 oz cooked shredded cabbage, 115 g/ 4 oz roughly mashed potato, 1 finely chopped spring onion, 2 lightly beaten eggs and salt and freshly ground pepper to taste and mix well. Heat some oil or butter in a frying pan. Cook spoonfuls of the mixture in small batches for about 2 minutes each side or until golden. Drain on kitchen paper. Serve hot. Serves 4–6.

## Garlic Pepper Cabbage

Finely shred ½ a small green cabbage. Heat 25 g/1 oz butter and 1 teaspoon oil in a heavy-based frying pan or wok. Add 2 teaspoons of garlic pepper seasoning and the cabbage. Stir-fry for 2–3 minutes or until tender. Serve hot. Serves 4–6.

# Cauliflower *with* Bacon

Cut 1 small cauliflower into florets. Steam or microwave until just tender. Heat 1 teaspoon of oil in a medium pan. Add 2 finely shredded bacon rashers and cook until browned. Add the cauliflower and 2 finely chopped spring onions and stir to combine. Serve hot. Serves 4–6.

# Hot Chilli Cauliflower

Cut 1 small cauliflower into florets. Steam or microwave until just tender. Mix together 40 g/1½ oz of melted butter, 1 tablespoon tomato paste, 2 tablespoons chopped fresh coriander and ¼ teaspoon chilli powder (or to taste) in a large bowl. Toss through the cauliflower. Serve hot. Serves 4–6.

# Cauliflower *with* Tomato Sauce

Cut 1 small cauliflower into medium florets. Steam or microwave cauliflower until just tender. Heat 1 tablespoon of oil in a medium pan. Add ½ teaspoon cracked black pepper, 1 teaspoon mixed Italian herbs and 1 crushed garlic clove. Cook for 1 minute. Add one 400 g/14 oz can chopped tomatoes. Bring to the boil, reduce the heat and simmer for 5 minutes or until reduced slightly. Pour the sauce over the vegetables and serve hot. Serves 4–6.

# Parmesan Cauliflower

Cut 1 small cauliflower into florets. Combine, in a bowl, 25 g/1 oz plain flour, 2 tablespoons finely grated Parmesan cheese and 1 teaspoon dried mixed herbs. Toss the florets in this mixture. Heat 2 tablespoons oil and 40 g/ 1½ oz of butter in a heavy-based frying pan. Gently cook the cauliflower in batches until just tender. Drain on kitchen paper. Serve hot. Serves 4–6.

# Tomato Pasta Salad

preparation time 20 minutes

total cooking time 12 minutes

serves 10

## INGREDIENTS

25 g/1 oz sun-dried tomatoes in
   oil, drained
1–2 garlic cloves, crushed
1 tablespoon balsamic vinegar
2 tablespoons oil, from the sun-
   dried tomatoes
120 ml/4 fl oz olive oil
500 g/1¼ lb pasta bows
500 g/1¼ lb fresh asparagus
250 g/9 oz cherry tomatoes
250 g/9 oz yellow plum tomatoes
5 tablespoons chopped flat-leaf parsley
salt and pepper
fresh basil leaves, to garnish

*1* Put the sun-dried tomatoes, garlic, vinegar, sun-dried tomato oil and olive oil in a food processor. Process for 20 seconds, or until the ingredients are thoroughly combined.

*2* Cook the pasta bows in a large pan of boiling, salted water for 10–12 minutes, or until just tender. Drain well.

*3* Plunge the asparagus spears into a bowl of boiling water. Leave for 2 minutes, until vibrant green in colour and slightly tender. Drain, then plunge into a bowl of iced water. When cold, drain and pat dry with kitchen paper. Cut into short lengths. Cut the cherry tomatoes and plum tomatoes in half lengthways.

*4* Assemble the salad while the pasta is still warm: combine the pasta, tomatoes, asparagus and parsley in a large serving bowl. Mix in the tomato dressing. Season with salt and pepper to taste. Garnish with basil leaves.

# Festive Salad

preparation time 15 minutes

total cooking time Nil

serves 8–10

## INGREDIENTS

½ lollo rosso lettuce
½ butterhead lettuce
150 g/5 oz bean sprouts, chopped
1 medium red pepper, seeded and cut
    into thin strips
1 red onion, thinly sliced
5 tablespoons coriander leaves
1 large tomato, chopped
1 orange, segmented
1 avocado, peeled, stoned
    and chopped
2 tablespoons coarsely chopped
    roasted macadamia nuts

Macadamia Nut Dressing
2 tablespoons macadamia nut oil
2 tablespoons olive oil
2 tablespoons red wine vinegar
1 teaspoon wholegrain mustard
½ teaspoon dried oregano
¼ teaspoon crushed black peppercorns
½ teaspoon salt

1 Tear the lettuces into bite-size pieces. Place in a large mixing bowl. Add the bean sprouts, red pepper, onion, coriander and tomato and toss well.

2 Arrange the salad on a large serving platter. Just before serving, top with the orange segments and avocado and sprinkle with the nuts.

3 To make the macadamia nut dressing, place the oils, vinegar, mustard, oregano, peppercorns and salt in a small, screwtop jar. Shake vigorously for 1 minute or until they are thoroughly combined and emulsified. Drizzle the dressing over the salad just before serving.

## Cook's File

Make your salad extra special by sprinkling it with crisp bacon bits, plain or garlic-flavoured croûtons, black olives, sun-dried tomatoes, capers, or even smoked oysters or dried fruits.

# *Mushroom Nut Roast*

preparation time 30 minutes

total cooking time 1 hour

serves 4–6

## INGREDIENTS

butter, for greasing
2 tablespoons olive oil
1 large onion, diced
2 garlic cloves, crushed
300 g/11 oz open cap mushrooms,
  finely chopped
200 g/7 oz unroasted cashew nuts
200 g/7 oz Brazil nuts
115 g/4 oz Cheddar cheese, grated
4 tablespoons freshly grated
  Parmesan cheese
1 egg, lightly beaten
2 tablespoons chopped chives
75 g/3 oz fresh wholemeal breadcrumbs
lemon wedges, to garnish
mixed salad, to serve

*1* Preheat the oven to 180°C/350°F/ Gas 4. Grease an 11 x 21 cm/ 4½ x 8½ inch loaf tin and line the base with greaseproof paper.

*2* Heat the oil in a frying pan. Add the onion, garlic and mushrooms and cook over a medium heat for 5 minutes, or until softened. Transfer to a large bowl and set aside to cool.

*3* Put the nuts into a food processor and process until finely chopped, but do not overprocess.

*4* Add the nuts, cheeses, egg, chives and breadcrumbs to the mushroom mixture and mix thoroughly. Spoon into the prepared loaf tin, pressing down firmly. Bake for 45 minutes, or until firm. Leave for 5 minutes, then turn out the roast, cut into slices, garnish with lemon wedges and serve with a mixed salad.

# Wild and Brown Rice Salad

preparation time 20 minutes

total cooking time 40 minutes

serves 6

## INGREDIENTS

*90 g/3½ oz wild rice*
*200 g/7 oz brown rice*
*1 medium red onion*
*1 small red pepper, seeded*
*2 celery sticks*
*2 tablespoons chopped parsley*
*4 tablespoons chopped pecan nuts*
*pitta or crusty bread, to serve (optional)*

*Dressing*
*4 tablespoons orange juice*
*4 tablespoons lemon juice*
*1 teaspoon finely grated orange rind*
*1 teaspoon finely grated lemon rind*
*5 tablespoons olive oil*

*1* Cook the wild rice in a pan of boiling water for 30–40 minutes, until just tender. Drain and allow to cool completely. Meanwhile, cook the brown rice in a pan of boiling water for 25–30 minutes, drain well and allow to cool completely.

*2* Chop the onion and red pepper finely. Cut the celery into thin slices. Combine them in a bowl, together with the parsley and the cooked rices. Place the pecans in a dry frying pan and stir over a medium heat for 2–3 minutes, until lightly toasted. Transfer to a plate to cool.

*3* To make the dressing, put the orange and lemon juices, rinds and the olive oil in a small screwtop jar and then shake well to combine.

*4* Pour the dressing over the salad and gently fold through. Add the pecans and gently mix through. Serve with pitta or crusty bread, if desired.

## Cook's File

Wild rice, despite its name, is not really a type of rice at all, but the seed of an aquatic grass that is indigenous to North America, where it was traditionally harvested by the Native Americans. A slightly different variety is grown in Asia. True wild rice is hard to find and is often very expensive, but worth it for the wonderful flavour and aroma. Cultivated types grown for the commercial market have somewhat less flavour, but are also less expensive. Be careful when preparing, as overcooking wild rice will diminish its flavour.

# *Mediterranean* *Salad*

preparation time 40 minutes

total cooking time 2 minutes

serves 8

## INGREDIENTS

1 medium aubergine

salt

2 tablespoons vegetable oil

250 g/9 oz cherry tomatoes, halved

2 small cucumbers, sliced

1 red onion, very thinly sliced

250 g/9 oz feta cheese, cut into 2 cm/
    ¼ inch cubes

75 g/3 oz stoned black olives

5 tablespoons finely chopped basil leaves

Dressing

5 tablespoons olive oil

1 tablespoon balsamic vinegar

1 garlic clove, crushed

1 tablespoon chopped oregano

*1* Cut the aubergine into 2.5 cm/1 inch cubes and spread out on a plate. Sprinkle with a little salt and let stand for 30 minutes. Rinse under cold water and pat dry with kitchen paper.

*2* Heat the oil in a shallow pan. Add the aubergine and cook, stirring, over a medium heat for 2 minutes, or until lightly browned and tender. Drain on kitchen paper and cool. Combine the aubergine, tomatoes, cucumbers, onion, cheese, olives and basil in a large bowl.

*3* To make the dressing, put all the ingredients in a small screwtop jar. Shake vigorously for 10 seconds. Add to the salad and toss until mixed well.

## *Cook's File*

Storage time: Both salad and dressing can be made ahead. Combine just before serving.

*Step 1*

*Step 2*

*Step 3*

# Warm Duck Salad

preparation time 15 minutes

total cooking time Nil

serves 4

## INGREDIENTS

1 large Chinese barbecued duck,
  chopped, warmed (see Cook's File)
275 g/10 oz can mandarin segments, drained
115 g/4 oz mangetout, trimmed
50 g/2 oz bean sprouts
50 g/2 oz canned water chestnuts,
  drained, rinsed and sliced
50 g/2 oz sliced spring onions

*Dressing*
4 tablespoons peanut oil
1 tablespoon cider or white wine vinegar
1 tablespoon honey, warmed
2 teaspoons grated fresh root ginger
1 teaspoon soy sauce
¼ teaspoon Chinese five-spice powder

*1* Half an hour before serving, place all the dressing ingredients in a small, screwtop jar and shake vigorously for 1 minute.

*2* Place the duck, drained mandarin segments, mangetout, bean sprouts, water chestnuts and spring onions in a large serving bowl. Add the dressing, toss gently and serve.

## Cook's File

Note: This unusual salad is quite delicious, has a festive air and has the advantage of being very easy to assemble at a time of year when the family cook is often hard-pressed. Any kind of Chinese duck from a supermarket or reliable take-away is suitable — crispy aromatic duck or Peking duck would both work well. Warm through in a steamer or the microwave. The mandarin segments make the perfect partnership because their slight citrus tang cuts through the richness of the duck.

Hint: Make sure that you use Chinese five-spice powder, not the very different Indian one.

# Penne Salad with Sun-dried Tomatoes

preparation time 20 minutes

total cooking time 10 minutes

serves 6

## INGREDIENTS

500 g/1¼ lb dried penne
3 tablespoons olive oil
150 g/5 oz sun-dried tomatoes in
   oil, drained
25 g/1 oz basil leaves
75 g/3 oz  stoned black olives, halved
2 teaspoons white wine vinegar
1 garlic clove, cut in half
50 g/2 oz Parmesan cheese, shaved,
   to garnish

*1* Cook the pasta in a large pan of lightly salted boiling water for 10 minutes, or until just tender. Drain, rinse under cold water and drain again. Place in a large serving bowl and toss with 1 tablespoon of the olive oil to prevent it from sticking together.

*2* Thinly slice the sun-dried tomatoes. Mix the basil leaves and sun-dried tomatoes into the pasta, together with the black olives.

*3* Place the remaining oil, the vinegar and garlic in a small screwtop jar and shake well. Leave for 5 minutes, then discard the garlic. Shake the dressing again and pour it over the salad. Toss gently to combine. Garnish with shavings of Parmesan and serve immediately.

## Cook's File

Note: Sun-dried tomatoes have a very intense, concentrated flavour and are surprisingly sweet. You may be able to obtain genuinely sun-dried tomatoes, but most commercial varieties are actually air-dried. They are available in packets or preserved in olive oil. The former should be soaked in hot water to soften them before cooking. The flavoured soaking water may be used in stocks and sauces. The oil in jars of sun-dried tomatoes is very flavoursome and may be used for cooking.

Hint: You can use any pasta shapes for this salad. Penne — quills — are good because they are chunky and hollow, so they 'trap' the other ingredients, but farfalle — bows, conchiglie — shells, fusilli — spirals, or rotelle — wheels, would all work just as well.

# Coleslaw

preparation time 10 minutes

total cooking time Nil

serves 6–8

## INGREDIENTS

150 g/5 oz white cabbage
150 g/5 oz red cabbage
2 medium carrots
3 spring onions
4 tablespoons mayonnaise
1 tablespoon white wine vinegar
½ teaspoon French mustard
salt and pepper

*1* Finely shred the cabbages, grate the carrots and finely chop the spring onions. Combine in a large bowl and toss together until well mixed.

*2* Whisk together the mayonnaise, vinegar and mustard until thoroughly combined and season to taste with salt and pepper. Add the dressing to the salad and toss gently to mix.

## Cook's File

Variation: A variety of other ingredients may be added to basic coleslaw to give it a special taste. For example, grate a crisp green eating apple, such as Granny Smiths, and stir it in with the dressing. For a stronger flavour, grate a small onion and use instead of the spring onions. For a fruitier taste, add 50 g/2 oz plump sultanas or chopped, dried, ready-to-eat apricots or prunes.

# Cottage Cheese Salad

preparation time 20 minutes

total cooking time 5 minutes

serves 4

### INGREDIENTS

1 sheet lavash tanoory bread
2 teaspoons vegetable oil
sweet paprika, to sprinkle
16 red oak leaf lettuce leaves
2 tablespoons chopped chives
500 g/1¼ lb cottage cheese
200 g/7 oz red grapes
1 medium carrot, grated
4 tablespoons alfalfa sprouts

1 Preheat the oven to 180°C/350°F/ Gas 4. Brush the lavash bread with the oil and sprinkle lightly with paprika. Cut in half lengthways, then across into 16 strips. Place on a baking tray and bake for 5 minutes, or until golden. Remove from the oven and cool on a rack.

2 Wash and dry the lettuce thoroughly. Mix together the chives and cottage cheese. Arrange the lettuce, cheese, grapes, grated carrot and alfalfa sprouts on individual serving plates, with four lavash crisps on the side. Serve immediately.

## Cook's File

Note: Cottage cheese originated in America and is made from the curds of skimmed milk. Its low fat content makes it a dieter's choice. It goes well with fruit.

Note: Lavash tanoory is a flat bread somewhat similar to pitta in texture and flavour.

---

# Nachos Salad

preparation time 20 minutes

total cooking time Nil

serves 4

### INGREDIENTS

425 g/15 oz can red kidney beans
1 large tomato, diced
120 ml/4 fl oz ready-made mild salsa
250 g/9 oz packet plain corn or
    tortilla chips
8 lettuce leaves, shredded
1 small avocado, peeled, stoned
    and sliced
1 tablespoon lemon juice
25 g/1 oz Cheddar cheese, grated

1 Empty the beans into a colander or strainer and rinse under cold running water. Drain well and place in a bowl. Add the diced tomato and salsa and mix thoroughly to combine.

2 Arrange a bed of corn or tortilla chips on individual serving plates and top with the lettuce then the bean mixture. Gently toss the avocado slices in the lemon juice and arrange them on top of the salad. Sprinkle with the grated cheese and serve immediately.

## Cook's File

Hint: Salsas are very quick and easy to make at home. For a sweet pepper salsa, place 1 red pepper and 1 yellow pepper under a preheated grill for 8–10 minutes, until the skins are charred and blistered. Remove with tongs, place on a work surface and cover with a tea towel. Meanwhile, dry-fry 1 teaspoon cumin seeds for about 1 minute, until they give off their aroma. Crush in a mortar with a pestle. When the peppers are cool enough to handle, make a hole in the base of each and squeeze the juices into a small bowl. Peel and seed the peppers and put the flesh in a food processor with the cumin seeds, 1 seeded fresh red chilli and 3 tablespoons chopped coriander. Process briefly until finely chopped. Mix together the spiced peppers, the pepper juices, 2 tablespoons olive oil and 1 tablespoon white wine vinegar and season to taste with salt and pepper. Store in the refrigerator.

# Farfalle Salad *with* Sun-Dried Tomatoes and Spinach

preparation time 20 minutes   total cooking time 12 minutes   serves 4–6

## INGREDIENTS

*500 g/1¼ lb dried farfalle or fusilli*

*3 spring onions*

*50 g/2 oz sun-dried tomatoes in oil,*
*   drained and cut into strips*

*500 g/1¼ lb spinach, stalks trimmed and*
*   leaves shredded*

*4 tablespoons toasted pine nuts*

*1 tablespoon chopped oregano*

*Dressing*
*4 tablespoons olive oil*
*1 teaspoon chopped fresh chilli*
*1 garlic clove, crushed*
*salt and pepper*

*1* Cook the pasta in a large pan of lightly salted boiling water for 8–10 minutes, until just tender. Drain the pasta and rinse well under cold water. Transfer to a large salad bowl.

*2* Trim the spring onions and chop finely. Add them to the pasta, together with the tomatoes, spinach, pine nuts and oregano.

*3* To make the dressing, put the olive oil, chilli and garlic in a small screwtop jar, season to taste with salt and pepper and shake until well combined. Pour the dressing over the top of the salad, toss well and serve immediately.

## Cook's File

Hint: Use tender baby spinach leaves in salads. Look for crisp, unblemished deep-green leaves with no discoloration or signs of slug damage. Store in a cool place for no more than two days before using. Wash thoroughly in several changes of cold water and shake dry.

Variation: Other more exotic leaves may be used in combination with the spinach to make the salad extra special. Try rocket, sorrel or roselle, all of which have a strong, pungent flavour. (Sorrel is very sour, so use it sparingly.) You could also use lamb's lettuce, sometimes known as mâche, purslane, young (pollution-free) dandelion leaves, nasturtium leaves, land cress or salad burnet.

# Watercress Salad

preparation time 35 minutes

total cooking time Nil

serves 4–6

## INGREDIENTS

500 g/1¼ lb watercress

3 celery sticks

1 cucumber

3 medium oranges

1 red onion, thinly sliced and separated
    into rings

30 g/1¼ oz chopped chives

50 g/2 oz chopped pecan nuts or walnuts

Dressing

4 tablespoons olive oil

4 tablespoons lemon juice

2 teaspoons grated orange rind

1 teaspoon wholegrain mustard

1 tablespoon clear honey

pepper

*1* To make the salad, wash and drain all the vegetables. Break the watercress into small sprigs, discarding the coarser stems. Cut the celery into thin 5 cm/2 inch long sticks. Peel, halve and seed the cucumber and cut into thin slices. Peel the oranges, remove all the white pith and cut the oranges into segments between the membranes. Chill in the refrigerator until needed.

*2* To make the dressing, put the olive oil, lemon juice, orange rind, mustard and honey in a screwtop jar and season to taste with pepper. Shake vigorously to combine and emulsify.

*3* Put the watercress sprigs, celery, cucumber, orange segments, onion and chives in a large serving bowl. Pour the dressing over and toss lightly to mix. Sprinkle with the pecans or walnuts and serve immediately.

## Cook's File

When buying watercress, the darker and larger the leaves, the better the cress. Watercress does not keep well, but will stay freshest if it is completely submerged in water and stored in the refrigerator. Sprigs of watercress look beautiful in green salads, and its slightly peppery flavour adds contrast. It also makes an excellent garnish for cold soups.

# Fish and Seafood

## Baked Salmon

preparation time 10 minutes

total cooking time 30 minutes, plus 45 minutes standing   serves 8

### INGREDIENTS

*2 kg/4½ lb whole salmon, cleaned, gutted*
*and scaled*
*2 spring onions, roughly chopped*
*3 sprigs fresh dill*
*½ lemon, thinly sliced*
*6 black peppercorns*
*oil, for brushing*
*60 ml/2 fl oz dry white wine*
*3 bay leaves*
*lemon slices, to serve*

*1* Preheat the oven to 180°C/350°F/ Gas 4. Rinse the salmon under cold running water and pat dry inside and out with kitchen paper. Stuff the cavity with the chopped spring onion, dill, lemon slices and peppercorns.

*2* Brush a large double-layered piece of aluminium foil with oil and lay the salmon on the foil. Sprinkle on the wine and arrange the bay leaves over the top. Fold the foil over and wrap up, covering the salmon tightly.

*3* Place in a shallow baking dish and bake for 30 minutes. Turn the oven off and leave the salmon in the oven for 45 minutes with the door closed.

*4* Undo the foil and carefully peel away the skin of the salmon on the top side. Carefully flip the salmon on to the serving plate and remove the skin from the other side. Pull out the fins and any visible bones. Serve at room temperature with lemon slices.

# Spaghetti *Creole*

preparation time 10 minutes

total cooking time 15 minutes

serves 6–8

## INGREDIENTS

500 g/1¼ lb dried spaghetti

50 g/2 oz butter

500 g/1¼ lb raw prawns, peeled
and deveined

75 ml/3 fl oz white wine

400 g/14 oz can peeled tomatoes,
drained and mashed

2 teaspoons curry powder

300 ml/11 fl oz double cream

2 tablespoons freshly grated
Parmesan cheese

salt and pepper

chopped parsley, to garnish

*1* Cook the spaghetti in a large pan of lightly salted boiling water for 10–12 minutes, or until just tender. Drain, rinse under warm water and drain thoroughly again. Return the spaghetti to the pan and cover.

*2* Meanwhile, melt the butter in a frying pan. Add the prawns and cook, stirring frequently, until they have just turned pink. Remove the prawns from the pan and set aside. Add the wine, tomatoes, curry powder, cream and grated cheese and season to taste with salt and pepper. Lower the heat and simmer for 10 minutes. Return the prawns to the pan and heat through for 1–2 minutes.

*3* Add the prawn sauce to the spaghetti and toss over a very low heat for 1–2 minutes, until warmed through. Serve immediately, garnished with parsley.

## Cook's File

Note: The dark vein that runs along the back of prawns is not harmful, but may taste unpleasant, so it should be removed.

# Sesame Prawns *with* Tangy Mint Chutney

preparation time 20 minutes  total cooking time 2 minutes per batch  serves 4

## INGREDIENTS

25 g/1 oz plain flour

50 g/2 oz dried breadcrumbs

115 g/4 oz sesame seeds

24 raw tiger prawns (about 1 kg/
2¼ lb), peeled and deveined,
with tails intact

1 egg, lightly beaten

oil, for deep-frying

Tangy Mint Chutney

25 g/1 oz mint leaves

8 tablespoons fruit chutney

2 tablespoons lemon juice

*1* Put the flour on a plate. Mix the breadcrumbs and sesame seeds on another plate. Toss the prawns in flour, dip in beaten egg and coat in the sesame seed mix.

*2* Heat the oil in a large pan. Fry the prawns over a medium heat for 2 minutes, or until golden brown. Remove with tongs or a slotted spoon. Drain on kitchen paper.

*3* Process all the ingredients for the tangy chutney in a food processor for 15 seconds, or until smooth. Serve as a dip for the prawns.

# Crystal Prawns

preparation time 15 minutes, plus marinating

total cooking time 20 minutes

serves 4

## INGREDIENTS

675 g/1½ lb medium raw prawns
2 spring onions, roughly chopped
2 teaspoons salt
5 teaspoons cornflour
1 egg white, lightly beaten
1 tablespoon oyster sauce
2 teaspoons dry sherry
1 teaspoon sesame oil
oil, for deep-frying
½ teaspoon crushed garlic
½ teaspoon finely grated fresh root ginger
115 g/4 oz sugar snap peas
   or mangetout
1 small red pepper, seeded and cut into
   thin strips

1 Peel and devein the prawns. Place the shells and heads, together with the spring onions, in a pan and cover with water. Bring to the boil and simmer, uncovered, for 15 minutes. Strain and reserve the stock and discard the shells, heads and spring onions.

2 Place the prawns in a glass bowl. Add 1 teaspoon of the salt and stir briskly for 1 minute. Rinse under cold, running water. Repeat twice, using ½ teaspoon salt each time. Rinse the prawns thoroughly the final time. Pat dry on kitchen paper.

3 Mix together 4 teaspoons of the cornflour and the egg white in a bowl. Add the prawns and marinate for 30 minutes in the refrigerator.

4 Combine 120 ml/4 fl oz of the reserved stock, the oyster sauce, sherry, remaining cornflour and the sesame oil in a small bowl. Heat the oil in a wok or deep heavy-based frying pan. Gently lower the prawns into the oil. Cook over a medium heat for 1–2 minutes, or until lightly golden. Remove from the oil with tongs. Drain on kitchen paper. Keep warm.

5 Pour off all but 2 tablespoons of the oil. Return the pan to the heat. Add the garlic and ginger and stir-fry for 30 seconds. Add the sugar snap peas or mangetout and pepper and stir-fry over a high heat for 2 minutes. Add the sherry sauce and cook, stirring, until it boils and thickens. Add the prawns and stir to combine. Serve immediately.

# Spanish Prawn Salad

preparation time 25 minutes

total cooking time Nil

serves 6

## INGREDIENTS

2 large oranges
1 small Cos lettuce
500 g/1¼ lb cooked tiger prawns, peeled
   and deveined, with tails intact
1 small red onion, finely sliced
2 tablespoons red wine vinegar
4 tablespoons olive oil
½ teaspoon finely grated orange rind
1 garlic clove, crushed
crusty bread, to serve

1 Cut a slice off each end of the oranges to where the flesh starts. Using a small knife, cut the skin away in a circular motion, cutting just deep enough to remove all the white membrane (reserve a little peel for grating). Separate the segments by cutting between the membranes and the flesh.

2 Wash and dry the lettuce thoroughly. Arrange the leaves on individual plates or a serving platter, top with the prawns, orange segments and onion rings.

3 Place the vinegar, olive oil, orange rind and garlic in a small screwtop jar and shake well. Drizzle over the salad and serve immediately with crusty bread.

## Cook's File

Choose firm prawns with crisp shells and a fresh, pleasant smell; stale prawns will be limp and dry. Frozen prawns are available, but should not be substituted for fresh prawns unless specified in recipes, as the thawed flesh tends to be slightly mushy.

# Tuna Steaks with Olive Paste

preparation time 15 minutes, plus 1 hour marinating

total cooking time 5 minutes

serves 6

### INGREDIENTS

5 tablespoons olive oil

2 tablespoons dry white wine

2 tablespoons lemon juice

6 tuna steaks (about 200 g/7 oz each)

2 tablespoons soured cream

Olive Paste

115 g/4 oz stoned black olives

2 teaspoons capers

1 garlic clove, crushed

1 tablespoon olive oil

1 tablespoon finely chopped parsley

*1* Combine the olive oil, white wine and lemon juice in a small screwtop jar and shake vigorously for 30 seconds. Place the tuna steaks in a single layer in a shallow ceramic or glass dish. Pour the marinade over and set aside in the refrigerator for 1 hour, turning the tuna over halfway through the marinating time.

*2* To make the olive paste, put the olives, capers, garlic and olive oil in a food processor and, using pulse action, process for 30 seconds, or until thoroughly combined. Transfer the paste to a bowl, cover with clear film and store in the refrigerator until required.

*3* Shortly before serving, stir the chopped parsley into the olive paste and set aside for at least 10 minutes at room temperature.

*4* Remove the tuna steaks from the dish and reserve the marinade. Place the steaks in a foil-lined grill pan and cook under a preheated grill on high heat for 2–3 minutes on each side, basting occasionally with the marinade.

*5* To serve, place one tuna steak on each individual plate, top with a tablespoon of olive paste and a teaspoon of soured cream. Serve immediately.

# Tuna Teriyaki

preparation time 10 minutes, plus marinating

total cooking time 10 minutes

serves 4

### INGREDIENTS

500 g/1¼ lb tuna fillet

Teriyaki Marinade

2 cm/¾ inch piece fresh root ginger, finely grated

2 tablespoons shoyu sauce

1 tablespoon lemon juice

2 tablespoons dry sherry

120 ml/4 fl oz fish stock

*1* Remove and discard all the skin from the tuna fillet. Cut the fillet into four even-size pieces.

*2* Combine all the marinade ingredients in a shallow dish. Place the tuna fillets in the marinade and set aside for at least 30 minutes. Turn the tuna during marinating time.

*3* Place the tuna on a foil-lined grill pan and cook under a preheated grill for 2–3 minutes on each side, until the flesh flakes. Baste during cooking, using all the marinade. Serve immediately.

## Cook's File

Note: Shoyu is Japanese soy sauce. Do not substitute Chinese soy sauce, which is very much stronger. There are several different types. Usukuchi is light coloured, delicately flavoured, but quite salty and is good for flavouring cooked dishes. Tamari is thick and rich in flavour. It is most often served as a dipping sauce. Some excellent ready-made teriyaki sauces are available from specialist foodstores and some supermarkets.

Hint: When the summer comes, this dish is an excellent choice for cooking over hot coals on the barbecue.

# Fresh Tuna with Herbs and Balsamic Vinegar

preparation time 5 minutes   total cooking time 10 minutes   serves 4

### INGREDIENTS

2 tablespoons olive oil
4 tuna steaks (about 200 g/7 oz each)
1 tablespoon chopped parsley
1 tablespoon chopped basil
2 tablespoons balsamic vinegar

*1* Heat the oil in a large, heavy-based frying pan. Add the tuna steaks to the pan in a single layer and cook on both sides over a medium heat for about 10 minutes, or until the fish is cooked through. (The cooking time will depend on the thickness of the tuna steaks. Test with a fork and if the flesh flakes easily, the tuna is cooked through.)

*2* Transfer the tuna steaks to a serving plate. Sprinkle with chopped parsley and basil and drizzle with balsamic vinegar. Serve immediately.

## Cook's File

Tuna is an oily fish and should be eaten as fresh as possible. Tuna steaks are usually cooked with the skin on.

# Fresh Tuna Rissoles

preparation time 20 minutes

total cooking time 10–15 minutes

serves 4

### INGREDIENTS

500 g/1¼ lb fresh tuna fillet
1 medium onion, finely chopped
115 g/4 oz mashed potato
1 tablespoon finely chopped pimiento
2 tablespoons finely chopped parsley
pepper
25 g/1 oz seasoned plain flour
1 egg, beaten
115 g/4 oz dried breadcrumbs
oil, for shallow-frying

*1* Skin the tuna fillet. Cut it into small pieces, then mince in a food processor or chop very finely.

*2* Put the tuna into a bowl. Add the onion, potato, pimiento and parsley, season with pepper and mix well. Mould spoonfuls of the mixture into rissoles.

*3* Coat the rissoles with the flour. Dip in beaten egg and roll in breadcrumbs.

*4* Heat the oil in a frying pan. Cook the rissoles, a few at a time, until golden, turning once. Drain on kitchen paper and serve immediately.

## Cook's File

Note: Fresh tuna is increasingly available, usually in the form of steaks and fillets. As there is no waste and because tuna is quite a substantial and filling fish, it is an economic buy. Although it is quite an oily fish, it has a tendency to dry out during cooking, so it should always be carefully prepared.

Variation: This recipe could also be prepared with bonito or even mackerel, which are both members of the same family as tuna.

# Trout *with* Almonds

preparation time 15 minutes

total cooking time 15 minutes

serves 4

## INGREDIENTS

4 trout (about 200 g/7 oz each), cleaned
    and scaled
25 g/1 oz plain flour
pepper
½ teaspoon dried dill leaves
¼ teaspoon dry mustard
5 tablespoons lemon juice
75 g/3 oz butter
50 g/2 oz blanched halved almonds
120 ml/4 fl oz dry white wine
lemon slices and sprigs of dill or parsley,
    to garnish

1 Using scissors, remove the fins from the trout and trim the tails. Wipe over the surface of the fish with damp kitchen paper to remove any loose scales. Season the flour with pepper to taste, the dill and dry mustard.

2 Brush the surface of the fish with lemon juice. Coat the trout all over in seasoned flour to form a crust. Shake off any excess flour.

3 Melt the butter in a large frying pan. Add the almonds and cook, stirring constantly, until golden. Remove from the heat. Drain the almonds on kitchen paper. Add the trout to the pan and cook over a medium heat until tender, turning once and taking care not to break them. Remove the trout from the pan and drain well on kitchen paper.

4 Add the remaining lemon juice and the wine to pan. Simmer, uncovered, over a high heat until the liquid has reduced by half. Add the almonds and pour over the fish. Serve immediately, garnished with lemon slices and dill or parsley sprigs.

# Smoked Trout *with* Kiwi Fruit Salad

preparation time 20 minutes

total cooking time Nil

serves 4

## INGREDIENTS

3 large smoked trout
2 kiwi fruit
1 large ripe avocado
juice and rind of 1 lime
1 tablespoon white wine vinegar
2 tablespoons hazelnut oil
assorted salad leaves, such as butterhead
    lettuce, Cos lettuce, frisée and radicchio
25 g/1 oz hazelnuts, finely chopped

1 Carefully remove the skin from the trout. Then carefully remove the fillets from each side. Cut each fillet into two pieces. Peel and slice the kiwi fruit. Peel, stone and slice the avocado.

2 Combine the lime juice, rind, vinegar and oil and mix thoroughly.

3 Wash and dry the salad leaves and arrange them on either a large serving platter or individual serving plates.

4 Arrange the smoked trout fillets, kiwi fruit and avocado on top of the salad leaves and lightly pour over the lime dressing. Sprinkle with the chopped hazelnuts and serve immediately.

## Cook's File

Hint: The delicate pale-green flesh of avocados discolours very quickly when it is exposed to the air, turning an unappetizing shade of grey. Only peel or slice avocados just before using them and immediately sprinkle the flesh with lemon or lime juice to prevent discoloration. All dishes containing avocado should be served within one hour of preparation and, preferably, as soon as they are ready.

# Fresh Tuna Fettuccine

preparation time 15 minutes

total cooking time 15–20 minutes

serves 8–10

## INGREDIENTS

*675 g/1¼ lb dried fettuccine*

*5 tablespoons olive oil*

*2 large, ripe tomatoes*

*115 g/4 oz fresh asparagus, cut into*
*    3 cm/1¼ inch lengths*

*500 g/1¼ lb tuna steaks*

*3 garlic cloves, crushed*

*2 onions, sliced*

*4 tablespoons finely sliced basil leaves*

*4 tablespoons chopped capers*

*1* Cook the fettuccine in lightly salted boiling water for 8–10 minutes, until tender. Drain and toss with 1 tablespoon of oil. Meanwhile, peel and chop the tomatoes.

*2* Cook the asparagus in a small pan of rapidly boiling water for 2 minutes, or until just tender. Drain, rinse under cold water and drain again.

*3* Heat 1 tablespoon of the remaining oil in a large frying pan. Add the tuna steaks and cook for 2 minutes on each side, or until golden brown on the outside but still moist on the inside.

Remove from the pan. Using a fork, shred the tuna and remove any bones. Set the flesh aside.

*4* Heat the remaining oil in a large pan. Add the garlic and onions and cook over a medium heat, stirring constantly, for 3 minutes, or until the onions are soft and translucent. Add the cooked fettuccine, asparagus, tuna, chopped tomato, basil and chopped capers and stir over a medium heat until all the ingredients are thoroughly combined and heated through. Serve immediately.

# Greek-*Style* Squid

preparation time 30 minutes

total cooking time 35 minutes

serves 6–8

## INGREDIENTS

*Stuffing*

*1 tablespoon olive oil*

*2 spring onions, chopped*

*5 tablespoons pine nuts*

*4 tablespoons currants*

*2 tablespoons chopped parsley*

*2 teaspoons finely grated lemon rind*

*350 g/12 oz cooked rice*

*1 egg, lightly beaten*

*1 kg/2¼ lb prepared medium squid*

*Sauce*

*1 tablespoon olive oil*

*1 onion, finely chopped*

*1 garlic clove, crushed*

*4 large ripe tomatoes, peeled*
*    and chopped*

*4 tablespoons red wine*

*1 tablespoon chopped oregano*

*1* Preheat the oven to 160°C/325°F/ Gas 3. Mix together the oil, onion, pine nuts, currants, parsley, lemon rind and rice in a bowl. Add enough beaten egg to moisten all the ingredients.

*2* Three-quarters fill each squid tube with the stuffing. Secure the end with a cocktail stick or a skewer. Place the squid in a single layer in a casserole dish.

*3* To make the sauce, heat the oil in a pan. Add the onion and garlic and cook over a low heat for 2 minutes, or until the onion is soft and translucent. Add the tomatoes, wine and oregano. Cover and cook over a low heat for 10 minutes.

*4* Pour the sauce over the squid. Cover and bake for 20 minutes, or until tender. Remove the cocktail sticks and slice thickly. Spoon the sauce over and serve.

# Sweet and Sour Fish

preparation time 20 minutes

total cooking time 30 minutes

serves 6–8

## INGREDIENTS

1.5 kg/3 lb 5 oz sea bream or 2 x 750 g/
  1 lb 10 oz sea bream
oil, for brushing
1 teaspoon finely chopped fresh
  root ginger
2 garlic cloves, crushed
2 spring onions, finely chopped
1 teaspoon sesame oil
2 teaspoons soy sauce
120 ml/4 fl oz ready-made sweet-and-sour
  sauce with vegetables

1 Preheat the oven to 180°C/350°F/
Gas 4. Place the fish on a sheet of
lightly oiled foil large enough to enclose it.

2 Mix together the ginger, garlic,
spring onions, sesame oil and soy
sauce in a small bowl. Rub the mixture
into the cavity and all over the fish.

3 Wrap the fish in the foil and place it
on a baking tray. Bake for 30 minutes,
or until tender. Meanwhile, heat the sweet-
and-sour sauce. Pour the sauce over the
fish just before serving.

## Cook's File

Hint: Fish should smell fresh, have bright
protruding eyes and be firm to the touch. Have
the fish cleaned and scaled at the
fishmonger's and cook it within two days of
buying. Before cooking, rinse and pat the fish
dry with kitchen paper both inside and out.
Using a sharp knife or kitchen scissors, trim
the fins and tail. Score the thickest part of the
flesh with a sharp knife for even cooking.

# Chilli Garlic Prawns

preparation time 10 minutes

total cooking time 4 minutes

serves 4–6

## INGREDIENTS

1 tablespoon chilli seasoning mix, or
  1–2 teaspoons chilli powder
2 tablespoons lemon juice
1 teaspoon sugar
4 tablespoons olive oil
1.5 kg/3 lb 5 oz raw tiger prawns, peeled
  and deveined, with tails intact
3 garlic cloves, thinly sliced

1 Mix together the chilli seasoning or
chilli powder, lemon juice, sugar and
2 tablespoons of the oil in a large bowl.
Add the prawns and toss well to coat.

2 Heat the remaining oil in a preheated
wok or large, heavy-based frying pan.
Add the garlic and prawns, stir-fry over a
high heat for 4 minutes, or until just cooked
through and pink. Serve.

## Cook's File

Note: The flesh of raw prawns is usually greyish
or brownish in colour, but the colour of the shell
will vary between different species. Look for
prawns with pale flesh. The longer they stand,
the darker they become. Prawns should have a
fresh salty smell and a firm shell. Prawns which
have been frozen often have a slightly softer
shell with spongy flesh. Frozen prawns should
always be thawed thoroughly before cooking.

# Grilled Oysters

preparation time 6 minutes

total cooking time 3 minutes

serves 4

## INGREDIENTS

120 ml/4 fl oz double cream

¼ teaspoon pepper sauce

2 teaspoons Worcestershire sauce

3 rashers bacon, rind removed finely
   chopped or minced

24 large fresh oysters in halfshells

1 tablespoon ground almonds

1 tablespoon dried breadcrumbs

*1* Mix together the cream, pepper and Worcestershire sauces and the bacon. Arrange the oysters on a large baking tray. Spoon the cream mixture evenly over each oyster. Combine the almonds and breadcrumbs and sprinkle the mixture over the oysters. Cook under a preheated grill for 3 minutes. Serve immediately.

# Seafood Sauce

preparation time 5 minutes, plus chilling

total cooking time Nil

makes 250 ml/8 fl oz

## INGREDIENTS

150 ml/5 fl oz soured cream

1 tablespoon tomato purée

2 tablespoons tomato ketchup

2 teaspoons lemon juice

1 teaspoon Worcestershire sauce

2 teaspoons chopped chives

¼ teaspoon hot pepper sauce (optional)

*1* Mix all the ingredients together in a small mixing bowl. Refrigerate, covered with clear film, for several hours or overnight. Serve with cooked seafood or serve as a dip.

## Cook's File

Hint: To make a quick prawn cocktail, arrange a bed of shredded lettuce in the base of 4 wine glasses. Mix 450 g/1 lb thawed frozen prawns with sufficient seafood sauce to coat and divide between the glasses.

# Poached Salmon Cutlets

preparation time 5 minutes

total cooking time 15 minutes

serves 4

### INGREDIENTS

*350 ml/12 fl oz fish stock*
*½ teaspoon salt*
*½ teaspoon crushed black peppercorns*
*pinch of ground nutmeg*
*120 ml/4 fl oz dry white wine*
*2 spring onions, finely chopped*
*4 salmon cutlets*
*6 tablespoons finely chopped parsley*

*1* Combine the fish stock, salt, peppercorns, nutmeg, wine and spring onions in a shallow medium-size pan. Bring to the boil over a low heat and boil for 1 minute.

*2* Place the salmon cutlets in the stock in a single layer. Cover and simmer for 10 minutes. Transfer the salmon to serving plates and keep warm.

*3* Boil the stock for another minute. Stir in 4 tablespoons of the parsley. Spoon the liquid over the salmon, sprinkle with the remaining parsley and serve.

# Salmon with Dill Mayonnaise

preparation time: 30 minutes, plus chilling   total cooking time 15–20 minutes   serves 4

### INGREDIENTS

*1.5 kg/3 lb 5 oz salmon*
*475 ml/16 fl oz fish stock*
*250 ml/8 fl oz mayonnaise*
*2 tablespoons finely chopped dill*
*pepper*
*sprig of dill, to garnish*

*1* Scale, wash and trim the salmon. Place it in a fish kettle or a large pan. Pour the fish stock over the salmon. Bring to the boil over a low heat and poach without turning for about 15 minutes, or until the flesh flakes easily when tested with a fork.

*2* Remove the salmon and set aside to cool. When it is cold, chill well in the refrigerator, preferably overnight.

*3* Mix together the mayonnaise and dill and season to taste with pepper. Transfer the mixture to a serving bowl and garnish with a sprig of fresh dill.

*4* Carefully skin the salmon on one side and serve from each side of the backbone with a spoon and fork.

## Cook's File

Note: If you can obtain wild salmon, do so, as it has a wonderful flavour that is far superior to farmed salmon and the flesh has a firmer texture. However, it is seasonal – generally between February and August – so you will probably have to compromise with either frozen wild or fresh farmed salmon for Christmas. It is sometimes sold by the name of the river where it was caught, such as Tay or Dee salmon.

# Paella

preparation time 30 minutes

total cooking time 45 minutes

serves 4

## INGREDIENTS

120 ml/4 fl oz white wine

1½ small red onions, finely chopped

12 mussels, scrubbed and beards removed

120 ml/4 fl oz olive oil

1 skinless chicken breast fillet, diced

275 g/10 oz raw prawns, peeled
and deveined

115 g/4 oz prepared squid, cut into rings

115 g/4 oz white fish fillet, cut into cubes

1 rasher bacon, rind removed and
finely chopped

4 garlic cloves, crushed

1 small red pepper, seeded and
finely chopped

1 tomato, peeled and chopped

50 g/2 oz fresh or frozen peas

90 g/3½ oz chorizo or peperoni,
thinly sliced

pinch of cayenne pepper

salt and pepper

200 g/7 oz long-grain rice

¼ teaspoon powdered saffron

475 ml/16 fl oz hot chicken stock

2 tablespoons finely chopped parsley

*1* Heat the wine and two-thirds of the onions in a large pan. Add the mussels, cover and cook over a high heat, shaking the pan frequently, for 3–5 minutes. After 3 minutes, start removing opened mussels and set aside. Discard any that remain unopened. Strain and reserve the cooking liquid.

*2* Heat half the oil in a large frying pan. Add the chicken pieces and cook for 5 minutes, or until golden brown. Remove from the pan and set aside. Add the prawns, squid and fish and cook for 1 minute. Remove and set aside.

*3* Heat the remaining oil. Add the remaining onion, the bacon, garlic and red pepper and cook for 5 minutes, or until the onion is soft. Add the tomato, peas, chorizo or peperoni and cayenne pepper and season to taste with salt and pepper. Add the reserved cooking liquid and stir in the rice.

*4* Blend the saffron with 120 ml/4 fl oz of the stock and add to the pan with the remaining stock. Mix and bring to the boil. Reduce the heat to low and simmer, uncovered, for 15 minutes without stirring.

*5* Place the chicken, prawns, squid and fish on top of the rice. Using a wooden spoon, gently push them into the rice. Cover and continue to cook over a

*Step 5*

low heat for 10–15 minutes, or until the rice is tender and the seafood is cooked through. If the rice is not quite cooked, add a little extra stock and cook for a few minutes more. Serve the paella in large bowls, topped with the mussels, in shells or half shells, and sprinkled with the chopped parsley.

# New Orleans Oysters

preparation time 10 minutes

total cooking time 4–6 minutes

serves 4

## INGREDIENTS

24 large oysters, shells removed

¼ teaspoon freshly ground
white pepper

¼ teaspoon freshly ground
black pepper

¼ teaspoon cayenne pepper

¼ teaspoon dried thyme

¼ teaspoon dried oregano

½ teaspoon paprika

¼ teaspoon dried basil

50 g/2 oz plain flour

120 ml/4 fl oz vegetable oil

40 g/1½ oz unsalted butter

sprigs of dill, to garnish

lemon wedges and mayonnaise, to serve

*1* Dry the oysters on kitchen paper. In a shallow dish, mix the white and black pepper, cayenne pepper, thyme, oregano, paprika and basil. Set aside 2 teaspoons of the spice mix. Add the flour to the remaining spice mix and stir thoroughly.

*2* Thread three oysters on to each of eight oiled skewers and coat with the spiced flour.

*3* Heat the oil and butter in a wide pan. Cook the oysters until golden, turning several times, for about 6 minutes. Drain on kitchen paper. Sprinkle with the reserved spice mix, garnish with dill and serve with lemon wedges and mayonnaise.

## Cook's File

Variation: For Oysters Mornay, melt 15 g/½ oz butter in a small pan and add 2 tablespoons plain flour. Stir over a low heat for 2 minutes. Gradually stir in 250 ml/8 fl oz milk and whisk until the mixture is smooth. Stir over a low heat for 2 minutes, or until the mixture boils and thickens. Add 25 g/1 oz grated Cheddar cheese, ½ teaspoon French mustard, and 1 teaspoon lemon juice and season to taste with salt and freshly ground white pepper. Stir until the mixture is smooth. Spoon the sauce over 24 oysters on half shells, sprinkle with extra grated cheese and cook under a preheated grill until lightly browned. Serves 2–4.

For Oysters Rockefeller, melt 15 g/½ oz butter in a medium-size pan. Add 4 tablespoons finely chopped onion and 1 crushed garlic clove and fry for 3 minutes, until the onion is soft and translucent. Remove from the heat and add 50 g/2 oz finely chopped cooked spinach (well drained) and 175 ml/6 fl oz soured cream. Season with salt and pepper to taste. Spoon the mixture over 24 oysters on half shells. Mix together 25 g/1 oz fine fresh breadcrumbs with 50 g/2 oz grated Cheddar cheese and sprinkle the mixture over the oysters. Cook the oysters under a preheated grill until the topping turns golden brown. Serves 2–4.

Hint: To open, grip the oyster firmly with your hand wrapped in a cloth. Insert a strong knife blade into the hinge between the two shells and twist to prise them open. Slide the blade of the knife along the inside of the upper shell to cut the muscle and lift off the upper shell. Slide the blade under the oyster to cut the muscle below.

# Seafood with Mango Salsa

preparation time 30 minutes, plus chilling

total cooking time 3 minutes

serves 6

## INGREDIENTS

*12 oysters on half shells*
*2 medium prepared squid (about*
 *275 g/10 oz)*
*15 g/½ oz butter*
*1 tablespoon lemon juice*
*1 tablespoon finely chopped parsley*
*12 unpeeled cooked prawns*

*Mango Salsa*
*1 large ripe mango*
*1 small fresh red chilli*
*1 lemon grass stalk*
*1 teaspoon finely chopped coriander*
*1 teaspoon finely grated fresh root ginger*

*Dill Vinaigrette*
*2 tablespoons white wine vinegar*
*120 ml/4 fl oz vegetable oil*
*1 teaspoon Dijon mustard*
*2 teaspoons finely chopped dill*
*2 teaspoons clear honey*
*salt and freshly ground white pepper*

*1* Remove any grit from the surface of the oyster flesh. Slice the squid into rings about 1 cm/½ inch wide.

*2* Melt the butter in a medium-size frying pan. Add the squid and lemon juice and cook over a medium heat, stirring constantly, for about 3 minutes, or until the squid are opaque. Stir in the parsley. Remove the mixture from the pan and set aside to cool. Chill the squid, together with the prawns and oysters, in the refrigerator until required.

*3* To make the mango salsa, peel the mango, cut the flesh away from the stone and then dice it into small cubes. Cut the chilli in half lengthways, remove the seeds and finely slice the flesh. Cut a 2 cm/¾ inch piece of the white part from the lemon grass stalk and chop finely.

*4* Mix together the mango, chilli, lemon grass, coriander and ginger in a small bowl and chill in the refrigerator for 1 hour. Remove from the refrigerator and allow the salsa to stand at room temperature for 10 minutes before serving.

*5* To make the dill vinaigrette, place the vinegar, oil, mustard, dill and honey in a small screwtop jar. Shake vigorously for 1 minute, or until all ingredients are well combined and emulsified. Season with salt and pepper to taste.

*6* To serve, divide the oysters, squid and prawns evenly among individual serving plates. Add a tablespoon of dill vinaigrette into bowls to accompany each plate, or hand a small jug of dressing separately for guests to help themselves. Add salsa to plates.

## Cook's File
Hint: It is easier to cut the mango flesh away from the stone, rather than to try to remove the stone from the fruit first.

---

# Grilled Mussels

preparation time 10 minutes

total cooking time 5–10 minutes

serves 2–4

## INGREDIENTS

*500 g/1¼ lb fresh mussels, scrubbed*
 *and beards removed*
*2 tablespoons lemon juice*
*1 garlic clove, crushed*
*1 small red chilli, seeded and finely chopped*
*3 tablespoons finely chopped parsley*

*1* Place the mussels in a pan of simmering water. Remove the mussels as the shells open. Discard any mussels that do not open after 5 minutes.

*2* Open out the mussels and loosen from the shells using scissors. Return them to half shells and discard empty ones.

*3* Mix together the lemon juice, garlic and chilli in a small bowl and spoon the mixture over the mussels. Place the mussels in a single layer on a grill rack or baking tray and cook under a preheated medium grill until heated through. Sprinkle the mussels with the parsley and serve immediately.

# Seafood Stew

preparation time 20 minutes

total cooking time 50 minutes

serves 4–6

## INGREDIENTS

275 g/10 oz raw prawns

4 tablespoons olive oil

2 medium onions, finely chopped

2 medium carrots, chopped

2 celery sticks, finely chopped

2 garlic cloves, crushed

6 medium tomatoes (about 1 kg/2¼ lb),
    peeled and chopped

120 ml/4 fl oz white wine

2 tablespoons tomato purée

1 kg/2¼ lb fish fillets, cut into 3 cm/
    1¼ inch cubes

salt and pepper

12 mussels, scrubbed and beards removed

2 tablespoons chopped parsley

1 tablespoon fresh thyme leaves

*1* Peel and devein the prawns, leaving the tails intact. Heat the oil in a large flameproof casserole. Add the onions and cook over a low heat, stirring frequently, for 10 minutes. Add the carrots, celery and garlic and cook, stirring, for 10 minutes.

*2* Add the tomatoes and 4 tablespoons of the wine. Bring to the boil, reduce the heat, cover and simmer for 20 minutes.

*3* Stir in the tomato purée and add the prawns. Cover and simmer for a further 3 minutes. Add the diced fish and season to taste with salt and pepper. Simmer for 2 minutes more.

*4* Place the mussels in a large pan. Add the remaining wine, the parsley and thyme. Cover and cook over a medium heat for 2–3 minutes, until the mussels have opened. Discard any that remain closed. Strain the cooking liquid into the tomato mixture and stir thoroughly. Arrange the mussels on top and serve.

## Cook's File

Hint: To remove all traces of grit from fresh mussels, immerse them in a bucket of salted water to which you have added a sprinkling of oatmeal or flour. Leave for at least 1 hour, preferably longer. The mussels will digest the oatmeal or flour, expelling any grit at the same time. It is still sensible to strain the liquid in which the mussels have been cooked before adding it to any sauces. Line a sieve with muslin to do this.

# Tomato Garlic Mussels

preparation time 15 minutes

total cooking time 15 minutes

serves 2–3

## INGREDIENTS

18 large fresh mussels, scrubbed and
    beards removed

25 g/1 oz butter

3 garlic cloves, crushed

3 large ripe tomatoes, chopped

1 tablespoon Worcestershire sauce

4 tablespoons apple juice

2 tablespoons tomato purée

*1* Prise open the mussel shells with a small knife. Discard the empty half shells and reserve the remainder.

*2* Melt the butter in a large pan. Add the garlic and cook for 1 minute. Add the tomatoes, Worcestershire sauce, apple juice and tomato purée and cook over a medium heat, stirring, for 2 minutes. Bring to the boil, reduce the heat, cover and simmer for 5 minutes. Add the mussels, cover and simmer for a further 5 minutes. Serve immediately.

# Lobster Thermidor

preparation time 25 minutes

total cooking time 10–15 minutes

serves 2

## INGREDIENTS

1 medium cooked lobster, cut in
    half lengthways
65 g/2½ oz butter
4 spring onions, finely chopped
2 tablespoons plain flour
½ teaspoon dry mustard
2 tablespoons white wine
250 ml/8 fl oz milk
3 tablespoons double cream
1 tablespoon chopped parsley
salt and pepper
50 g/2 oz Gruyère cheese, grated
lemon slices, to garnish

1 Remove the lobster meat and set aside. Wash the half shells and set aside. Crack the legs and prise the meat from them. Remove the intestinal vein and soft body matter and discard. Slice the lobster meat into 2 cm/¾ inch pieces, cover and refrigerate.

2 Melt 50 g/2 oz of the butter in a frying pan. Add the spring onions and cook for 2 minutes or until soft. Add the flour and mustard and cook, stirring, for 1 minute. Gradually stir in the wine and milk. Cook, stirring until the mixture boils and thickens. Simmer for 1 minute. Stir in the cream, parsley and lobster meat and season with salt and pepper.

3 Spoon the lobster mixture into the half shells, sprinkle with the cheese and dot with the remaining butter. Cook under a preheated grill for 2 minutes, or until lightly browned. Garnish with lemon slices and serve immediately.

# Lobster Mornay

preparation time 25 minutes

total cooking time 5–10 minutes

serves 2

## INGREDIENTS

1 medium cooked lobster
300 ml/11 fl oz milk
1 slice onion
1 bay leaf
6 black peppercorns
25 g/1 oz butter
2 tablespoons plain flour
salt and freshly ground white pepper
pinch of nutmeg
2 tablespoons cream
50 g/2 oz Cheddar cheese, grated
sprigs of dill, to garnish

1 Using a sharp knife, cut the lobster in half lengthways. Lift the meat from the tail and body of the lobster. Crack the legs and prise the meat from them. Remove the intestinal vein and soft body matter and discard. Cut the meat into 2 cm/¾ inch pieces, cover and refrigerate. Wash the shell halves, drain, dry and reserve.

2 Put the milk, onion, bay leaf and peppercorns in a small pan and bring to the boil. Remove from the heat, cover and leave to infuse for 15 minutes. Strain and reserve the flavoured milk.

3 Melt the butter in a large pan. Add the flour and cook, stirring, for 1 minute. Remove the pan from the heat and gradually add the flavoured milk, whisking until smooth. Cook over a medium heat, whisking until the mixture boils and thickens. Season with salt, pepper and nutmeg. Stir in the cream.

4 Fold the lobster meat through the sauce. Divide the mixture between the half shells and sprinkle with cheese. Place under a preheated grill for 2 minutes, or until the cheese has melted. Serve garnished with dill sprigs.

# Hot Seafood Mornay

preparation time 25 minutes

total cooking time 25 minutes

serves 10–12

## INGREDIENTS

25 g/1 oz butter

2 tablespoons plain flour

2 tablespoons dry white wine

1 tablespoon lemon juice

1 tablespoon tomato purée

250 ml/8 fl oz single cream

2 teaspoons wholegrain mustard

½ teaspoon crushed black peppercorns

500 g/1¼ lb scallops

1 kg/2¼ lb white fish fillets

1 kg/2¼ lb raw prawns, peeled
    and deveined

175 g/6 oz croûtons

115 g/4 oz Gruyère cheese, grated

2 tablespoons flaked almonds

lime slices and sprigs of dill, to garnish

*1* Preheat the oven to 220°C/425°F/ Gas 7. Melt the butter in a small pan. Add the flour and cook over a low heat, stirring constantly, for 1 minute or until the flour mixture is lightly golden.

*2* Mix together the wine, lemon juice and tomato purée and add to the pan, stirring until smooth. Gradually stir in the cream. Cook, stirring constantly, over a medium heat for 3 minutes, or until boiling and thick. Remove from the heat, stir in the mustard and peppercorns and set aside to cool.

*3* Rinse the scallops, remove the vein, leaving the coral intact, and drain well. Cut the fish into 3 cm/1¼ inch cubes.

Combine the fish, seafood, sauce, three-quarters of the croûtons and 25 g/1 oz of the cheese in a large bowl and mix well.

*4* Spoon the mixture into a shallow ovenproof dish and sprinkle with the remaining croûtons, the remaining cheese and the almonds. Bake for 20 minutes, or until golden and cooked through. Serve garnished with lime slices and dill.

## Cook's File

To make croûtons, cut off the crusts from 6 thick slices of bread. Cut the bread into 1 cm/½ inch cubes. Scatter on a foil-lined tray and bake in a preheated oven, 180°C/350°F/ Gas 4, for 15 minutes or until golden.

# Steamed Fish with Ginger

preparation time 45 minutes, plus marinating

total cooking time 12 minutes

serves 4

## INGREDIENTS

675 g/1¼ lb snapper or sea bass, cleaned
    and scaled
2 tablespoons finely grated fresh
    root ginger
2 teaspoons dry sherry
2 tablespoons soy sauce
2 tablespoons peanut oil
2 teaspoons sesame oil
2 spring onions, thinly sliced diagonally
50 g/2 oz pine nuts, toasted
1 rasher bacon, rind removed diced
    and cooked until crisp (optional)

*1* Wash the fish, removing any remaining loose scales, and pat dry inside and out with kitchen paper. Place the fish: on a large heatproof dish and sprinkle with the ginger, sherry and soy sauce. Set aside to marinate for 30 minutes in the refrigerator.

*2* Place a trivet in a wok and put the fish dish on top. Carefully pour 1.5–2 litres/2½–3½ pints boiling water into the wok. Cover and steam the fish over a rolling boil for 10 minutes.

*3* Test with a fork to see if the flesh flakes easily. Turn off the heat.

*4* Heat the peanut and sesame oils in a small, heavy-based pan until very hot. Carefully remove the fish in its dish from the wok. Scatter the sliced spring onions over the fish and very carefully pour the hot oil over them. Garnish with pine nuts and diced bacon, if desired. Serve at once.

# Baked Fish with Spices

preparation time 15 minutes

total cooking time 30 minutes

serves 2

## INGREDIENTS

2 x 300 g/11 oz white fish, such as sole
1 onion, chopped
1 garlic clove, crushed
1 teaspoon chopped fresh root ginger
1 teaspoon chopped lemon rind
2 tablespoons tamarind sauce
1 tablespoon soy sauce
1 tablespoon peanut oil

*1* Preheat the oven to 180°C/350°F/ Gas 4. Make deep slashes on each side of the fish with a sharp knife. Place the fish on 2 large sheets of foil.

*2* Put the chopped onion, garlic, ginger, lemon rind, tamarind sauce, soy sauce and peanut oil in a food processor and process until the mixture is smooth.

*3* Spread the spice mixture evenly over both sides and on the inside of both the fish.

*4* Wrap the foil loosely around each fish and secure to make neat parcels. Place in an ovenproof dish and bake for 30 minutes, or until the fish is just cooked through. Serve the parcels so that they can be unwrapped at the table.

# Spaghetti *alla* Marinara

preparation time 40 minutes

total cooking time 50 minutes

serves 4–6

## INGREDIENTS

2 tablespoons olive oil

1 onion, finely chopped

1 carrot, finely chopped

1 red chilli, seeded and chopped

3 garlic cloves, crushed

400 g/14 oz can tomatoes, drained
  and crushed

250 ml/8 fl oz white wine

1 teaspoon sugar

pinch of cayenne pepper

120 ml/4 fl oz fish stock

12 fresh mussels, scrubbed and
  beards removed

25 g/1 oz butter

115 g/4 oz squid rings

115 g/4 oz white fish fillets, cut into cubes

200 g/7 oz raw prawns, peeled
  and deveined

25 g/1 oz parsley, chopped

200 g/7 oz can clams, drained

375 g/13 oz dried spaghetti

*Step 1*

*Step 2*

*Step 3*

*1* Heat the oil in a medium-size pan. Add the onion and carrot and cook over a medium heat, stirring frequently, for 10 minutes, or until lightly browned. Add the chilli, 2 of the garlic cloves, tomatoes, 120 ml/4 fl oz of the white wine, the sugar and cayenne pepper. Simmer, uncovered, stirring occasionally, for 30 minutes.

*2* Meanwhile, heat the remaining wine, the stock and the remaining garlic in a large pan. Add the mussels, cover and cook over a high heat, shaking the pan occasionally, for 3–5 minutes. After 3 minutes start removing the opened mussels. After 5 minutes discard any unopened mussels. Strain and reserve the cooking liquid.

*3* Melt the butter in a frying pan. Add the squid rings, fish and prawns and stir-fry for 2 minutes. Remove from the pan, set aside and keep warm.

*4* Add the reserved mussel cooking liquid, parsley, cooked fish and seafood and the clams to the tomato sauce. Reheat gently.

*5* Cook the pasta in a large pan of lightly salted boiling water for 8–10 minutes, until just tender. Drain, combine the sauce and pasta and serve.

## Cook's File

Hint: The tomato sauce may be made ahead and stored, covered in the refrigerator. Complete the dish just before serving.

# Moules

## Marinière

preparation time 15 minutes

total cooking time 30–35 minutes

serves 4

### INGREDIENTS

24 *fresh mussels, scrubbed and*
   *beards removed*
3 *onions, chopped*
1 *celery stick, chopped*
250 *ml/8 fl oz white wine*
350 *ml/12 fl oz fish stock*
4 *sprigs of parsley*
1 *sprig of thyme*
1 *bay leaf*
50 *g/2 oz butter*
2 *garlic cloves, crushed*
1 *teaspoon plain flour*
*sprigs of dill, to garnish*
*crusty bread, to serve*

1 Put the mussels, one-third of the onions, the celery and wine in a large pan and bring rapidly to the boil. Cover and cook, shaking the pan frequently, for 3 minutes. After 3 minutes start removing mussels from the pan as they open.

2 Pull away the empty half shells and discard. Set aside the mussels attached to the other shell halves, cover and keep warm. After 5 minutes discard any unopened mussels.

3 Strain and reserve the cooking liquid and discard the vegetables.

4 Put the fish stock, parsley, thyme and bay leaf in a pan and bring to the boil. Reduce the heat, cover and simmer for 10 minutes. Remove the herbs.

5 Melt the butter in a large pan. Add the garlic and the remaining onions and cook over a low heat for 5–10 minutes, or until the onion is soft, but not browned.

Stir in the flour. Add the reserved liquid and simmering fish stock. Bring to the boil and simmer, uncovered, for 10 minutes.

6 Place the mussels in four soup bowls. Ladle the liquid over the mussels and garnish with dill sprigs. Serve immediately with crusty bread.

## Cook's File

Hint: To prepare mussels, rinse them several times under cold running water. Scrub each mussel shell with a stiff brush to remove any dirt and sand. Pull out the beard from between the shell halves and scape off any barnacles with a knife. Discard any mussels with damaged shells or any that do not close immediately when sharply tapped with a knife.

*Step 1*

*Step 2*

*Step 5*

# Sole Véronique

preparation time 45 minutes

total cooking time 20 minutes

serves 4

## INGREDIENTS

*40 g/1½ oz butter, plus extra for greasing*

*12 sole fillets, skinned*

*250 ml/8 fl oz fish stock*

*4 tablespoons white wine*

*1 shallot, thinly sliced*

*1 bay leaf*

*6 black peppercorns*

*2 sprigs of parsley*

*1 tablespoon plain flour*

*120 ml/4 fl oz milk*

*4 tablespoons single cream*

*salt and pepper*

*115 g/4 oz seedless white grapes, peeled*

*1* Preheat the oven to 180°C/350°F/ Gas 4. Lightly grease a shallow ovenproof dish. Roll up the fish fillets with the skinned side on the inside and secure with cocktail sticks. Place side-by-side in a single layer in the prepared dish.

*2* Mix together the fish stock, white wine, shallot, bay leaf, peppercorns and parsley and pour the mixture over the fish. Cover with greased foil and bake for 15 minutes, or until the flesh flakes easily when tested with a fork. Using a slotted spoon, carefully transfer the fish rolls to another dish and keep warm. Reserve the cooking liquid.

*3* Pour the cooking liquid into a saucepan, bring to the boil and boil for about 2 minutes, or until reduced by about half. Strain through a fine sieve or through clean muslin and reserve.

*4* Melt the butter in a small pan, add the flour and cook, stirring constantly, for 1 minute, or until pale and foaming. Remove from the heat. Mix the milk, cream and reserved cooking liquid. Gradually stir into the pan. Return to the heat and bring to the boil, stirring constantly, until thickened. Season to taste, stir in the grapes and heat through. Pour the sauce over the fish and serve immediately.

# Mixed Seafood Salad

preparation time 1 hour, plus refrigeration

total cooking time 12 minutes

serves 8

## INGREDIENTS

20 cooked king prawns

12 cooked Dublin Bay prawns

120 ml/4fl oz white wine

pinch of dried thyme

pinch of dried tarragon or a bay leaf

salt and freshly ground white pepper

20 scallops, with roe attached

400 g/14 oz skinless salmon or trout fillets

6 hard-boiled eggs

150 g/5 oz mixed lettuce leaves

2 tablespoons coarsely chopped fresh
   flat-leaf parsley

2 avocados, peeled, stoned and sliced

2 tablespoons lemon juice


Dill Vinaigrette

120 ml/4 fl oz extra virgin olive oil

2 tablespoons white wine vinegar

1 teaspoon sugar

2 teaspoons Dijon mustard

1 tablespoon chopped fresh dill


Green Goddess Dressing

2 egg yolks

2 teaspoons Dijon mustard

3 tablespoons lemon juice

250 ml/8 fl oz olive oil

4 anchovy fillets, chopped

1 clove garlic, crushed

50 ml/2 fl oz soured cream

15 g/½ oz chopped fresh mixed herbs

*1* Peel and devein the prawns. Put the Dublin Bay prawns on their backs. Cut below the base of the head to remove and discard the head piece. Using scissors, cut down either side of the undershell, pull back and remove the flesh in one piece.

*2* Put the water in a pan and add the wine, herbs and a pinch of salt and pepper. Bring to the boil, then reduce the heat and simmer for 5 minutes. Add the scallops and poach for 1–2 minutes, or until they have just turned white, then remove with a slotted spoon and drain on kitchen paper. Add the fish fillets and poach until cooked and just tender; remove with a slotted spoon and drain on kitchen paper. Break into large pieces.

*3* To make the dill vinaigrette, combine all the ingredients and whisk until blended, then season to taste.

*4* Combine the prawns, Dublin Bay prawns, scallops and fish in a bowl. Pour the dill vinaigrette into the bowl, cover and refrigerate for 1 hour. Peel and slice the eggs, reserving 2 yolks.

*5* To make the dressing, process the egg yolks, Dijon mustard and 2 tablespoons of lemon juice in a food processor or blender for 30 seconds, or until light and creamy. With the motor running, add the oil in a thin, steady stream, increasing the flow as the mayonnaise thickens. Add 2–4 teaspoons of lemon juice, the anchovy fillets, garlic, soured cream and fresh herbs. Season with salt and pepper and pulse for 30 seconds to combine the mixture well.

*6* Place half of the lettuce leaves in the base of a deep serving bowl. Arrange about half of the seafood on the lettuce, reserving the dill vinaigrette. Sprinkle with half of the parsley, top with half of the avocado and drizzle with half of the lemon juice. Then finish with half the sliced eggs, including the extra whites. Season with salt and pepper to taste.

*7* Repeat the layers and season to taste again. Drizzle with the reserved dill vinaigrette. Crumble the reserved egg yolks over the top of the salad and serve with the green goddess dressing.

# Traditional Christmas Dinner

**Menu**

**Starter**
*Watercress Soup*

**Main**
*Redcurrant Glazed Roast Turkey*

**Accompaniment**
*Golden Roast Potatoes*

**Dessert**
*Ice-Cream Fruit Bombe*

**Sweet treat**
*Mini Choc-Rum Puddings*

## Watercress Soup

preparation time 40 minutes

total cooking time 15 minutes

serves 8

### INGREDIENTS

*1 large onion*
*4 spring onions*
*450 g/1 lb watercress*
*115 g/4 oz butter*
*40 g/1½ oz plain flour*
*600 ml/1 pint chicken stock*
*475 ml/16 fl oz water*
*soured cream and sprigs of watercress,*
  *to garnish*

*1* Roughly chop the onion, spring onions and watercress. Melt the butter in a large heavy-based pan. Add the onion, spring onions and watercress and cook over a low heat, stirring, for 3 minutes, or until the vegetables have softened. Stir in the flour.

*2* Mix together the stock and water and gradually add to the pan, stirring until the mixture is smooth. Stir constantly over a medium heat for 10 minutes, or until the mixture boils and thickens. Boil for 1 minute further. Remove from heat and set aside to cool.

*3* Place the mixture in small batches in a food processor. Process for 15 seconds, or until the mixture is smooth. Return the soup to the pan and gently heat through. Serve warm, garnished with soured cream and watercress.

*Step 1*

*Step 2*

*Step 3*

# Redcurrant Glazed Roast Turkey

preparation time 1 hour 30 minutes

total cooking time 2 hours

serves 8

## INGREDIENTS

2.75 kg/6 lb turkey breast joint
4 tablespoons redcurrant jelly
2 tablespoons golden syrup
4 tablespoons brown sugar
40 g/1½ oz butter, melted
250 ml/8 fl oz water

Gravy
2 tablespoons plain flour
175 ml/6 fl oz chicken stock

Apple Stuffing
20 g/¼ oz butter
1 medium onion, finely chopped
1 large green apple, finely chopped
2 spring onions, finely chopped
4 slices dry bread, grated
1 tablespoon chopped chives
2 teaspoons lemon juice

1 Preheat the oven to 180°C/350°F/ Gas 4. Trim the turkey of excess fat. Mix together the redcurrant jelly, syrup and sugar in small bowl. Brush the turkey all over with the melted butter and place on a roasting rack in a deep roasting tin. Pour the water into the base of the tin.

2 Cover the turkey with foil and roast for 40 minutes. Remove from the oven and brush liberally with the jelly mixture. Roast, uncovered, for a further 20 minutes. Repeat the process once more. Remove the turkey from the oven, transfer to a carving board and leave, covered with foil, in a warm place 10 minutes before slicing.

3 To make the gravy, sprinkle the flour evenly over a baking tray. Place under a hot grill until golden. Add the flour to the cooking juices and cook, stirring, over a low heat for 2 minutes. Gradually add the stock, stirring until the mixture is smooth. Stir constantly over a medium heat for 5 minutes, or until boiling and thickened, then boil a further 1 minute. Remove from the heat.

4 To make the stuffing, melt the butter in a medium-size, heavy-based pan. Add the onion and apple and cook over a medium heat, stirring, until golden brown. Add the remaining ingredients and stir until well combined. Serve hot with the turkey and gravy.

## Cook's File
Wine suggestions: A soft, full-bodied Shiraz complements turkey.

# Golden Roast Potatoes

preparation time 20 minutes

total cooking time 1 hour

serves 8

## INGREDIENTS

8 medium potatoes
50 g/2 oz butter, melted
4 tablespoons olive oil
½ teaspoon paprika

1 Preheat the oven to 200°C/400°F/ Gas 6. Wash and peel the potatoes. Boil the potatoes for 5 minutes. Drain and pat dry with kitchen paper.

2 Using the prongs of a fork, scrape the potatoes to form a rough surface. Place them in a shallow ovenproof dish. Mix together the melted butter and oil and brush over the potatoes. Sprinkle with paprika. Roast for 20 minutes.

3 Remove from the oven and brush with the butter mixture. Roast for a further 20 minutes. Repeat this process and roast for a further 15 minutes. Serve hot with Redcurrant Glazed Roast Turkey.

## Cook's File
Hint: Use even-sized, floury potatoes for the best results.

Variation: Substitute rosemary for the paprika.

# Ice-Cream Fruit Bombe

preparation time 20 minutes, plus soaking and freezing

total cooking time Nil

serves 8

## INGREDIENTS

*300 g/11 oz mincemeat*

*75 g/3 oz dried figs, finely chopped*

*4 tablespoons rum*

*115 g/4 oz flaked almonds*

*4 eggs*

*200 g/7 oz caster sugar*

*350 ml/12 fl oz double cream*

*175 ml/6 fl oz buttermilk*

*figs and almonds, to decorate*

1 Mix together the mincemeat, figs and rum in a small bowl. Cover with clear film and set aside to macerate overnight. Place the almonds on a baking tray and toast under a preheated grill until golden. Beat the eggs in a large bowl with an electric mixer for 5 minutes, or until thick and pale.

2 Gradually add the sugar, beating constantly until it has dissolved and the mixture is pale yellow and glossy. Mix together the cream and buttermilk and gradually add to the eggs. Beat for a further 5 minutes.

3 Using a metal spoon, fold in the mincemeat mixture and almonds. Pour into a deep 2 litre/3½ pint freezerproof pudding basin and cover with foil. Place in the freezer overnight.

4 To serve, push a flat-bladed knife between the pudding basin and bombe to allow air in. Place a serving plate on top of the basin and, holding the basin and plate firmly, invert. Gently ease the bombe on to the serving plate. Decorate with figs and almonds and cut into wedges to serve.

*Step 2*

*Step 3*

*Step 4*

# Mini Choc-rum Puddings

preparation time 50 minutes, plus setting

total cooking time 5 minutes

makes about 20

**INGREDIENTS**

250 g/9 oz moist chocolate
   cake, crumbled
4 tablespoons ground nuts
1 tablespoon golden syrup
1 tablespoon rum
50 g/2 oz butter, melted
4 tablespoons mincemeat
150 g/5 oz dark chocolate, chopped
15 g/½ oz vegetable shortening
50 g/2 oz white chocolate, chopped
1 tablespoon double cream

*1* Mix together the cake crumbs, nuts, syrup, rum, butter and mincemeat in a large bowl. Using a metal spoon, stir until the mixture comes together. Roll 2 heaped teaspoons of the mixture at a time into balls. Place them on a tray and refrigerate until firm.

*2* Place the dark chocolate and shortening in a medium-size heatproof bowl set over a pan of simmering water. Stir until the chocolate and shortening have melted and the mixture is smooth. Cool slightly.

*3* Using two forks, dip the mincemeat balls into the melted chocolate. Drain off excess and place the balls on a tray. Refrigerate until firm.

*4* Place the white chocolate and cream in a small heatproof bowl set over a pan of simmering water. Stir until the chocolate has melted and the mixture is smooth. Cool slightly. Spoon ½ teaspoon of the mixture on top of each ball, allowing it to run down the sides. Refrigerate until set. Serve with coffee.

*Step 1*

*Step 2*

*Step 3*

Menu

# Winter Welcome

*Menu*

# Vegetable Timbales with Tomato Sauce

preparation time 1 hour

total cooking time 20 minutes

serves 6

## INGREDIENTS

1 tablespoon olive oil, plus extra
  for greasing
1 garlic clove, crushed
1 small red pepper, seeded and chopped
115 g/4 oz button mushrooms chopped
3 spring onions, finely chopped
225 g/8 oz freshly cooked arborio rice
50 g/2 oz Cheddar cheese, grated
2 tablespoons grated Parmesan cheese
crushed black peppercorns
15 g/½ oz butter

Tomato Sauce
2 teaspoons olive oil
3 large ripe tomatoes, finely chopped
2 tablespoons tomato purée
2 teaspoons balsamic vinegar

## Cook's File

Storage time: Timbales can be assembled
3 hours ahead. Reheat gently.

*1* Lightly grease six 120 ml/4 fl oz timbale moulds with oil. Heat the oil in a large, heavy-based pan. Add the garlic, pepper, mushrooms and spring onions. Stir over a medium heat for 2–3 minutes, or until softened. Add the rice, cheeses, pepper to taste and butter. Stir until the cheese melts.

*2* Spoon the mixture into the prepared moulds; pack it in tightly to give the timbales shape. (No further cooking is necessary.) Place a knife down the side of each mould and carefully ease the timbales out. Cover with foil and keep warm.

*3* To make the sauce, heat the oil in a medium-size heavy-based pan. Add the tomatoes and purée and cook over a medium heat, stirring, for 3 minutes, or until the tomatoes are very soft. Stir in the vinegar. Place the timbales on serving plates and spoon the sauce around.

*Step 1*

*Step 2*

# Roast Lamb *with* Sage and Tarragon

preparation time  15 minutes  total cooking time 1¼ hours  serves 6

## INGREDIENTS

2 kg/4½ lb leg of lamb

4 tablespoons roughly chopped
  sage leaves

2 tablespoons roughly chopped
  tarragon leaves

1 garlic clove

1 medium onion, chopped

1 tablespoon vegetable oil

2 tablespoons plum sauce

250 ml/8 fl oz white wine

4 tablespoons chicken stock

*1* Preheat the oven to 180°C/350°F/ Gas 4. Using a small, sharp knife, trim the meat of excess fat. Put the sage, tarragon, garlic, onion, oil and plum sauce in a food processor. Using the pulse action, process for 30 seconds, or until the mixture is smooth.

*2* Place the meat on a rack in a deep roasting tin. Rub the meat all over with the sage mixture. Add a little water to the base of the tin to prevent burning. Roast for 1¼ hours or until cooked. Remove from the oven, place on a carving platter and cover loosely with foil and leave in a warm place for 10 minutes before slicing.

*3* Place the roasting tin over a medium heat. Add the wine and stock to the cooking juices, stirring well to incorporate the sediment from the base of the tin. Bring to the boil, reduce the heat and simmer for 5 minutes. Pour a little gravy over the lamb to serve and hand the rest separately. Serve with Peppery Sprouts and Baby Squash.

## Cook's File

Wine suggestions: With this menu you could serve a Chardonnay or chilled pale sherry with the first course, a Cabernet Sauvignon with the Roast Lamb and a sweet dessert wine, such as Sauternes, with the Caramel Soufflé Gâteau. Alternatively, drink Cabernet Sauvignon or claret throughout the meal, but not with dessert, as the sweet creaminess of the cake would be overwhelmed by the strong-flavoured wine. Some people find Champagne or other sparkling wine a pleasant way to finish a special meal.

Hint: The lamb is already strongly flavoured with herbs, so the popular accompaniment of mint sauce would not be appropriate, but you could serve it with redcurrant jelly.

*Step 1*

*Step 2*

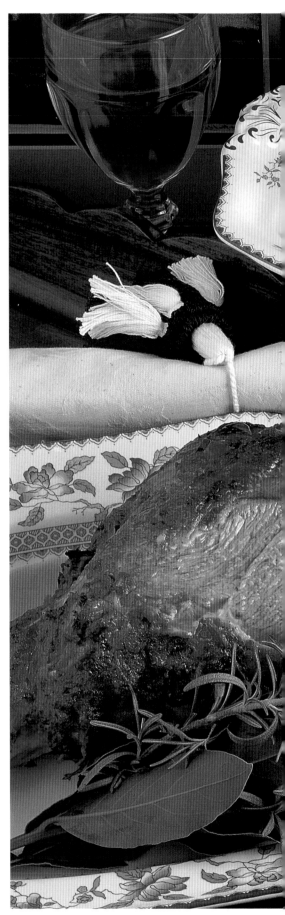

# Peppery Sprouts *and* Baby Squash

preparation time 15 minutes

total cooking time 10 minutes

serves 6

### INGREDIENTS

2 rashers bacon
12 small Brussels sprouts
12 baby pattypan squash
1 tablespoon pine nuts
1 teaspoon crushed black peppercorns

*1* Remove the rind from the bacon and cut the bacon into thin strips. Trim any rough outer leaves from the Brussels sprouts and cut in half lengthways.

*2* Cook the bacon in a medium-size, heavy-based pan until browned. Stir in the sprouts and squash and cook for 2 minutes. Cover tightly and cook over a medium heat for 5–10 minutes, or until the vegetables are just tender.

*3* Add the pine nuts and peppercorns to the pan and mix gently to combine. Cover the pan and cook for a further 30–40 seconds. Remove from the heat and serve immediately with Roast Lamb with Sage and Tarragon.

## Cook's File

Variation: Frozen Brussels sprouts may be used instead of fresh. Three medium courgettes, sliced, can also be used to replace either of the vegetables in this recipe.

Hint: Be careful not to overcook vegetables. For the best taste, texture, colour and nutritional value, cook vegetables only until they are just tender. Never add baking soda to green vegetables, as this seriously depletes their vitamin content.

# Caramel Soufflé Gâteau

preparation time 1½ hours, plus chilling

total cooking time 35 minutes

makes one 20 cm round cake

## INGREDIENTS

150 g/5 oz butter, plus extra for greasing

130 g/4½ oz caster sugar

1 tablespoon muscovado sugar

1 tablespoon glucose syrup

2 eggs, lightly beaten

2 teaspoons vanilla essence

175 g/6 oz self-raising flour, sifted

120 ml/4 fl oz buttermilk

2 tablespoons cocoa powder, sifted

2 x 400 g/14 oz cans pear slices, drained
    and juice reserved

Mousse

50 g/2 oz butter

4 tablespoons brown sugar

2 tablespoons golden syrup

2 teaspoons gelatine

2 eggs, separated

475 g/16 fl oz double cream, whipped to
    firm peaks

*1* Preheat the oven to 180°C/350°F/ Gas 4. Brush a deep, 18 cm/7 inch round cake tin and a deep, 23 cm/9 inch square cake tin with melted butter. Line the bases and sides with greaseproof paper and brush with melted butter.

*2* Beat the butter, caster sugar, muscovado sugar and glucose with an electric mixer until light and creamy. Gradually add the eggs, beating thoroughly after each addition. Add the vanilla essence and beat until combined. Transfer the mixture to a large bowl.

*3* Using a metal spoon, fold in the sifted flour alternately with the buttermilk. Stir until just combined and the mixture is smooth.

*4* Spoon half the mixture into the round tin and smooth the surface. Spoon half the remaining mixture over half of the base of the square tin. Combine the remaining mixture with the cocoa and stir until smooth. Spread evenly over the remaining half of the square tin. Bake the round cake for 30 minutes and the square cake for 20 minutes, or until a skewer comes out clean when inserted in the centre of the cakes. Leave the cakes in the tins for 10 minutes before turning on to wire racks to cool.

*5* To make the mousse, put the butter, sugar, 120 ml/4 fl oz of the reserved pear juice and the syrup in a medium-size, heavy-based pan. Cook over a low heat without boiling, stirring until the sugar has completely dissolved. Sprinkle over the gelatine and stir until dissolved. Remove from the heat and cool slightly. Whisk in the egg yolks.

*6* Transfer the mixture to a large bowl. Put the egg whites in a small, clean, dry bowl. Using an electric mixer, beat the egg whites until stiff peaks form. Using a metal spoon, gradually fold the egg whites and cream into the butter mixture. Set aside.

*7* Line a deep, 20 cm/8 inch springform tin with foil, leaving an extra 2 cm/ ¾ inch at the top. Trim the edges of the square cake. Cut the chocolate half and the vanilla half into 27 even squares each. Place alternate colours in two rows around the inside of the lined tin and press against the side. Carefully place the round cake in the centre, gently easing it into the base.

*8* Lay the pear slices overlapping each other on top of the cake base. Top with the mousse mixture. Cover and chill in the refrigerator overnight. Cut into wedges to serve.

## Cook's File

Storage time: You need to cook and assemble this dish one day before serving.

Hint: Decorate the cake as desired with whipped cream and a few pear slices or chocolate leaves.

*Step 3*

*Step 4*

*Step 5*

*Step 7*

*Step 8*

# Seafood Celebration

# Honey Basil Prawns

preparation time 20 minutes, plus marinating

total cooking time 5 minutes

serves 6

## INGREDIENTS

12 medium raw tiger prawns
2 tablespoons finely chopped basil
2 teaspoons clear honey
1 tablespoon soy sauce
1 teaspoon rice vinegar

## Cook's File

Variation: Fresh scallops are a good alternative to tiger prawns.

Hint: To prevent burning, soak bamboo skewers in water for 30 minutes.

Wine suggestions: Sauvignon Blanc is the first choice for this menu. However, a crisp young Sémillon or Chardonnay would also marry well. Alternatively, serve a cold beer or a glass of Champagne with the appetiser. Try an aged, sweet Rhine Riesling or a liqueur Muscat with the dessert torte.

*1* Peel and devein the prawns, leaving the tails intact.

*2* Whisk together the the basil, honey, soy sauce and rice vinegar in a small bowl for 2 minutes, or until combined. Transfer the marinade to a large shallow dish, add the prawns and mix well to ensure that they are thoroughly coated. Cover with clear film and marinate in the refrigerator for 30 minutes.

*3* Thread one prawn on to each of 12 skewers. Cover the ends of the skewers with small pieces of foil to prevent them from charring during cooking.

*4* Place the prawns on a cold grill tray and cook under a preheated medium grill for 2–3 minutes on each side, or until the prawns have just turned pink. Remove from the grill. transfer to a serving platter and serve immediately.

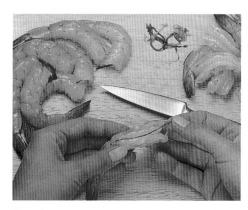
*Step 1*

*Step 3*

# Soufflé Oysters

preparation time 25 minutes   total cooking time 20 minutes   serves 6

## INGREDIENTS

18 oysters in the half shells
25 g/1 oz butter
1 tablespoon self-raising flour
120 ml/4 fl oz milk
2 teaspoons wholegrain mustard
1 egg, separated

## Cook's File

Storage time: Assemble the oysters several hours in advance and store in the refrigerator. Bake just before serving.

Wine suggestions: Try a small glass of stout, such as Guinness — a truly traditional accompaniment to oysters. Alternatively, you could simply serve Champagne or a very dry white wine with the oysters.

*1* Preheat the oven to 180°C/350°F/ Gas 4. Line a 33 x 28 cm/13 x 11 inch baking tray with foil. Place the oysters on the tray and remove any grit from the surface.

*2* Melt the butter in a small heavy-based pan. Sir in the flour and cook over a low heat, stirring, for 2 minutes, or until the mixture is lightly golden. Gradually add the milk, stirring until the mixture is smooth. Cook, stirring constantly over a medium heat for 5 minutes, or until the mixture boils and thickens. Boil for a further 1 minute and then remove from the heat. Set aside to cool. Stir in the mustard and egg yolk and transfer to a bowl.

*3* Place the egg white in a small, clean dry bowl. Beat with an electric mixer until firm peaks form. Using a metal spoon, fold the egg white in a figure-of-eight movement into the milk mixture.

*4* Spoon heaped teaspoons of the mixture on to each oyster. Bake for 15 minutes, or until the topping is slightly puffed and golden brown. Transfer to a serving plate and serve immediately.

*Step 4*

# Oysters with Pine Nuts and Bacon

preparation time 25 minutes   total cooking time 20 minutes   serves 6

## INGREDIENTS

18 oysters in the half shells
2 rashers bacon
2 tablespoons pine nuts, roughly chopped
3 teaspoons Worcestershire sauce
1 tablespoon finely chopped chives
lemon wedges, to garnish

*1* Preheat the oven to 180°C/350°F/ Gas 4. Line a 33 x 28 cm/13 x 11 inch baking tray with foil. Place the oysters on the tray. Remove any grit from the surface of the oyster flesh.

*2* Cook the bacon in a small heavy-based pan over a medium heat until browned. Add the pine nuts and Worcestershire sauce and stir until well combined. Remove the pan from the heat.

*3* Spoon the mixture evenly on to each oyster. Sprinkle with the chives. Bake for 5–10 minutes, or until heated through. Transfer to a warm serving platter, garnish with lemon wedges and serve immediately with the Soufflé Oysters.

# Salmon Cutlets *with* Vanilla Glaze

preparation time 40 minutes   total cooking time 30 minutes   serves 6

## INGREDIENTS

6 salmon cutlets (about 200 g/7 oz each)
4 tablespoons lemon juice
2 tablespoons water
50 g/2 oz butter, diced
2 tablespoons finely
  chopped chives

Vanilla Glaze
250 ml/8 fl oz white wine vinegar
4 tablespoons water
1 vanilla pod
1 tablespoon brown sugar
2 tablespoons sugar
1 teaspoon grated lemon rind

*1* Preheat the oven to 180°C/350°F/ Gas 4. Remove any scales from the fish. Place the salmon in a single layer in an ovenproof dish. Mix together the lemon juice and water and pour the mixture over the fish. Top with the diced butter.

*2* Cover with foil and bake for about 20 minutes, or until the fish flakes easily when tested with a fork.

*3* Meanwhile, make the glaze: Combine all the ingredients in a medium-size heavy-based pan. Cook over a low heat without boiling, stirring until the sugar has dissolved. Bring to the boil, reduce the heat and simmer for 5 minutes, or until the glaze has reduced by half. Remove from the heat and discard the vanilla pod.

*4* Place the salmon cutlets on individual serving plates, sprinkle with the chives and spoon over the glaze. Serve immediately with Onion Potato Cake.

## Cook's File

Note: Vanilla pods are available from health food shops, delicatessens and supermarkets.

Variation: If salmon cutlets are not available, you can use rainbow trout fillets or your own favourite fish.

Wine suggestions: Serve a chilled Pouilly Fumé, a crisp Chardonnay, a young Beaujolais or a mature claret.

*Step 1*

*Step 2*

# Onion Potato Cake

preparation time 40 minutes

total cooking time 50 minutes

makes one 17cm/6½ inch round cake

### INGREDIENTS

115 g/4 oz butter, melted, plus extra for greasing
4 large potatoes, peeled
1 large red onion
2 garlic cloves, crushed
2 egg yolks
40 g/1½ oz fine, dry breadcrumbs
50 g/2 oz freshly grated Parmesan cheese
crushed black peppercorns

*1* Preheat the oven to 180°C/350°F/Gas 4. Brush a deep, 17 cm/ 6½ inch round springform cake tin with melted butter. Line the base and sides with greaseproof paper and brush with melted butter. Using a sharp knife, cut the potatoes and onion into wafer-thin slices.

*2* Mix together the butter, garlic and egg yolks in a small bowl. Whisk thoroughly until well combined. Lay the potato slices overlapping each other over the base of the prepared tin. Brush liberally with the butter mixture. Top with a few onion rings. Mix together the breadcrumbs, cheese and peppercorns and sprinkle the mixture over the onion rings.

*3* Repeat this layering process until all the ingredients are used, finishing with a breadcrumb and cheese layer. Bake for 40 minutes. Increase the oven temperature to 220°C/425°F/Gas 7 and bake for a further 10 minutes. Allow to stand for 10 minutes in the tin before transferring to a board. Carefully remove the cake from the tin. Cut into wedges and serve.

## Cook's File

Storage time: This dish can be eaten hot or cold. Prepare several hours in advance and bake just before serving.

Variation: For a different flavour add chopped shallots and a little chopped fresh rosemary to the potato layers before cooking.

# Chocolate and Mascarpone Torte

preparation time 1 hour, plus setting  total cooking time 45 minutes  makes one 20 cm/8 inch round cake

## INGREDIENTS

115 g/4 oz butter, plus extra for brushing

90 g/3½ oz caster sugar

50 g/2 oz icing sugar, sifted

2 eggs, lightly beaten

1 teaspoon vanilla essence

2 tablespoons instant coffee powder

1 teaspoon hot water

175 g/6 oz self-raising flour

50 g/2 oz cocoa powder

1 teaspoon bicarbonate of soda

250 ml/8 fl oz buttermilk

1 tablespoon vegetable oil

Filling

350 ml/12 fl oz double cream,
    whipped to stiff peaks

50 g/2 oz icing sugar, sifted

1 teaspoon vanilla essence

250 g/9 oz mascarpone cheese

Chocolate Collar

115 g/4 oz dark chocolate, chopped

2 teaspoons cocoa powder, sifted

2 teaspoons drinking chocolate

1 Preheat the oven to 180°C/350°F/ Gas 4. Brush a deep, 20 cm/8 inch round cake tin with melted butter. Line the base and sides with greaseproof paper and brush with melted butter.

2 Beat together the butter, caster sugar and icing sugar with an electric mixer until light and creamy. Gradually add the eggs, beating thoroughly after each addition. Add the vanilla essence. Mix together the coffee powder and water and beat into the mixture until well combined.

Transfer the mixture to a large bowl. Using a metal spoon, fold in the remaining dry ingredients alternately with the remaining liquids. Stir until just combined and the mixture is smooth.

3 Pour the mixture into the prepared tin and smooth the surface. Bake for 45 minutes, or until a skewer comes out clean when inserted into the centre of the cake. Leave the cake in the tin for 10 minutes before turning on to a wire rack to cool completely.

4 To make the filling, combine the cream, icing sugar, vanilla essence and mascarpone in a bowl. Using a metal spoon, fold together until the mixture is smooth and free of lumps.

5 To assemble the cake, using a serrated knife, cut the cake horizontally into three even layers. Place one layer on a serving plate. Spread the surface evenly with one-third of the filling. Continue layering the cake with the remaining cake and one-third of the filling, with a cake layer on top.

6 To make the chocolate collar, put the dark chocolate in a small heatproof bowl set over a pan of simmering water and stir until the chocolate has melted and is smooth. Cool slightly. Spread the chocolate evenly over a 70 x 7.5 cm/ 28 x 3 inch strip of baking parchment, using a flat-bladed knife. Allow to semi-set. Smooth the surface.

7 When the chocolate is firm enough to stand, but soft enough to bend, wrap the collar around the cake and seal the ends. Pour the remaining filling on top and smooth the surface. Leave to set. Peel off the paper. Mix together the sifted cocoa and drinking chocolate and use to dust the top of the cake.

## Cook's File

Variation: For a marbled chocolate collar, melt 50 g/2 oz white chocolate in a heatproof bowl set over a pan of simmering water. Spoon it alternately with the melted dark chocolate on to the parchment strip and swirl the two colours together with a fork.

Step 2

Step 4

Step 5

Step 6

Step 7

# Brasserie *Style*

*Menu*

**Appetiser**
*Caraway Pikelets with Smoked Trout*
**Starter**
*Warm Goat's Cheese Salad*
**Main**
*Lamb Cutlets with Tomato-mint Relish*
**Accompaniment**
*Green Bean Salad*
**Dessert**
*Chestnut Truffle Terrine*

# Caraway Pikelets *with* Smoked Trout

preparation time 15 minutes

total cooking time 20 minutes

makes 30

## INGREDIENTS

*50 g/2 oz wholemeal self-raising flour*
*½ teaspoon caraway seeds*
*40 g/1½ oz butter*
*1 egg, lightly beaten*
*5 tablespoons milk*
*2 tablespoons soft cream cheese*
*115 g/4 oz smoked trout, sliced*
*sprigs of marjoram, dill or parsley and*
   *lemon wedges, to garnish*

## Cook's File

Storage time: The batter can be made a day in advance. Store, covered, in the refrigerator. Cook and assemble just before serving.

Wine suggestions: A chilled mellow Chardonnay goes very well with smoked fish, and could be drunk throughout this meal. On a richer note, try a liqueur Muscat with the dessert.

*1* Sift the flour into a medium-size bowl and tip the bran into it. Add the caraway seeds. Make a well in the centre. Melt 15 g/½ oz of the butter and whisk with the egg and milk. Add to the dry ingredients. Using a wooden spoon, stir until well combined, but do not overbeat.

*2* Grease a large heavy-based pan with a little of the remaining butter. Allow 1 teaspoon of mixture for each pikelet, cooking four or five at a time. Cook until bubbles appear on the surface, then turn to brown the other side. Cool on a wire rack. Repeat until all the mixture is used.

*3* To assemble, spread a little cream cheese on each pikelet and top with a piece of smoked trout. Make piles of four or five on each plate. Garnish with a sprig of marjoram, dill or parsley and a piece of lemon. Serve at room temperature.

*Step 2*

*Step 3*

# *Warm*  *Goat's Cheese Salad*

preparation time 15 minutes

total cooking time 15 minutes

serves 6

## INGREDIENTS

*6 slices wholemeal bread*

*2 x 115 g/4 oz goat's cheese logs*

*115 g/4 oz mixed salad leaves*

*1 tablespoon tarragon vinegar*

*4 tablespoons olive oil*

*½ teaspoon wholegrain mustard*

*1* Preheat the oven to 180°C/350°F/ Gas 4. With a plain pastry cutter, cut a circle out of each slice of bread that will just fit a slice of goat's cheese. The bread must not extend beyond the cheese or it will burn. Place the bread on a baking tray and cook for 10 minutes.

*2* Cut each cheese log into three discs. Place a disc of cheese on each bread circle. Arrange a bed of salad leaves on small serving plates.

*3* Cook the cheese under a preheated grill for 5 minutes, or until it turns golden and bubbles.

*4* Meanwhile, make the dressing. Put the tarragon vinegar, olive oil and mustard in a small screwtop jar and shake vigorously for 1 minute or until thoroughly combined. Drizzle the salad leaves with the dressing, place a cheese round on top and serve immediately.

## *Cook's File*

Note: Goat's cheese is available from supermarkets and delicatessens. Most French varieties — *chèvre* — are usually sold in a log shape. Those labelled *chèvre* or *chèvre pur* are made entirely from goat's milk. *Mi-chèvre* may contain only 25 per cent goat's milk.

*Step 1*

*Step 2*

*Step 3*

# Lamb Cutlets *with* Tomato-mint Relish

preparation time 20 minutes, plus 1 hour standing  total cooking time 15 minutes  serves 6

## INGREDIENTS

*12 lamb cutlets (about 75 g/3 oz each)*
*1 tablespoon olive oil*
*sprigs of rosemary, to garnish*

*Tomato-mint Relish*
*3 medium tomatoes*
*2 teaspoons brown sugar*
*4 teaspoons cider vinegar*
*1 spring onion, finely chopped*
*2 teaspoons finely chopped mint*

*1* First, make the relish. Mark a small cross on the top of each tomato. Place in a bowl of boiling water for 1–2 minutes, then plunge immediately into cold water. Peel the skin down from the cross. Cut the tomatoes in half and gently squeeze the seeds out. Remove any remaining seeds with a teaspoon. Chop the tomatoes finely.

*2* Put the tomatoes, sugar, vinegar and spring onion in a small pan over a medium heat. Bring to the boil, reduce the heat slightly and simmer for 5 minutes. Remove from the heat, transfer to a small bowl and leave to stand at room temperature for at least 1 hour. Stir in the mint just before serving.

*3* Trim any excess fat from each cutlet. Using a small sharp knife, scrape the bone until it is clean and trim the meat to a neat disc. Heat the oil in a frying pan. Add the cutlets and cook over a high heat for 2 minutes on each side to seal, then for a further minute on each side. Transfer to individual serving plates, garnish with rosemary and serve with the relish.

*Step 1*

*Step 2*

*Step 3*

# Green Bean Salad

## INGREDIENTS

*425 g/15 oz can haricot or cannellini beans*
*2 tablespoons lemon juice*
*4 tablespoons olive oil*
*1 garlic clove, crushed*
*150 g/5 oz fresh green beans*

*1* Drain the canned beans then place in a food processor. Using the pulse action, process for 1 minute or until a smooth purée.

*2* Put the lemon juice, olive oil and garlic in a small screwtop jar and shake vigorously for 1 minute, or until combined. Add 2 tablespoons of the lemon juice mixture to the bean purée and process briefly to combine. Transfer to a bowl, cover with clear film and store in the refrigerator until required.

*3* Top and tail the green beans. Place them in a medium-size pan and just cover with water. Bring to the boil and cook for 3 minutes, or until tender. Plunge into cold water, then drain. Pat dry with kitchen paper. Place the green beans in a medium-size bowl and toss with the remaining dressing. To serve, pile the green beans on individual serving plates and top with 2 tablespoons of the bean purée. Serve with Lamb Cutlets with Tomato-mint Relish.

## Cook's File

Storage time: Make the bean purée one day ahead. Cook the beans just before serving.

Hint: You can use any type of green beans, such as dwarf French beans.

*Step 1*

*Step 2*

*Step 3*

# Chestnut Truffle Terrine

preparation time 20 minutes, plus 1½ hours refrigeration

total cooking time 15 minutes

serves 6

## INGREDIENTS

225 g/8 oz unsweetened chestnut purée
1 tablespoon sugar
25 g/1 oz butter, softened
200 g/7 oz dark chocolate, chopped
75 ml/3 fl oz cream
75 g/ 3 oz white chocolate, chopped
1 tablespoon cream, extra
fresh seasonal fruit, to serve

*1* Line a 15 x 7.5 cm/6 x 3 inch, 475 ml/ 16 fl oz capacity mini-loaf tin with foil.

*2* Place the chestnut purée, sugar and butter in a medium mixing bowl. Using an electric mixer, beat until light and creamy. Cover with clear film; leave at room temperature until required.

*3* Place the dark chocolate and cream in a small heatproof bowl. Set over a pan of simmering water; stir until the chocolate has melted and the mixture is smooth. Remove from the heat; cool slightly. Pour half the chocolate mixture into the prepared tin and gently tap the tin on a work surface to eliminate air bubbles and level the surface. Refrigerate until set. Cover the remaining mixture with clear film and leave at room temperature until required.

*4* Place the white chocolate and extra cream in a small heatproof bowl. Set over a pan of simmering water; stir until the chocolate has melted and the mixture is smooth. Remove from the heat; cool slightly. Spread over the dark chocolate layer in the tin. Gently tap the tin on a work surface to level the surface. Refrigerate until set.

*5* Spread the chestnut mixture in an even layer on top of the white

chocolate. Refrigerate. Gently reheat the remaining dark chocolate mixture. Spread on to the chestnut layer and chill until set.

*6* To serve, cut the terrine into 12 thin slices; place two slices on each plate, with fresh seasonal fruit such as mango, kiwi fruit or berries.

## Cook's File

Storage time: Prepare this dish up to two days ahead. Store in the refrigerator.

Hint: To make cutting easier, hold a knife under hot water, dry thoroughly and slice. Repeat between slices to ensure a clean cut.

# Vegetarian Delight

*Menu*

# Parmesan-herb Lace Biscuits

preparation time 10 minutes

total cooking time 1 minute each batch

makes 32

## INGREDIENTS

75 g/3 oz Parmesan cheese
1 tablespoon finely chopped parsley
1 tablespoon finely chopped chives
¼ teaspoon paprika

## Cook's File

Storage time: Make these biscuits up to one hour before serving.

Wine suggestions: A rich Cabernet Sauvignon or a spicy Shiraz would go beautifully with this meal. If you prefer white wine, an Australian Chardonnay would suit. You could also serve a sparkling wine or good-quality pink Champagne with the appetiser. Finish the dinner with your favourite liqueur.

*1* Finely grate the Parmesan. Place the Parmesan, parsley, chives and paprika in a small bowl and mix to combine. Place level teaspoons of the mixture in flat piles 5 cm/2 inches apart on a non-stick baking tray. (Cook only a few at a time.)

*2* Cook the cheese mixture under a preheated grill for 1 minute, until golden and bubbling. Watch carefully that the cheese does not burn.

*3* Remove from the grill and let the biscuits cool on the tray for 5 minutes. Lift off carefully with a flat-bladed knife or spatula. Store in an airtight container layered between sheets of absorbent paper for up to 1 hour.

*Step 1*

*Step 3*

# Mushrooms with Garlic and Red Pepper Sauces

preparation time 30 minutes, plus chilling  total cooking time 2 minutes each batch  serves 8

## INGREDIENTS

675 g/1½ lb button mushrooms

40 g/1½ oz plain flour

3 eggs

65 g/2½ oz dried breadcrumbs

1 small red pepper, halved and seeded

250 ml/8 fl oz olive oil

2 egg yolks

1 teaspoon Dijon mustard

1 tablespoon lemon juice

1 small garlic clove, crushed

2 tablespoons plain yogurt

2 teaspoons finely chopped parsley

vegetable oil, for deep-frying

1 Wipe the mushrooms with damp kitchen paper to remove any grit. Place the flour in a large plastic bag, add the mushrooms and shake until they are evenly coated. Place the eggs in a medium-size bowl and beat lightly. Dust the excess flour from the mushrooms. Divide the mushrooms in half and coat the first half with the egg. Repeat with the second half.

2 Place the breadcrumbs in a large plastic bag. Add half the egg-coated mushrooms and shake to coat. Place the crumbed mushrooms in a large bowl. Repeat with the remaining mushrooms. Chill in the refrigerator for 1 hour.

3 Brush the red pepper with oil. Grill, skin side up, until black, then wrap it in a damp tea towel until cool. Rub off the skin and place the flesh in a food processor or blender. Process to a smooth paste. Place the egg yolks, mustard and half the lemon juice in a medium-size mixing bowl. Beat with an electric mixer for 1 minute.

*Step 1*

*Step 2*

*Step 3*

Add the oil, about 1 teaspoon at a time, beating constantly until the mixture is thick and creamy. Add the oil in a steady stream as the mayonnaise thickens. Continue beating until all the oil is added, then add the remaining lemon juice. Divide mayonnaise between two bowls. Stir the garlic, yogurt and parsley into one and the pepper purée into the other.

4 Heat the vegetable oil in a medium-size heavy-based pan. Gently lower batches of the mushrooms into the oil. Cook over a medium heat for 1 minute, or until golden brown. Remove the mushrooms with a slotted spoon and drain on kitchen paper. To serve, arrange the mushrooms on individual serving plates with a spoonful of each sauce.

# Onion and Olive Tart

preparation time 1 hour, plus chilling

total cooking time 1 hour 25 minutes

serves 8

## INGREDIENTS

115 g/4 oz wholemeal plain flour

115 g/4 oz plain flour

130 g/4½ oz butter, diced

4–5 tablespoons iced water

1 kg/2¼ lb medium white onions

1 tablespoon French mustard

250 ml/8 fl oz soured cream

3 eggs, lightly beaten

50 g/2 oz stoned black olives,
    thinly sliced

sprig of marjoram, to garnish

## Cook's File

Storage time: This tart can be made up to one day ahead. Store in the refrigerator and reheat gently to serve.

*Step 1*

*Step 4*

*1* Sift the flours into a large bowl and tip in the bran. Add 115 g/4 oz of the butter. Using your fingertips, rub the butter into the flour for 1 minute, or until mixture is fine and crumbly. Add almost all the water and mix to a firm dough, adding more water if necessary. Turn on to a lightly floured surface and knead for 1 minute, or until smooth. Roll out the pastry to fit a 23 cm/9 inch flan tin. Line the tin with the pastry, trim the edges and chill in the refrigerator for 30 minutes.

*2* Preheat the oven to 180°C/350°F/ Gas 4. Cut a sheet of greaseproof paper to cover the pastry-lined tin. Spread a layer of dried beans or rice evenly over the paper. Bake for 10 minutes. Remove the tin from the oven and discard the paper and beans or rice. Return the tin to the oven for a further 10 minutes or until the pastry is lightly golden. Set aside to cool.

*3* Peel and the slice onions into 1 cm/ ½ inch rings. Melt the remaining butter in a large heavy-based pan. Add the onions and cook, stirring frequently, over a low heat for 45 minutes. Set aside to cool.

*4* Spread the mustard over the pastry base. Put the soured cream and eggs in a medium-size bowl and whisk together. Spread the onions over the mustard and pour the egg mixture over them. Scatter the olives on top. Bake for 35 minutes, until the top is golden and the filling has set. Allow to stand for 5 minutes. Garnish with marjoram and serve.

# Spinach and Avocado Salad with Warm Mustard Vinaigrette

preparation time 15 minutes   total cooking time 2 minutes   serves 8

## INGREDIENTS

30 spinach leaves (about 115 g/4 oz)

1 oak leaf lettuce (feuille de chêne)

2 medium avocados

4 tablespoons olive oil

2 teaspoons sesame seeds

4 teaspoons lemon juice

2 teaspoons wholegrain mustard

*1* Wash and thoroughly dry the spinach and lettuce leaves. Tear the leaves into bite-size pieces. Place in a large serving bowl and toss to mix. Peel and stone the avocados and cut the flesh into thin slices. Scatter them over the leaves.

*2* Heat 1 tablespoon of the oil in a small heavy-based pan. Add the sesame seeds and cook, stirring constantly, over a low heat until they just start to turn golden and give off their aroma. Remove from the heat immediately and allow to cool slightly.

*3* Add the remaining oil, the lemon juice and mustard to the pan and stir well to combine. While still warm, pour the dressing over the salad and toss gently to coat the leaves. Serve immediately.

Step 1

Step 2

Step 3

# Pecan Blondies *with* Chocolate Fudge Sauce

preparation time 30 minutes   total cooking time 35 minutes   serves 8

## INGREDIENTS

melted butter or oil, for greasing
115 g/4 oz self-raising flour
50 g/2 oz plain flour
150 g/5 oz caster sugar
115 g/4 oz shelled pecan nuts, chopped
115 g/4 oz butter, diced
115 g/4 oz white chocolate, diced
1 teaspoon vanilla essence
2 eggs, lightly beaten
whipped cream and 2 large bananas,
   peeled and sliced, to serve

Chocolate Fudge Sauce
115 g/4 oz dark cooking chocolate
5 tablespoons double cream
1 teaspoon vanilla essence

*Step 2*

*Step 3*

*Step 4*

*1* Preheat the oven to 180°C/350°F/ Gas 4. Brush a shallow 28 x 18 cm/ 11 x 7 inch rectangular cake tin with melted butter or oil. Line the base and sides with greaseproof paper and brush with melted butter or oil. Sift the flours into a large bowl. Add the sugar and pecans and make a well in the centre.

*2* Put the butter and chocolate in a medium-size heatproof bowl set over a pan of simmering water. Stir until the chocolate and butter have melted and the mixture is smooth. Cool slightly.

*3* Add the butter mixture, vanilla essence and eggs to the well in the bowl of dry ingredients. Using a wooden spoon, gradually draw together, then stir until well combined, but do not overbeat. Pour the mixture into the prepared tin and smooth the surface. Bake for 30 minutes,

or until a skewer comes out clean when inserted in the centre of the cake. Leave the cake in the tin for 10 minutes, then turn out on to a wire rack to cool completely.

*4* To make the chocolate fudge sauce, put the chocolate in a small bowl. Place the cream in a small pan and bring to just below boiling point. Pour the hot

cream over the chocolate and stir until the chocolate has melted and the mixture is smooth and thoroughly combined. Add the vanilla essence and stir to mix well.

*5* To serve, cut the crusts from the Pecan Blondies. Serve on individual plates with whipped cream, sliced bananas and chocolate fudge sauce.

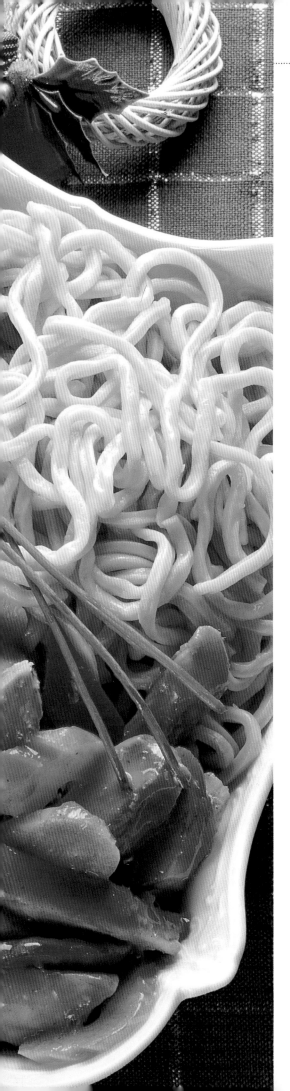

# Christmas Leftovers

## Devilled Turkey Stir-fry

preparation time 10 minutes    total cooking time 7 minutes    serves 4–6

### INGREDIENTS

1 red pepper, seeded
1 green pepper, seeded
1 celery stick
1 carrot, thinly sliced
2 tablespoons peanut oil
450 g/1 lb strips cooked turkey
2 tablespoons mango chutney
1 tablespoon Worcestershire sauce
1 tablespoon Dijon mustard
chives, to garnish

*1* Cut the red and green peppers into thin strips. Slice the celery diagonally. Cut the carrot into thin slices.

*2* Heat the oil in a preheated wok or frying pan. Add the peppers, celery and carrot and stir-fry over a medium heat for 5 minutes. Add the chopped, cooked turkey and stir-fry for 1 minute.

*3* Mix together the chutney, Worcestershire sauce and mustard in a small bowl. Pour the chutney mixture over the ingredients in the pan. Cook, stirring constantly, for 1 minute, until well coated and heated through. Garnish with chives and serve immediately.

### Cook's File

Variation: You could use diced cooked chicken in place of turkey.

Hint: Serve with boiled rice or noodles.

# Pork and Apple Triangles

preparation time 15 minutes

total cooking time 20 minutes

makes 12

## INGREDIENTS

melted butter or oil, for greasing

400 g/14 oz roast pork, finely diced

2 peeled apples, coarsely grated

1 tablespoon currants

2 teaspoons curry paste

3 sheets ready-rolled puff pastry, thawed
  if frozen

1 egg, lightly beaten

sprig of marjoram, sage or parsley,
  to garnish

apple sauce, to serve (optional)

*1* Preheat the oven to 220°C/425°F/
Gas 7. Brush two 33 x 28 cm/
13 x 11 inch baking trays with melted
butter or oil. Mix together the pork, apple,
currants and curry paste.

*2* Cut each pastry sheet into four
squares. Divide the pork mixture into
12 portions. Place 1 portion diagonally
along one half of a square to within 1 cm/
½ inch of the edge.

*3* Brush the edge of the pastry with a
little beaten egg. Fold the opposite
corner over the filling to form a triangle.
Press gently to seal the edges and trim with
a pastry wheel. Repeat the filling and
folding process with the remaining
ingredients to make 12 triangles.

*4* Arrange the triangles on the prepared
baking trays and brush with the
beaten egg to glaze. Bake for 20 minutes,
or until the triangles are puffed up and
well browned. Serve immediately if serving
warm or let cool and serve cold, garnished
with sprigs of marjoram, sage or parsley
and with apple sauce, if desired.

# Vietnamese

## Chicken Salad

preparation time 30 minutes

total cooking time 5 minutes

serves 4

## INGREDIENTS

1–2 tablespoons vegetable oil

350 g/12 oz white radish, shredded

1 celery stick, shredded

1 medium onion, thinly sliced

1 large carrot, grated

3 spring onions, shredded

250 g/9 oz cooked chicken, shredded

lettuce leaves

2 tablespoons crushed roasted peanuts

fresh herbs, such as mint and parsley

Dressing

50 ml/2 fl oz nuoc mam or light soy sauce

4 tablespoons lime or lemon juice

4 tablespoons vegetable oil

2 teaspoons sugar

1 garlic clove, crushed

*1* Heat the oil in a preheated wok or heavy-based frying pan. Add the white radish and celery and stir-fry over a medium heat for about 2 minutes, until the vegetables are softened. Add the onion and stir-fry for 1 further minute. Remove the pan from the heat and set aside to cool.

*2* To make the dressing, put the nuoc mam or soy sauce, lime or lemon juice, oil, sugar and garlic in a screwtop jar and shake vigorously for 1 minute, until combined and emulsified.

*3* Mix together the white radish, celery, onion, carrot, spring onions and chicken in a medium-size bowl. Pour the dressing on to the salad and toss lightly to mix. Arrange a bed of lettuce leaves on individual serving plates and top with the chicken salad. Garnish with crushed peanuts and herbs and serve immediately.

# Scottish

## Stovies

preparation time 15 minutes

total cooking time 50 minutes

serves 4–6

### INGREDIENTS

40 g/1½ oz butter

2 large onions, coarsely chopped

1 kg/2¼ lb potatoes, thickly sliced

1 teaspoon salt

¼ teaspoon pepper

250 ml/8 fl oz water

115 g/4 oz shredded cooked lamb or
   other leftover roast meat

1 tablespoon finely chopped parsley

*1* Melt the butter in a medium-size, heavy-based pan. Add the onions and cook over a low heat for 5 minutes, or until lightly golden. Add the potatoes, salt and pepper and toss until well coated.

*2* Add the water and cover with a tight-fitting lid. Simmer gently for 35 minutes, shaking the pan occasionally to prevent the potatoes from sticking or burning.

*3* Add the meat and parsley to the pan and shake the pan gently. Simmer, covered, for a further 10 minutes. Transfer to a warm dish and serve immediately.

## Cook's File

The name "stovies" refers to being cooked on the stove. This dish can also be cooked successfully in a casserole in the oven. Any leftover meat of your choice can be used in this dish to replace the lamb. It can also be made without using meat at all, and is then known as Potato Stovies. Any type of potatoes may be used, including new ones. The cooking time will vary according to the type of potatoes chosen for the dish. It is often served with glasses of ice-cold buttermilk.

*Step 1*

*Step 2*

*Step 3*

# Tossed Beef/Lamb Salad

preparation time 20 minutes, plus chilling

total cooking time Nil

serves 4–6

## INGREDIENTS

200 g/7 oz green beans, trimmed

1 red onion

1 large carrot

10 cherry tomatoes

250 g/9 oz thinly sliced medium-rare
  cooked beef or lamb

4 tablespoons olive oil

1 teaspoon sesame oil

2 tablespoons lime juice

¼ teaspoon sugar

1 fresh red chilli, seeded and chopped

2 teaspoons chopped mint leaves

90 g/3½ oz watercress

4 tablespoons coriander leaves

1 Cut the beans diagonally into
3 cm/1¼ inch lengths. Using a sharp
knife, thinly slice the onion and cut the
carrot into fine matchstick strips. Cut the
tomatoes in half. Combine the beans,
onion, carrot, tomatoes and beef or lamb
in a large bowl.

2 Place the olive oil, sesame oil, lime
juice, sugar, chilli and mint in a
screwtop jar. Shake vigorously for
1 minute, until combined and emulsified.
Pour the dressing over the salad and mix
well. Cover with clear film and chill in the
refrigerator for 2 hours. Remove the bowl
from the refrigerator and allow to stand at
room temperature for 30 minutes before
assembling and serving.

3 Arrange the watercress around the
outer edge of a large serving platter.
Spoon the dressed salad mixture into the
centre. Sprinkle with the coriander leaves
and pour any remaining dressing over the
salad. Serve immediately.

# Turkey Leftovers

Roast turkey is a seasonal dish for most people and is often served only at Christmas. If the thought of days of cold turkey is all a bit overwhelming, here are some tasty alternatives.

## Turkey  Empanadas

Heat 1 tablespoon vegetable oil in a frying pan. Add 1 small finely chopped onion and 1 crushed garlic clove. Cook over a medium heat for 2 minutes, then add 2 teaspoons paprika, 1 teaspoon ground cumin and ½ teaspoon ground cinnamon and stir until fragrant. Add 2 tablespoons sherry, 400 g/14 oz can tomatoes, puréed and 400 g/14 oz finely chopped turkey. Simmer for about 10 minutes, or until thick. Remove from the heat, stir in 50 g/2 oz chopped stoned green olives, 3 chopped hard-boiled eggs and 1 tablespoon chopped parsley, and season. Transfer to a bowl and allow to cool. With a pastry cutter, cut 18 12 cm/4½ inch circles from 4½ sheets of ready-rolled shortcrust pastry. Place 2 tablespoons of the mixture on one half of each circle, brush the edge lightly with water and fold the pastry over to enclose the filling. Press the edges with a fork to seal. Deep-fry the empanadas in batches for about 2–3 minutes on each side, or until golden brown. Drain on kitchen paper and serve. Makes 18.

## Turkey San Choy Bow

Soak 8 small iceberg lettuce leaves in cold water. Soak 5 dried Chinese mushrooms in hot water for 15 minutes, or until soft. Drain, discard the stems and chop the caps finely. Heat 1 teaspoon sesame oil and 2 teaspoons vegetable oil in a pan. Add 2 crushed garlic cloves, 1 tablespoon grated fresh root ginger and 115 g/4 oz sliced canned baby corn and toss over the heat. Add 300 g/11 oz diced cooked turkey, the mushrooms, 115 g/4 oz chopped water chestnuts, 115 g/4 oz beansprouts, 2 chopped spring onions, 1 tablespoon chopped coriander, 1 teaspoon sugar and 1 tablespoon each oyster and soy sauces. Toss well to heat. Drain the lettuce and pat dry. Spoon the filling into each lettuce cup and serve. Serves 4.

## Leek, Turkey and Sweetcorn Soup

Melt 25 g/1 oz butter in a large pan and add 1 thinly sliced leek. Cook over a medium heat until soft. Add 900 ml/1½ pints chicken stock and 425 g/15 oz can creamed sweetcorn. Season with salt and pepper. Bring to the boil, reduce the heat and simmer for 5 minutes. Add 250g/9 oz shredded cooked turkey. Serves 4.

# Potato *and* Apple Salad

Cut 4 spring onions into thin strips and fry in 1 tablespoon vegetable oil until crisp. Boil 675 g/1½ lb new potatoes until just tender. Drain and allow to cool, then cut in half. Cut an unpeeled red apple into thin wedges and toss with 1 tablespoon lemon juice. Boil 2 thickly sliced courgettes until tender, then drain and refresh in cold water. For the dressing, combine 120 ml/4 fl oz mayonnaise, 4 teaspoons wholegrain mustard, 1 tablespoon Dijon mustard and 5 teaspoons lemon juice. Season to taste. Cut 400 g/14 oz turkey meat into thin strips and toss with the potatoes, apple, courgettes, 2 tablespoons chopped parsley and the dressing until combined. Top with the crispy spring onion. Serves 6.

*LEFT TO RIGHT Turkey Empanadas; Leek, Turkey and Sweetcorn Soup; Potato and Apple Salad; Turkey Filo Parcels; and Turkey San Choy Bow*

# Turkey Filo Parcels

Preheat the oven to 180°C/350°F/Gas 4. Melt 25 g/1 oz butter in a large pan. Add 200 g/7 oz sliced mushrooms and 4 diced bacon rashers. Cook over a high heat until the mushrooms are tender and there is no liquid left. Stir in 350 g/12 oz diced, cooked turkey, 150 g/5 oz ricotta cheese, 2 sliced spring onions and 4 tablespoons shredded basil. Season to taste with pepper. Cover 24 sheets of filo pastry (thawed, if frozen) with a damp tea towel. Working with 3 sheets at a time, brush each layer with melted butter. Cut the pastry into 3 strips. Place 1 tablespoon of the filling at the end of each strip and fold the pastry over to form a triangle. Continue folding until you reach the end of the pastry. Repeat with the remaining pastry and filling. Place on a baking tray, brush with butter and sprinkle with sesame seeds. Bake for 35 minutes, or until crisp. Makes 24.

# Ham Leftovers

A 7 kg/15½ lb ham serves about 20 people. But don't worry, leftover ham can be kept wrapped in a damp tea towel in the refrigerator for up to 10 days. Here are plenty of ways of using it up.

## Ham and Cider Casserole

Preheat the oven to 200°C/400°F/Gas 6. Melt 25 g/1 oz butter in a heavy-based pan. Add 1 chopped onion and fry for 2–3 minutes, until tender. Add 2 sliced leeks and continue frying until the leeks are cooked through. Add 2 crushed garlic cloves and stir briefly. Place the onion and leek mixture in the base of an ovenproof dish and scatter over 400 g/14 oz — 8 slices — chopped ham; season to taste with pepper and pour over 7 tablespoons cider. Spoon 300 g/11 oz can rinsed drained haricot beans over and around the ham and sprinkle with 4 tablespoons breadcrumbs and 1 tablespoon freshly grated Parmesan cheese. Dot with 25 g/1 oz butter and bake for 20 minutes. Serves 4.

## Split Pea and Ham Soup

Rinse 500 g/1¼ lb yellow split peas in cold water, then drain. Place the peas, a leftover ham bone, 2 chopped carrots, 2 chopped celery sticks, 1 large chopped onion, 2 bay leaves and 3 litres/5¼ pints water in a pan, cover and bring to the boil. Reduce the heat and simmer, partly covered, for about 2 hours, or until the peas are tender. Skim off any scum that rises to the surface. Remove the ham bone, cut the meat from the bone and chop finely. Remove and discard the bay leaves. Process the soup in a food processor until a smooth purée, adding a little more water if needed, then stir in the ham. Season to taste with salt and pepper. Serves 8.

## Ham and Leek Pie

Preheat the oven to 200°C/400°F/Gas 6. Boil 2 medium peeled potatoes until just tender. Drain and then slice. Melt 25 g/1 oz butter in a frying pan. Add 2 sliced leeks and cook until golden. Add 300 g/11 oz ham, cut into large cubes, and toss to combine. Place the potato slices in the base of a greased 23 cm/9 inch pie dish and top with the ham and leek mixture. Mix together 5 tablespoons double cream, 2 lightly beaten eggs and 2 tablespoons chopped parsley and pour into the dish. Sprinkle with 50 g/2 oz grated cheese. Dampen the edge of the pie dish with a little water. Place 1 sheet ready-rolled puff pastry, thawed if frozen, on top, trim the edges and press down to seal. Cut two slits in the top of the pastry and decorate with any trimmings. Bake for 40 minutes, or until golden. Serves 6–8.

# Layered Cob

Place 2 red peppers under a preheated grill, and grill, turning occasionally until the skin blackens and blisters. Cool under a tea towel or in a plastic bag, then peel away the skin; seed and cut the flesh into slices. Slice 500 g/1¼ lb aubergines and grill until golden on both sides. Briefly steam 400 g/14 oz spinach until wilted. Allow to cool, then squeeze out any excess liquid. Cut the top off a 23 cm/9 inch cob loaf, leaving a wide opening and reserving the top. Scoop out the white bread with a spoon, leaving a 1 cm/½ inch shell. Mix together 2 tablespoons vegetable oil and 2 crushed garlic cloves and brush the mixture over the inside of the bread shell and the "lid". Place half the aubergine slices in the base of the bread shell and layer the red pepper on top, then 150 g/5 oz sliced ham. Mix together 450 g/1 lb ricotta cheese, 2 tablespoons chopped parsley and 4 tablespoons grated Parmesan cheese and season to taste with salt and pepper. Top the ham with the ricotta mixture. Spread the spinach leaves over the top, then add the remaining aubergines. Place the "lid" on top and wrap tightly with clear film. Place a plate on top, weigh it down with some cans and leave overnight. Serves 6–8.

# Ham, Bean and Tomato Salad

Top and tail 200 g/7 oz green beans, such as French beans, and 200 g/7 oz sugar snap peas. Cut the beans diagonally into 4 cm/1½ inch lengths. Add the beans, peas and 200 g/7 oz frozen broad beans to a medium-size pan of boiling water and cook for 1 minute. Drain and refresh in cold water. Discard the outer skin from the broad beans. Cut 200 g/7 oz sliced ham into thin strips. Mix together the ham, beans and peas, 250 g/9 oz cherry tomatoes, cut in half, 75 g/3 oz cashew nuts, 2 tablespoons chopped parsley and 2 tablespoons snipped chives in a large bowl. To make the dressing, put 4 tablespoons olive oil, 2 tablespoons cider vinegar, ½ teaspoon sugar and 2 tablespoons chopped mint in a screwtop jar and shake vigorously for 1 minute, or until combined and emulsified. Pour the dressing over the ham mixture, season to taste with salt and pepper and toss lightly to mix. Serves 6.

*LEFT TO RIGHT Ham and Cider Casserole; Layered Cob; Split Pea and Ham Soup; Ham and Leek Pie (in front); and Ham; Bean and Tomato Salad (behind)*

# Chicken and Asparagus Frittata

preparation time 10 minutes

total cooking time 20 minutes

serves 4

### INGREDIENTS

25 g/1 oz butter
4 spring onions, finely chopped
6 eggs, lightly beaten
250 ml/8 fl oz milk
2 teaspoons wholegrain mustard
350 g/12 oz diced, cooked chicken
salt and pepper
8 canned asparagus spears, drained
75 g/3 oz Gruyère cheese, grated
mixed salad, to serve

*1* Melt the butter in a large frying pan. Add the spring onions and cook, stirring constantly, for 1 minute, or until soft and translucent.

*2* Whisk together the eggs, milk and wholegrain mustard. Stir in the chicken and season to taste with salt and pepper. Pour the egg mixture over the spring onions and cook over a low heat for about 15 minutes or until the frittata is set.

*3* Arrange the asparagus on top of the frittata and sprinkle with the grated cheese. Place under a preheated grill and cook for 2 minutes, or until the cheese is melted and golden. Serve with a crisp mixed salad.

## Cook's File

Hint: Cook the frittata in a frying pan with a flameproof handle. If you do not have one, cover the handle with foil to prevent charring under the grill or slide the frittata out of the pan into a gratin dish.

Frittata can be served hot or cold. Cut it into wedges for lunch boxes.

# Pan-fried Pudding *with* Coffee Cream

preparation time 6 minutes

total cooking time 25 minutes

serves 6

## INGREDIENTS

*350 ml/12 fl oz double cream*
*4 tablespoons roasted coffee beans*
*3 eggs yolks*
*4 tablespoons caster sugar*
*50 g/2 oz butter*
*6 wedges Christmas pudding*
*berry fruits, to serve (optional)*

1 Put the cream and coffee beans in a small pan and cook over a low heat, stirring occasionally, for about 10 minutes or until just below boiling point. Remove the pan from the heat and set aside to cool completely. Strain.

2 Beat together the egg yolks and sugar in a small bowl with an electric mixer until light and creamy. Add the coffee-flavoured cream and stir with a wooden spoon until thoroughly combined.

3 Strain the mixture into a small, heavy-based pan and cook over a low heat, stirring constantly, for 8 minutes or until the mixture coats the back of a wooden spoon. Do not allow it to boil. Remove the pan from the heat and cover with clear film or a circle of greaseproof paper. (The covering should be touching the coffee cream to prevent a skin from forming on top.)

4 Melt the butter in a large non-stick frying pan. Add the Christmas pudding slices and cook for 2 minutes on each side, or until golden and just heated through. Serve with the coffee cream and berry fruits, if desired.

## Cook's File

Variation: If you prefer a vanilla-flavoured cream, replace the coffee beans with a vanilla pod.

Variation: Dust the pudding wedges with flour, dip in beaten egg and coat with finely crushed cornflakes before frying.

# Puddings and Desserts

## Ice-Cream Christmas Pudding

preparation time 20 minutes, plus standing and overnight freezing

total cooking time 4 minutes    serves 8–10

### INGREDIENTS

175 g/6 oz mixed dried fruit

115 g/4 oz glacé cherries, cut into quarters

50 g/2 oz candied apricots, chopped

50 g/2 oz candied pineapple, chopped

2 teaspoons finely chopped
 candied ginger

2 teaspoons grated orange rind

2 tablespoons orange liqueur

1 tablespoon brandy

2 litres/3½ pints vanilla ice
 cream, softened

4 tablespoons chocolate chips

50 g/2 oz chopped pecan nuts

Chocolate Sauce

120 ml/4 fl oz water

25 g/1 oz cocoa powder, sifted

50 g/2 oz butter

2 tablespoons soft brown sugar

115 g/4 oz plain chocolate, chopped

1 tablespoon brandy

1 Mix together all the fruit, the orange rind, liqueur and brandy in a bowl. Set aside for 20 minutes, stirring occasionally.

2 Using a metal spoon, break up the ice cream in a large mixing bowl. Add the fruit mixture, chocolate chips and nuts and stir until well mixed.

3 Line a 2 litre/3½ pint pudding basin or freezerproof bowl with clear film. Spoon in the ice cream mixture and smooth the surface. Cover with clear film and freeze overnight.

4 To make the sauce, put the water, cocoa, butter and sugar in a small pan. Stir over a low heat for 4 minutes, or until the mixture boils and the sugar is dissolved. Remove from the heat, add the chocolate and stir until melted. Stir in the brandy. Unmould the ice cream, cut into wedges and serve with chocolate sauce.

# Plum

## Pudding

preparation time 30 minutes, plus 3 hours standing

total cooking time 5 hours 20 minutes

makes 2.75 litre/5 pint pudding

## INGREDIENTS

*melted butter, for greasing*

*900 g/2 lb mixed dried fruit*

*75 g/3 oz finely chopped dried dates*

*115 g/4 oz currants*

*115 g/4 oz chopped dried apricots*

*175 g/6 oz glacé cherries, cut in half*

*250 g/9 oz butter*

*115 g/4 oz soft brown sugar*

*2 tablespoons golden syrup*

*175 ml/6 fl oz water*

*1 teaspoon bicarbonate of soda*

*50 g/2 oz chopped pecan nuts*

*3 eggs, lightly beaten*

*150 g/5 oz self-raising flour, sifted*

*75 g/3 oz plain flour, sifted*

*2 teaspoons mixed spice*

*½ teaspoon ground ginger*

*5 tablespoons whisky*

*cream, ice cream or brandy butter,*
*  to serve*

1 Grease a 2.75 litre/5 pint pudding basin with melted butter and line the base with baking parchment. Mix together the dried fruit, dates, currants, apricots, cherries, butter, sugar, syrup and water in a large heavy-based pan and cook over a low heat, stirring constantly, for 10 minutes, or until the butter has melted and the sugar has dissolved. Bring to the boil, reduce the heat and simmer, stirring occasionally, for 6 minutes. Remove the pan from the heat, stir in the bicarbonate of soda and set aside to cool completely.

2 Transfer the fruit mixture to a large mixing bowl. Stir in the pecans, eggs, flours, spices and whisky and mix well. Spoon the mixture into the prepared basin and smooth the surface. Place a piece of baking parchment over the top of the pudding mixture, cover with foil, then with the pudding basin lid. Alternatively, cover

with a double layer of foil firmly tied in place with string.

3 Place the basin on a trivet in a large pan. Add enough boiling water to come two-thirds of the way up the side of the basin. Cover with a tight-fitting lid and boil steadily for 5 hours, topping up with boiling water as required.

4 Remove the basin from the pan and let cool completely. Remove the parchment and foil and cover tightly with clear film. Store the pudding in the refrigerator for up to six weeks.

5 To serve, remove the clear film and cover the surface of the pudding with baking parchment, foil and a lid. Simmer on a trivet in a large pan of boiling water for 2 hours. Unmould and serve with cream, ice cream or brandy butter.

*Step 1*

*Step 2*

# Red Fruit Pudding

preparation time 20 minutes, plus standing and chilling

total cooking time 13 minutes

makes one 20 cm/8 inch pudding

## INGREDIENTS

*425 g/15 oz can blueberries in syrup,
  drained and syrup reserved*

*425 g/15 oz can blackberries in syrup,
  drained and syrup reserved*

*150 g/5 oz sugar*

*1 medium dessert apple, peeled and
  coarsely grated*

*300 g/11 oz frozen raspberries, thawed*

*15 thick slices of bread, crusts removed*

*strawberries, blueberries, raspberries
  and blackberries, thawed, if frozen,
  to decorate*

*mascarpone cheese or double cream, to
  serve (optional)*

**1** Pour the fruit syrups into a medium-size pan. Add the sugar to the pan and stir over a low heat for 3 minutes, or until the sugar dissolves. Bring to the boil, reduce the heat and simmer for 10 minutes. Remove the pan from the heat.

**2** Mix together the blueberries, blackberries, apple and raspberries in a large mixing bowl.

**3** Cut the bread in half diagonally into triangles. Arrange approximately half the bread over the base and sides of a deep 20 cm/8 inch cake tin. Brush the bread on the base with 4 tablespoons of the fruit syrup. Spoon half the fruit into the tin and pour one-third of the remaining syrup over it. Place a layer of bread on the fruit. Top with the remaining fruit and one-third of the syrup. Place the remaining bread on top and cover with the remaining syrup.

**4** Stand the tin on a plate with a lip. Cover the pudding with clear film, top with a plate and a weight. Set aside for 1 hour. Remove the plate and weight and chill overnight in the refrigerator. Carefully turn out the pudding on to a serving plate and decorate with the berries. Serve the pudding with mascarpone cheese or double cream, if desired.

# Baked Mango Cheesecake

preparation time 20 minutes, plus chilling

total cooking time 45 minutes

serves 6–8

## INGREDIENTS

butter, for greasing
250 g/9 oz digestive biscuits, crushed
4 tablespoons desiccated coconut
115 g/4 oz butter, melted
500 g/1¼ lb cream cheese
4 tablespoons caster sugar
2 teaspoons grated orange rind
175 g/6 oz can mango pulp
4 eggs, lightly beaten
1 large mango, sliced and 250 ml/8 fl oz
    double cream, whipped, to decorate

Topping
175 g/6 oz can mango pulp
2 tablespoons sugar
1 teaspoon gelatine
4 tablespoons soured cream

1 Preheat the oven to 180°C/350°F/ Gas 4. Lightly grease a 20 cm/8 inch round springform tin with butter.

2 Place the biscuit crumbs and desiccated coconut in a small bowl and add the melted butter. Stir until well combined. Press the mixture evenly over the base and side of the prepared tin and smooth the surface.

3 Beat together the cream cheese, sugar and orange rind in a small bowl with an electric mixer until light and creamy. Add the mango pulp and beat well. Gradually add the eggs, beating thoroughly after each addition.

4 Pour the mixture into the prepared tin, spreading it evenly over the base. Bake for 40 minutes. Remove the tin from the oven and allow to cool completely.

5 To make the topping, put the mango pulp and sugar in a small pan. Sprinkle over the gelatine and stir over a very low heat for 1 minute, until the sugar dissolves and the mixture boils. Simmer, uncovered, for 4 minutes, stirring occasionally. Remove the pan from the heat.

Transfer the mixture to a small bowl and set aside to cool. Stir in the soured cream.

6 Spread the cake with the topping and chill for several hours in the refrigerator. Decorate with sliced mango and pipe with whipped cream to serve.

# Macerated Fruits *with* Creamed Ricotta

preparation time 12 minutes   total cooking time 6 minutes, plus chilling   serves 4

## INGREDIENTS

4 tablespoons water
1 tablespoon lemon juice
90 g/3½ oz caster sugar
1 cinnamon stick
1 tablespoon crème de fraises de bois or
   crème de framboise liqueur
250 g/9 oz strawberries, cut into quarters
250 g/9 oz blueberries
1 orange, segmented
strips of orange rind and bay leaves,
   to decorate

Creamed Ricotta
200 g/7 oz fresh ricotta cheese
4 tablespoons soured cream
4 tablespoons icing sugar, sifted
1 teaspoon grated lemon rind

*1* Put the water, lemon juice, sugar and cinnamon stick in a small pan. Stir over a low heat for 2 minutes, without boiling, until the sugar dissolves. Brush any sugar crystals from the side of the pan with a wet brush. Bring to the boil, reduce the heat and simmer, uncovered, for 4 minutes without stirring.

*2* Remove from the heat and stir in the liqueur. Put the strawberries, blueberries and orange in a bowl. Pour the syrup over the fruit and set aside to cool. Cover with clear film and chill overnight.

*3* To make the creamed ricotta, beat together the cheese, soured cream, icing sugar and lemon rind with an electric mixer until creamy. Discard the cinnamon; decorate the fruit with orange rind and bay leaves and serve with creamed ricotta.

# Crispy Pavlova *with* Fruit and Cream

preparation time 12 minutes

total cooking time 1½ hours

Serves 6

## INGREDIENTS

*melted butter or oil, for greasing*

*1 tablespoon cornflour, sifted, plus extra*
*for dusting*

*4 egg whites*

*¼ teaspoon cream of tartar*

*200 g/7 oz caster sugar*

*1 teaspoon lemon juice or vinegar*

*350 ml/12 fl oz double cream, whipped*

*1 banana, peeled and sliced*

*6 strawberries, cut into quarters*

*2 kiwi fruit, peeled and sliced*

*175 g/6 oz can passion fruit pulp*

*1* Preheat the oven to 150°C/300°F/ Gas 2. Brush a 33 x 28 cm/ 13 x 11 inch baking tray with melted butter or oil. Line the base with greaseproof paper and brush with melted butter or oil. Dust lightly with cornflour and shake off any excess. Using an 18 cm/ 7 inch pan lid or plate as a template, mark a circle in the centre of the prepared tray.

*2* Put the egg whites in a small, dry bowl. Add the cream of tartar and beat with an electric mixer until stiff peaks form. Gradually add the sugar, beating

constantly until the mixture is thick and glossy. Fold in the cornflour and lemon juice or vinegar with a metal spoon.

*3* Spread the meringue on the circle on the prepared tray. Bake for 1½ hours, or until pale and crisp. Cool on the tray in the oven, with the door slightly ajar. Transfer to a serving plate.

*4* Spread or pipe the cream over the meringue and decorate with banana slices, strawberries and kiwi fruit. Drizzle with the passion fruit pulp and serve.

# Mocha

## Ice Cream

preparation time 20 minutes, plus freezing

total cooking time 10–15 minutes

makes 2 litres

## INGREDIENTS

*40 g/1½ oz espresso coffee beans*

*700 ml/24 fl oz double cream*

*250 g/9 oz dark cooking*
 *chocolate, chopped*

*175 g/6 oz caster sugar*

*6 egg yolks*

*250 ml/8 fl oz milk*

*frosted rose petals, to decorate*

*1* Chill an ice-cream maker or line a 20 x 30 cm/8 x 12 inch rectangular tin with clear film and freeze.

*2* Put the coffee beans and cream in a medium-size pan and stir over a medium heat until the mixture reaches just below boiling point. Add the chocolate and remove the pan from the heat. Set the pan aside for 1–2 minutes before stirring the mixture.

*3* Whisk together the sugar and egg yolks in a large bowl until slightly thickened, then whisk in the milk. Gradually add the coffee mixture, together with the beans. Whisk until smooth. Carefully strain the beans from the mixture and discard them.

*4* Return the coffee-cream mixture to the pan and stir over a low heat until the mixture thickens and will coat the back of a spoon. Remove the pan from the heat and set aside to cool.

*5* Place the mixture in the ice-cream machine and churn until firm or pour it into the prepared tin and freeze until just firm. Transfer to a large bowl and beat with an electric mixer until thick. Return the mixture to the tin, cover with clear film and refreeze until firm. Repeat, beating once more before transferring to a container for storage in the freezer. Serve the ice cream in scoops decorated with frosted rose petals.

## Cook's File

Note: To frost rose petals, lightly whisk 1 egg white. Dip the required quantity of clean, pollution free, dry petals in the egg white, then sprinkle with caster sugar. Shake off the excess sugar and place on a tray, lined with greaseproof paper, to dry.

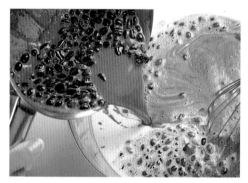

*Step 3*

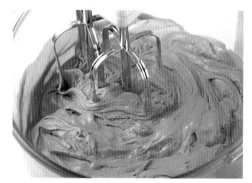

*Step 5*

# White Chocolate Citrus Gâteau

preparation time 1 hour, plus cooling

total cooking time 30 minutes

serves 8–10

## INGREDIENTS

50 g/2 oz butter, melted and cooled, plus
    extra for brushing
115 g/4 oz plain flour
4 eggs
115 g/4 oz caster sugar

*Filling*
2 tablespoons cornflour
5 tablespoons water
5 tablespoons lemon juice
5 tablespoons orange juice
1 teaspoon finely grated lemon rind
1 teaspoon finely grated orange rind
5 tablespoons caster sugar
2 egg yolks
20 g/¼ oz butter

*Topping*
200 g/7 oz white chocolate, chopped
120 ml/4 fl oz cream
50 g/2 oz butter

*Decoration*
1 large lemon
250 ml/8 fl oz water
90 g/3½ oz caster sugar
200 g/7 oz white chocolate, melted

*1* Preheat the oven to 180°C/350°F/
Gas 4. Brush two shallow 20 cm/
8 inch round cake tins with melted butter
and line the bases and sides with baking
parchment. Sift the flour three times on to
a sheet of greaseproof paper. Beat together
the eggs and sugar with an electric mixer
for 6 minutes, until thick, pale and
increased in volume.

*2* Using a metal spoon, fold in the flour
in two batches quickly and lightly
until the ingredients are just combined.
Add the melted butter with the second
batch, discarding any white sediment.
Spread evenly into the prepared tins and
bake for 20 minutes, until lightly golden
and springy to the touch. Leave in the tins
for 2 minutes before turning out on to a
wire rack to cool.

*3* To make the filling, blend the
cornflour with a little of the water to
a smooth paste. Place the remaining water,
the lemon and orange juice and rind and
the sugar in a small pan and stir over a
medium heat, without boiling, until the
sugar has dissolved. Add the cornflour
mixture, stirring constantly until the
mixture boils and thickens. Cook, stirring,
for another minute. Remove from the heat
and stir in the egg yolks and butter.
Transfer to a bowl, cover the surface with
clear film and set aside to cool completely.

*4* To make the topping, put the
chocolate, cream and butter in a
small pan and stir over a low heat until
melted. Transfer to a medium bowl. Cover
the surface with clear film and set aside to
cool completely, preferably overnight. Do
not refrigerate. Beat with an electric mixer
until soft peaks form.

*5* To make the decoration, peel wide
strips of rind from the lemon and
remove all the white pith. Cut star shapes
from the rind using a small cutter. Put the
water and sugar in a small pan and stir over
a medium heat until the sugar is completely
dissolved. Add the lemon rind and bring to
the boil. Reduce the heat and simmer for
5 minutes. Remove the rind with tongs and
place on a wire rack to drain and cool.
Spread melted chocolate about 1 cm/½ inch
thick on a smooth work surface. When just
set, shave wide curls from the chocolate
using a sharp, flat-bladed knife.

*6* To assemble the gâteau, cut the
cakes in half horizontally with a
serrated knife. Place one cake layer on a
serving plate. Spread the cake evenly with
the filling. Continue layering the cake and
filling, ending with a cake layer on top.
Spread the top and sides of the cake with
the topping and decorate with white
chocolate curls and lemon rind stars.

*Step 2*

*Step 3*

## Cook's File

Storage time: The cake may be made up to a day in advance. The gâteau may be assembled up to 8 hours in advance. Store in the refrigerator or a cool place.

Step 5

Step 6

# Crêpes

## Suzette

preparation time 30 minutes

total cooking time 35 minutes

serves 4–6

## INGREDIENTS

*Crêpe Batter*
115 g/4 oz plain flour
2 teaspoons caster sugar
2 eggs, lightly beaten
250 ml/8 fl oz milk
15 g/½ oz butter, melted
1 tablespoon brandy
vegetable oil, for greasing

*Suzette Sauce*
50 g/2 oz butter
4 tablespoons sugar
1 tablespoon grated orange rind
1 tablespoon grated lemon rind
250 ml/8 fl oz orange juice
4 tablespoons lemon juice
4 tablespoons Grand Marnier
cream or ice cream, to serve

*1* To make the batter, place all the ingredients in a food processor. Using the pulse action, process for 40 seconds or until the ingredients are combined and the mixture is free of lumps. Transfer the mixture to a bowl or jug and stand, covered with clear film, for 1 hour. The crêpe batter should be about the consistency of pouring cream — if it thickens on standing, thin it with a little extra milk or water.

*2* To cook the crêpes, lightly oil a 10 cm/4 inch crêpe pan and heat. Pour in 2–3 tablespoons of batter and immediately swirl it evenly over the base. Cook over a medium heat for 1 minute, or until the underside is golden. Flip the crêpe over with a palette knife and cook the other side. Transfer to a plate, cover with greaseproof paper and keep warm. Repeat

the process with the remaining batter, greasing the pan when necessary. Stack the crêpes on the plate, interleaving them with greaseproof paper.

*3* To make the sauce, melt the butter in a pan. Add the sugar and cook over a medium heat, stirring constantly, until caramelized. Add the orange and lemon rind and juice and the Grand Marnier and simmer, uncovered, for 10 minutes.

*4* Preheat the oven to 200°C/400°F/ Gas 6. Fold the crêpes into quarters

and arrange them on the base of an ovenproof dish, overlapping to form an attractive pattern. Pour the sauce over them. Bake for 10–15 minutes and serve warm with cream or ice cream. This batter can be used for all sweet crêpe recipes.

## Cook's File

Hint: Crêpes can be flambéed at the table. Heat 2 tablespoons Grand Marnier, brandy or orange liqueur in small pan or Turkish coffee pot. Carefully light at the table and pour the flaming liquid over the crêpes.

# Rich Chocolate *Mousse*

preparation time 20 minutes

total cooking time 5 minutes

serves 4

## INGREDIENTS

*250 g/9 oz dark chocolate*

*3 eggs*

*4 tablespoons caster sugar*

*2 teaspoons dark rum*

*250 ml/8 fl oz double cream, whipped to*
*soft peaks*

*1* Place the chocolate in a small heatproof bowl set over a pan of simmering water and stir until the chocolate has melted and the mixture is smooth. Set aside to cool. Beat together the eggs and sugar with an electric mixer for 5 minutes, or until thick, pale and increased in volume.

*2* Transfer the mixture to a large bowl. Using a metal spoon, fold the melted chocolate and rum into the egg mixture, then fold in the whipped cream. Work quickly until the mixture is just combined.

*3* Spoon the mousse into four ramekins or small dishes. Refrigerate for 2 hours, or until the mousse has set. Decorate with chocolate leaves, if desired (see below).

## Cook's File

Storage time: Chocolate mousse will keep for two days in the refrigerator. Cover the surface with clear film to prevent a skin forming.

Note: To make chocolate leaves, melt the required amount of dark chocolate. Then, with a clean paintbrush, paint melted chocolate evenly over firm, well-defined leaves, such as rose, oak or ivy. Lay aside to set. Gently peel away the leaf (not the chocolate) when firm. Keep refrigerated until needed.

*Step 1*

*Step 2*

*Step 3*

# Cheesecakes

## Basic

 *Cheesecake*

Preheat the oven to 180°C/350°F/Gas 4. To make the base, brush a 20 cm/8 inch round springform tin with melted butter or oil and line with nonstick baking parchment. Finely crush 250 g/9 oz digestive biscuits and stir in 1 teaspoon mixed spice, if liked, and 90 g/3½ oz melted butter until well combined. Spoon into the tin, and press over the base and side. Refrigerate for 20 minutes, or until firm.

To make the filling, beat 500 g/1¼ lb cream cheese with an electric mixer until smooth. Add 115 g/4 oz caster sugar, 1 teaspoon vanilla essence and 1 tablespoon lemon juice and beat until smooth. Add 4 eggs, one at a time, beating well after each addition. Pour over the crust and bake for 45–50 minutes, or until just firm.

For the topping, mix 250 ml/8 fl oz soured cream, 1 teaspoon vanilla essence, 1 tablespoon lemon juice and 1 tablespoon caster sugar in a bowl. Carefully spread over the hot cheesecake. Sprinkle with ground nutmeg and return to the oven for a further 7 minutes. Allow to cool and refrigerate until firm. Serves 8–10.

This cheesecake has a soft creamy centre and can be made without the soured cream topping, but will then need to be cooked for a further 5–10 minutes. The beauty of a basic baked cheesecake recipe is that it can be decorated with a huge variety of toppings depending on the occasion.

## Golden

*Mango*

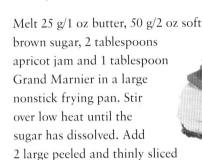

Melt 25 g/1 oz butter, 50 g/2 oz soft brown sugar, 2 tablespoons apricot jam and 1 tablespoon Grand Marnier in a large nonstick frying pan. Stir over low heat until the sugar has dissolved. Add 2 large peeled and thinly sliced mangoes and simmer gently for 3–4 minutes, but don't allow the mango to become mushy. Cool almost completely, then arrange the mango slices on top of the cheesecake while it is still in the tin. Reduce any remaining syrup by simmering for a further 2–3 minutes, then brush or drizzle over the mango. Chill for about an hour in the tin.

## Caramel

*Cheesecake*

Put 50 g/2 oz butter, 50 g/2 oz soft or dark brown sugar, 120 ml/4 fl oz condensed milk and 120 ml/4 fl oz double cream in a pan and stir over low heat until the butter has melted and the sugar dissolved. Bring to the boil, reduce the heat and simmer gently for 5–10 minutes, stirring continuously to prevent the caramel catching on the bottom of the pan. Remove from the heat, cool almost completely and carefully spread over the cheesecake while still in the tin. Refrigerate in the tin for about an hour, or until just set.

# Strawberries and Cream

Omit the soured cream topping. Whip 350 ml/ 12 fl oz double cream to firm peaks and remove the cooled cheesecake from the tin. Spoon cream over the cheesecake. Decorate with halved fresh strawberries. Spoon over the pulp of 2 passionfruit or simply dust with icing sugar.

# Blueberry Marmalade

Combine 120 ml/4 fl oz water, 200 g/7 oz caster sugar and 2 tablespoons lemon juice in a pan and stir over low heat without boiling until the sugar has dissolved. Add 400 g/ 14 oz blueberries and 4 cinnamon sticks. Boil, reduce the heat and simmer until reduced and thickened. Cool slightly and serve over cheesecake wedges.

# Fruit Salad Frenzy

Arrange thin slices of fresh kiwi fruit, halved strawberries, fresh whole blueberries, thin slices of mango and halved black and green grapes over the top of the cheesecake. Heat 4–5 tablespoons redcurrant jelly in a small pan and add 2–3 teaspoons brandy. Simmer for 1–2 minutes and then brush over the fruit on the cheesecake. Allow to set before removing from the tin.

Canned fruits need to be well drained. The extra liquid in these may begin to weep and discolour the cheesecake if it is left to stand for too long.

# Double Chocolate

Fold 50 g/2 oz plain chocolate chips into the cheesecake filling before baking. Omit the soured cream topping and allow the cheesecake to cool. Put 200 g/7 oz chopped plain chocolate and 250 ml/8 fl oz soured cream in a pan and whisk over low heat until the chocolate has melted and the mixture is smooth. Leave to cool slightly, then spread evenly over the cheesecake while still in the tin.

Refrigerate until set, release from the tin and decorate with white, milk and dark chocolate curls.

# Rich Cherry

Drain a large can or jar of stoned sour cherries and place on kitchen paper to absorb any remaining juice. Arrange the cherries over the cheesecake while it is still in the tin. Put 6 tablespoons sieved blackberry or mulberry jam and 2–3 tablespoons kirsch or cherry brandy in a small pan and simmer over low heat for 2–3 minutes, or until smooth and a little reduced. Cool slightly, then brush liberally over the cherries.

It may be necessary to reheat the jam if it begins to thicken quickly. The setting time depends on the consistency of the jam used. Allow to set before removing from the tin.

# English *Trifle*

preparation time 25 minutes, plus chilling

total cooking time 10 minutes

serves 6

## INGREDIENTS

*4 slices Madeira cake or trifle sponges*
*4 tablespoons sweet sherry or Madeira*
*250 g/9 oz raspberries, thawed if frozen*
*4 eggs*
*2 tablespoons caster sugar*
*2 tablespoons plain flour*
*475 ml/16 fl oz milk*
*¼ teaspoon vanilla essence*
*120 ml/4 fl oz double cream*

*To Decorate*
*4 tablespoons flaked almonds*
*raspberries, thawed if frozen*

*1* Put the cake in a serving bowl and sprinkle with the sherry. Scatter the raspberries over the top and crush them into the sponge with the back of a spoon.

*2* Mix together the eggs, sugar and flour. Heat the milk, stir it into the egg mixture and pour into a clean pan. Cook over a medium heat until the custard thickens and will coat the back of a spoon. Stir in the vanilla essence, cover the surface with clear film and leave to cool.

*3* Pour the custard over the raspberries and leave to set in the refrigerator. Whip the cream and spoon it over the custard. Decorate with almonds and raspberries and refrigerate until needed.

# Zuppa *Inglese*

preparation time 35 minutes, plus chilling

total cooking time 10 minutes

serves 6

## INGREDIENTS

*melted butter or oil, for brushing*
*475 ml/16 fl oz milk*
*1 vanilla pod, split lengthways*
*4 egg yolks*
*90 g/3½ oz caster sugar*
*2 tablespoons plain flour*
*300 g/11 oz Madeira cake, cut into*
*    1 cm/½ inch slices*
*5 tablespoons rum*
*1 tablespoon water*
*25 g/1 oz chocolate, grated or shaved*
*50 g/2 oz flaked almonds, toasted*

*1* Brush a 1.5 litre/2½ pint serving dish with melted butter or oil. Put the milk and vanilla pod in a pan and heat gently until bubbles appear around the edge of the pan. Whisk together the egg yolks, sugar and flour until thick and pale.

*2* Discard the vanilla pod and gradually whisk the warm milk into the egg mixture and blend well. Pour the custard into a clean pan and cook over a medium heat, stirring constantly, until the custard boils and thickens.

*3* Line the base of the prepared dish with one-third of the cake slices. Mix the rum with the water and brush the mixture on to the cake slices. Spread one-third of the custard over the cake, top with cake slices and brush with rum mixture. Repeat this process, finishing with a layer of custard. Cover and chill in the refrigerator for at least 3 hours.

*4* Sprinkle the trifle with grated or shaved chocolate and toasted flaked almonds just before serving.

# Chocolate Fudge Puddings

preparation time 40 minutes, plus standing

total cooking time 40 minutes

serves 6

## INGREDIENTS

*melted butter, for brushing*
*150 g/5 oz plain chocolate,*
*  roughly chopped*
*120 ml/4 fl oz milk*
*65 g/2½ oz day-old*
*  white breadcrumbs*
*25 g/1 oz unsalted butter*
*1 tablespoon sugar*
*2 eggs, separated*
*25 g/1 oz walnuts, finely chopped*
*½ teaspoon vanilla essence*

*Hot Chocolate Sauce*
*175 g/6 oz plain chocolate,*
*  roughly chopped*
*150 ml/5 fl oz double cream*

*1* Brush six dariole moulds or ramekins with melted butter. Line the bases with baking parchment. Place the chocolate and milk in a medium-size pan and stir over a medium heat until combined. Remove from the heat and stir in the breadcrumbs. Set aside to stand for 20 minutes, then transfer to a bowl.

*2* Preheat the oven to 180°C/350°F/ Gas 4. Beat together the butter and sugar until light and creamy. Gradually add the egg yolks, beating well after each addition. Fold into the chocolate mixture and stir in the walnuts and vanilla essence.

*3* Beat the egg whites with an electric mixer until stiff peaks form. Fold them into the chocolate mixture. Spoon the mixture into the prepared dishes. Place them in a roasting tin and pour in enough boiling water to come halfway up the sides of the dishes. Lightly grease a sheet of foil and rest it on top of the dishes. Bake for 35 minutes, or until just set. Leave to stand for 5 minutes before turning out on to serving plates.

*4* To make the hot chocolate sauce, place the chocolate and cream in a small heatproof bowl set over a pan of simmering water. Stir until the chocolate melts and the mixture is smooth. Pour the hot chocolate sauce over the puddings and serve immediately.

## Cook's File

Hint: Serve the puddings dusted with a combination of sifted icing sugar and cocoa powder, if desired. The sauce can be served separately in a jug.

*Step 2*

*Step 3*

# Orange Praline Torte with Marsala Sauce

preparation time 1 hour   total cooking time 1 hour 10 minutes   serves 6

## INGREDIENTS

115 g/4 oz unsalted butter, plus extra
    for greasing
90 g/3½ oz caster sugar
1 teaspoon grated orange rind
2 eggs
50 g/2 oz white chocolate, melted
    and cooled
120 ml/4 fl oz freshly squeezed
    orange juice
165 g/5½ oz self-raising flour
2 tablespoons Marsala
300 ml/½ pint double cream

Orange Custard
4 tablespoons custard powder
4 tablespoons caster sugar
250 ml/8 fl oz milk
250 ml/8 fl oz orange juice

Praline
115 g/4 oz pecan nuts or almonds, toasted
200 g/7 oz caster sugar

Marsala Cream Sauce
350 ml/12 fl oz double cream
5 tablespoons Marsala
2 teaspoons clear honey
1 tablespoon cornflour

*1* Preheat the oven to 180°C/350°F/ Gas 4. Grease and line the base of a deep, 20 cm/8 inch round tin. Cream together the butter, sugar and orange rind until light and fluffy. Add the eggs, one at a time, beating well after each addition. Beat in the chocolate.

*2* Mix together the orange juice and 2 tablespoons water. Use a metal spoon to fold in spoonfuls of flour alternately with spoonfuls of diluted juice. Spoon into the prepared tin, smooth the surface and bake for 35–40 minutes, or until a skewer comes out clean when inserted into the centre. Transfer to a wire rack to cool.

*3* To make the orange custard, put the custard powder and sugar in a pan. Set over a low heat and gradually stir in the milk until smooth. Add the orange juice and cook, stirring constantly, until the mixture boils and thickens. Cover the surface with clear film to prevent a skin forming and leave to cool.

*4* Cut the cake horizontally into four layers. Brush one layer with a little Marsala, spread with a third of the orange

custard, top with another cake layer and continue brushing with Marsala and spreading with custard until complete. Beat the cream into firm peaks and then spread over the cake. Chill until needed.

*5* To make praline, line a baking tray with non-stick baking parchment and scatter with a single layer of pecans or almonds. Put the sugar in a small pan with 4 tablespoons water and stir over a low heat until the sugar has dissolved. Bring to the boil, reduce the heat and simmer, without stirring, for about 8 minutes, or until a rich caramel colour. Immediatel, pour the mixture over the nuts on the tray and leave to cool. When set, break into pieces, process or crush and then arrange decoratively over the cake.

*6* To make the Marsala cream sauce, put the cream and Marsala in a small pan and simmer over a low heat for 5 minutes. Remove from the heat and add the honey. Mix the cornflour with 1 tablespoon water, then stir into the sauce. Cook, stirring constantly, until the sauce boils and thickens. Remove the pan from the heat and cool slightly. Serve the sauce warm or chilled with the sliced torte.

Step 1

Step 2

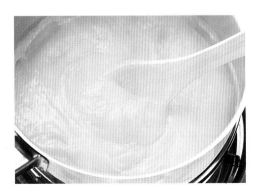

Step 3

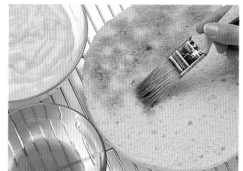

Step 4

Step 5

Step 6

# White Chocolate Puffs *with* Dark Chocolate Sauce

preparation time 40 minutes    total cooking time 35 minutes    serves 4–6

## INGREDIENTS

175 ml/6 fl oz water

50 g/2 oz butter

90 g/3½ oz plain flour

3 eggs, beaten

4 tablespoons custard powder

1 tablespoon caster sugar

350 ml/12 fl oz milk

150 g/5 oz white chocolate, chopped

1 tablespoon Grand Marnier

Chocolate Sauce

115 g/4 oz plain chocolate, chopped

120 ml/4 fl oz cream

*1* Preheat the oven to 200°C/400°F/ Gas 6. Line a baking tray with baking parchment. Put the water and butter in a pan, bring to the boil and remove from the heat. Add the flour and stir over a medium heat until the mixture forms a smooth ball. Allow to cool slightly. Place the mixture in a food processor. With the motor running, gradually add the eggs to form a smooth thick paste. Spoon 2 heaped teaspoons of the mixture on the prepared tray 5 cm/ 2 inches apart. Sprinkle with water. Bake for 10 minutes, then reduce the temperature to 180°C/350°F/Gas 4 and bake for a further 12–15 minutes, or until the dough is puffed up. Cut a slit in each. Turn off the oven and cool for 5 minutes.

*2* Put the custard powder and sugar in a pan and gradually stir in the milk until smooth. Stir over a low heat until the mixture boils and thickens. Remove the pan from the heat and add the chocolate and liqueur, stirring until melted. Cover the surface with clear film and cool.

*Step 1*

*Step 2*

*Step 3*

*3* Stir the custard until smooth and spoon into a piping bag with a 1 cm/ ½ inch plain nozzle. Pipe the custard into each puff through the slit.

*4* To make the chocolate sauce, put the chocolate and cream in a pan and stir over a low heat until melted. Serve the puffs warm with the chocolate sauce.

# Champagne Fruit Salad

preparation time 1 hour 20 minutes

total cooking time 20 minutes

serves 6–8

## INGREDIENTS

350 ml/12 fl oz Champagne
5 tablespoons caster sugar
300 g/11 oz lychees
4 nectarines
450 g/1 lb strawberries
double cream or ice cream, to serve

*1* Place 250 ml/8 fl oz of the Champagne and the sugar in a small pan and stir over a low heat, without boiling, until the sugar has completely dissolved. Bring to the boil, reduce the heat slightly and simmer for 10 minutes. Transfer to a jug and cool to room temperature.

*2* Halve the lychees and remove the skins and stones. Cut the nectarines in half around the stone and gently prise one half away. Cut around the stone to remove the flesh from the other half. Cut each nectarine into 12 slices. Hull and halve the strawberries. Combine the fruit in a serving bowl.

*3* Pour the cooled Champagne syrup over the fruit and chill in the refrigerator for 1 hour, stirring occasionally. To serve, pour the remaining Champagne over the fruit. Serve with thick cream or good vanilla ice cream.

## Cook's File

Storage time: The fruit salad may be refrigerated for up to 3 hours. Add extra Champagne just before serving.

Variation: Peaches may be used instead of nectarines and rambutans instead of lychees.

*Step 1*

*Step 2*

*Step 3*

# Chocolate Baskets *with* Honeycomb Ice Cream

preparation time 40 minutes, plus freezing  total cooking time 2–3 minutes  serves 8

## INGREDIENTS

*4 x 50 g/2 oz chocolate-coated*
*honeycomb bars*
*2 litres/3½ pints vanilla ice cream*
*200 g/7 oz plain chocolate, broken*
*into pieces*
*long chocolate curls, to*
*decorate (optional)*

*1* Place eight small upturned drinking tumblers or glass jars on a work surface. Cut some freezer wrap into eight 14 cm/5½ inch square sheets. Using a sharp knife, roughly chop the chocolate-coated honeycomb bars into bite-size pieces and set aside.

*2* Soften the ice cream slightly and transfer to a large bowl. Stir in the chocolate-coated honeycomb pieces. Return the mixture to the ice cream container or a freezerproof plastic tub and freeze until firm.

*3* Place the chocolate in a small heatproof bowl set over a pan of simmering water. Stir until the chocolate has melted and the mixture is smooth. Remove the bowl from the heat. Working with one sheet at a time, spread a circle of melted chocolate on the prepared pieces of freezer wrap. Drape each square over a glass or jar, chocolate side out.

*4* Allow the chocolate to set, then carefully peel away the freezer wrap (not the chocolate). Scoop the honeycomb ice cream into the chocolate cups. Decorate with long chocolate curls, if desired, and serve immediately.

Step 1

Step 2

Step 3

Step 4

## Cook's File

Storage time: This ice cream can be kept for one month in the freezer.

Note: Freezer wrap is heavier than standard clear film. It is available in most supermarkets. Alternatively, you could use squares of foil.

Hint: In a very warm house, the chocolate baskets may need to be refrigerated in order to set.

# Lemon Meringue Pie

preparation time 30 minutes, plus chilling

total cooking time 50 minutes

serves 8

## INGREDIENTS

150 g/5 oz plain flour
2–3 tablespoons icing sugar
115 g/4 oz butter, diced
3 tablespoons iced water

*Filling*
4 tablespoons cornflour
4 tablespoons water
250 ml/8 fl oz lemon juice
2 teaspoons finely grated lemon rind
150 g/5 oz caster sugar
4 egg yolks
25 g/1 oz butter, diced

*Topping*
4 egg whites
150 g/5 oz caster sugar

*1* Preheat the oven to 180°C/350°F/ Gas 4. Sift the flour and icing sugar into a large bowl, add the butter and rub in with the fingertips for 2 minutes, or until the mixture is fine and crumbly. Add almost all the water and mix to a firm dough, adding more liquid if necessary. Turn on to a lightly floured surface and knead lightly until smooth. Roll between 2 sheets of clear film until large enough to cover the base and side of a 23 cm/9 inch round flan tin. Line the tin with the pastry, trim and crimp the edges and set aside to rest in the refrigerator for 20 minutes.

*2* Place a sheet of greaseproof paper in the pastry-lined tin and spread with dried beans or rice. Bake for 10 minutes. Remove from the oven and discard the paper and beans. Return the tin to the oven for another 10 minutes, or until the pastry is lightly golden. Leave to cool.

*3* To make the filling, mix the cornflour with a little of the water to make a smooth paste. Put the remaining water, lemon juice and rind and sugar in a small pan. Stir over a low heat, without boiling, until the sugar dissolves. Stir in the cornflour mixture. Stir over a moderate heat until the mixture boils and thickens. Simmer, stirring, for 1 minute more. Remove the pan from the heat and whisk in the egg yolks and butter. Transfer the mixture to a bowl, cover the surface with clear film and cool.

*4* Finally, make the topping. Preheat the oven to 150°C/300°F/Gas 2. Beat the egg whites in a small, dry mixing bowl with an electric mixer until soft peaks form. Gradually beat in the sugar and continue beating until it has dissolved.

*5* Pour the cold filling into the cold pastry case. Spread with the meringue so that it covers the filling completely and form peaks. Bake for 20 minutes or until lightly browned. Serve hot or cold.

*Step 1*

*Step 3*

*Step 5*

# Glazed Berry Tart

preparation time 35 minutes, plus chilling

total cooking time 35 minutes

serves 4–6

## INGREDIENTS

115 g/4 oz plain flour
90 g/3½ oz butter
2 tablespoons icing sugar
1–2 tablespoons water

*Filling*
3 egg yolks
2 tablespoons caster sugar
2 tablespoons cornflour
250 ml/8 fl oz milk
1 teaspoon vanilla essence
250 g/9 oz strawberries, halved, thawed
   if frozen
115 g/4 oz blueberries, thawed
   if frozen
115 g/4 oz raspberries, thawed
   if frozen
150 g/5 oz redcurrant jelly

*Step 1*

*Step 3*

*Step 4*

*1* Preheat the oven to 180°C/350°F/ Gas 4. Put the flour, butter and icing sugar in a food processor and, using the pulse action, process for 15 seconds, or until fine and crumbly. Add almost all the water and process for 20 seconds, or until the mixture comes together, adding more water if necessary. Turn on to a lightly floured surface and knead lightly until smooth. Roll out the pastry to fit a 20 cm/ 8 inch round fluted flan tin. Line the tin with the pastry and trim the edges. Chill in the refrigerator for 20 minutes.

*2* Cut a sheet of greaseproof paper to cover the pastry-lined tin. Spread a layer of dried beans or rice evenly over the paper. Bake for 15 minutes. Remove from the oven and discard the paper and rice. Return the tart to the oven for 15 minutes, or until lightly golden.

*3* To make the filling, whisk together the egg yolks, sugar and cornflour until pale. Heat the milk in a small pan until just below boiling point, then remove from the heat. Gradually add the milk to the egg mixture, beating constantly. Strain the mixture into a clean pan. Stir over a low heat for 3 minutes, or until it boils and thickens. Remove from the heat and add the vanilla essence. Transfer to a bowl, cover with clear film and cool.

*4* Spread the filling in the cooled pastry case. Top with concentric circles of strawberries, blueberries and raspberries. Warm the redcurrant jelly in a small pan until it melts. Brush the jelly over the fruit with a pastry brush.

## Cook's File

Hint: Cook pastry up to a day ahead and fill up to 4 hours before serving.

# Red Wine Jelly *with* Frosted Fruits

preparation time 20 minutes, plus chilling

total cooking time 5 minutes

serves 4

## INGREDIENTS

600 ml/1 pint good red wine
rind and juice of 1 orange
rind of 1 lemon
2 cinnamon sticks
90 g/3½ oz caster sugar, plus extra
   for frosting
5 teaspoons gelatine
1 egg white
about 225 g/8 oz mixed blackcurrants and
   redcurrants or mixed seedless grapes

*1* Put the wine, orange and lemon rind, cinnamon and sugar in a small pan. Heat gently until the sugar has dissolved. Put the orange juice in a small bowl, sprinkle with the gelatine and set aside for 2 minutes. Put the small bowl into a larger bowl of hot water; leave to soften slightly. Then stir with a fork until the gelatine has completely dissolved.

*2* Stir the dissolved gelatine into the wine mixture. Pour through a muslin-lined sieve into a dampened 1.5 litre/ 2½ pint mould. Chill in the refrigerator for about 3 hours until set.

*3* Meanwhile, whisk the egg white lightly in a bowl. Put 1–2 tablespoons caster sugar in another bowl. Dip the fruit first into the egg white and then into the sugar, shaking off the excess. Place on a tray lined with non-stick paper to dry. To serve, turn out the jelly on to a serving plate and serve with the fruit.

*Step 1*

*Step 2*

# Berry

*Nests*

preparation time 30 minutes, plus cooling

total cooking time 1 hour 15 minutes

makes 12

## INGREDIENTS

4 egg whites
small pinch of cream of tartar
200 g/7 oz caster sugar
350 ml/12 fl oz double cream
2 teaspoons icing sugar
4 teaspoons brandy
fresh mixed berries

*1* Line a large baking tray with non-stick baking parchment and preheat the oven to 150°C/300°F/Gas 2.

*2* Beat together the egg whites and cream of tartar until soft peaks form, then gradually beat in the sugar. Continue beating until the mixture is stiff and glossy.

*3* Fit a piping bag with a medium-sized star nozzle and use to pipe tightly coiled spirals of meringue — about 8 cm/3 inches in diameter — on to the prepared tray. Pipe rings on the top edges of the rounds to form nests.

*4* Bake for 30 minutes. Reduce the oven temperature to 120°C/250°F/Gas ½ and bake for a further 45 minutes. Turn the oven off and allow the nests to cool in the oven with the door ajar. Whip the cream, together with the icing sugar and brandy. Pile into the nests and top with the mixed berries of your choice.

## Cook's File

Note: The cream of tartar will help to dry the meringues, making them crisp and crunchy. These nests are also delicious served with a simple coulis of puréed fresh berries, perhaps sweetened with a little icing sugar.

*Step 2*

*Step 3*

*Step 4*

# Black Forest Pavlova

preparation time 1 hour, plus soaking

total cooking time 1 hour 10 minutes, plus cooling

serves 8–10

## INGREDIENTS

350 g/12 oz canned or bottled, stoned
 sour or morello cherries, drained
4 tablespoons cherry brandy
2 cinnamon sticks
6 cloves
cornflour, for dusting
6 egg whites
275 g/10 oz caster sugar
2 tablespoons cocoa powder
450 g/1 lb plain chocolate, chopped
600 ml/1 pint double cream
fresh stoned sweet cherries to
 decorate (optional)

*1* Put the cherries, cherry brandy, cinnamon sticks and cloves in a bowl, cover with clear film and leave for several hours or overnight.

*2* Preheat the oven to 150°C/300°F/ Gas 2 and line three baking trays with non-stick baking parchment. Draw a 20 cm/8 inch circle on each sheet and sprinkle lightly with cornflour. Beat the egg whites with an electric mixer until stiff peaks form. Add the sugar gradually, beating well after each addition. Continue beating until the mixture is thick and glossy and all the sugar is dissolved. Beat in the cocoa powder.

*3* Spread the meringue mixture evenly over the circles on the prepared trays. Bake for 1 hour, or until crisp, and then turn the oven off and leave the meringues inside until completely cool.

*4* Put 200 g/7 oz of the chocolate and 4 tablespoons of the cream in a small heatproof bowl set over a pan of simmering water. Stir until the chocolate has melted and the mixture is smooth. Remove from the heat and allow to cool slightly before spreading it evenly over one side of the three meringue discs, almost up to the edge.

*5* Beat the remaining cream until firm peaks form and then spread a third of it over one of the meringue discs. Top with half the drained cherries. Place a second meringue layer on top and top with half the remaining cream and all the remaining cherries. Put the last meringue on top and spread with the remaining cream.

*6* Melt the remaining chocolate and spread in a thin layer over a cool smooth work surface. Using the edge of a sharp knife at a 45° angle, scrape thin strips of chocolate (scrape away from your body to be safe). The strips will curl as they come away. If the chocolate breaks it has set too hard and needs to be re-melted. Decorate the pavlova with a heap of fresh cherries, if desired, and chocolate curls.

## Cook's File

Storage time: The meringue discs can be made a day in advance. Store in an airtight container, but assemble the pavlova just before serving. The cherries can be left to soak for several days. Store, covered, in the refrigerator. The longer they soak, the better the flavour will be. Chocolate curls can be refrigerated between two sheets of greaseproof paper for up to 2 weeks or frozen for up to 6 months.

Variation: When available, stoned fresh cherries can be used. Add 2 tablespoons water and 1 tablespoon sugar to the brandy mixture and simmer the cherries over a low heat for about 5 minutes, instead of just leaving to macerate. Cool and drain before using.

*Step 1*

*Step 2*

*Step 3*

*Step 4*

*Step 5*

*Step 6*

# Simple Citrus Sorbet

preparation time 30 minutes, plus freezing

total cooking time 5–10 minutes

serves 6–8

### INGREDIENTS

*1 tablespoon gelatine*
*350 ml/12 fl oz cold water*
*120 ml/4 fl oz boiling water*
*200 g/7 oz sugar*
*250 ml/8 fl oz lemon, orange, grapefruit or*
*lime juice (or a combination), strained*
*citrus leaves or citrus rind, to decorate*

*1* Sprinkle the gelatine over 120 ml/ 4 fl oz of the cold water in a medium-size pan. Stand for 10 minutes. Add the boiling water and stir over a low heat until the gelatine is dissolved.

*2* Add the sugar and stir without boiling until the sugar is dissolved. Remove from the heat.

*3* Add the remaining cold water and the juice. Chill in the refrigerator, then pour into freezer trays and freeze for 2–3 hours, until just firm.

*4* Scrape or scoop the frozen mixture into chilled dessert dishes or wine glasses. Decorate with small citrus leaves or shreds of citrus rind.

# Kiwi Fruit Sorbet

preparation time 30 minutes, plus freezing

total cooking time 5–10 minutes

serves 4–6

### INGREDIENTS

*6 large kiwi fruit, peeled and chopped*
*5 tablespoons sugar*
*250 ml/8 fl oz water*
*2 egg whites*

*1* Put the kiwi fruit, sugar and water in a pan. Stir over a low heat, without boiling, until the sugar has dissolved. Bring to the boil, lower the heat and simmer for 5–10 minutes until soft. Remove from the heat and cool slightly. In a food processor, process in batches until smooth.

*2* Beat the egg whites with an electric mixer until firm peaks form. Fold them into the fruit mixture. Pour the mixture into a freezer tray and freeze for 3–4 hours, until slushy. Transfer to a bowl and beat with an electric mixer until smooth. Freeze overnight.

# Passion Fruit and Orange Sorbet

preparation time 15 minutes, plus freezing

total cooking time Nil

makes about 1 litre/1¼ pints

### INGREDIENTS

*750 ml/1¼ pints orange juice*
*175 ml/6 fl oz passion fruit pulp*
*90 g/3½ oz caster sugar*
*2 tablespoons Grand Marnier*
*2 egg whites*
*candied orange and mint, to decorate*

*1* Mix the orange juice, passion fruit pulp, sugar and liqueur. Beat the egg whites with an electric mixer until soft peaks form.

*2* Using a metal spoon, gradually fold the egg whites into the orange juice mixture. Pour into an ice-cream maker and chill and churn for about 30 minutes.

*3* Scoop into a chilled bowl and garnish with candied oranges and mint.

*4* To make by hand, pour the mixture into freezer trays. Freeze until just firm around edges. Scrape into a bowl and beat until light and fluffy. Return to the trays and freeze for 3 hours or until firm.

# Pecan Pie with Bourbon Cream

preparation time 30 minutes, plus chilling   total cooking time 1¼ hours   serves 6

## INGREDIENTS

*175 g/6 oz plain flour*
*115 g/4 oz butter, diced*
*2–3 tablespoons iced water*

*Filling*
*225 g/8 oz pecan nuts*
*3 eggs, lightly beaten*
*50 g/2 oz butter, melted and cooled*
*175 g/6 oz brown sugar*
*175 ml/6 fl oz golden syrup*
*1 teaspoon vanilla essence*
*pinch of salt*

*Bourbon Cream*
*250 ml/8 fl oz double cream*
*1 tablespoon icing sugar*
*2 teaspoons Bourbon whiskey*

*1* Preheat the oven to 180°C/350°F/ Gas 4. Place the flour and butter in a food processor. Process, using the pulse action for 20 seconds, or until the mixture is fine and crumbly. Add almost all the water, and process briefly until the mixture comes together, adding more water if necessary. Turn on to a lightly floured surface and knead lightly until smooth.

*2* Roll out the pastry to a 35 cm/14 inch circle. Line a 23 cm/9 inch flan tin with the pastry, trim the edges and chill in the refrigerator for 20 minutes. Pile the pastry trimmings together and roll out on baking parchment to a rectangle about 3 mm/⅛ inch thick. Chill.

*3* Cut a sheet of greaseproof paper large enough to cover the pastry-lined tin. Spread a layer of dried beans or rice evenly over the paper. Bake for 15 minutes. Remove the tin from the oven and discard the paper and rice. Return to the oven for a further 15 minutes, or until lightly golden. Remove from the oven and set aside to cool completely.

*4* To make the filling, spread the pecans over the pastry base. Whisk together the eggs, butter, brown sugar, golden syrup, vanilla essence and salt until thoroughly combined. Pour the mixture over the nuts.

*5* Using a fluted pastry wheel or small sharp knife, cut narrow strips from half the pastry rectangle. Cut out small stars with a biscuit cutter from the remaining pastry. Place decoratively over the filling. Bake for 45 minutes, until firm. Set aside to cool completely.

*6* To make the Bourbon cream, whisk together the cream and icing sugar with an electric mixer until soft peaks form. Fold in the Bourbon with a metal spoon until it is just combined with the cream. Serve with the pie.

## Cook's File

Storage time: The pie may be made up to a day in advance and refrigerated until required.

Note: The pecan is native to North America and is much used in the cooking of the American South, as is Bourbon.

# Cakes and Baking

## Traditional Christmas Cake

preparation time 1 hour

total cooking time 3–3½ hours

makes 20 cm/8 inch square cake

### INGREDIENTS

225 g/8 oz unsalted butter
225 g/8 oz soft brown sugar
4 eggs, lightly beaten
1 teaspoon vanilla essence
4 teaspoons orange marmalade
4 teaspoons golden syrup
1.25 kg/2¼ lb mixed dried fruit
225 g/8 oz plain flour, sifted
50 g/2 oz self-raising flour, sifted
2 teaspoons mixed spice, sifted
1 teaspoon ground cinnamon, sifted
120 ml/4 fl oz rum, brandy or port

Royal Icing
4 egg whites
625 g/1 lb 6 oz icing sugar, sifted
2 teaspoons lemon juice

Decoration
1 metre/1 yard ribbon
selection of small cake ornaments

1 Preheat the oven to 150°C/300°F/ Gas 2. Line the base and sides of a deep, 20 cm/8 inch square cake tin with greaseproof paper.

2 Beat the butter and sugar in a small bowl until light and creamy. Gradually add the eggs, beating well after each addition. Add the vanilla essence, orange marmalade and golden syrup and beat until the ingredients are combined.

3 Transfer the mixture to a large mixing bowl and stir in the fruit. Using a metal spoon, fold in the flours, mixed spice and cinnamon alternately with the liquid. Stir until the ingredients are just combined and the mixture is almost smooth. Spoon into the prepared tin and smooth the surface with a wetted hand.

4 Tap the tin gently on a work surface to settle the mixture. Wrap a double thickness of brown paper around the tin and secure with a paper clip. Bake for 3–3½ hours, or until a skewer comes out clean when inserted into the centre. Leave the cake overnight before turning out.

5 To make the icing, beat the egg whites in a clean, dry mixing bowl with an electric mixer for 30 seconds. Add the icing sugar, a tablespoon at a time, beating continuously on low speed until the mixture is very stiff and forms peaks. Blend in the lemon juice. Cover with a damp cloth or clear film.

6 Place the cake on a large plate or a cake board. Using a flat-bladed knife, cover with icing, reserving 2 tablespoons for decoration. Use a knife to work the icing into fluffy peaks. Set aside for 2 hours.

7 Wrap a ribbon around the cake and secure with a dot of icing. Trim the excess and tie into a bow. Place a dot of icing on the back of the bow, place over the ribbon join and secure with a pin (remove the pin when the icing is firm). Secure ornaments on the cake with icing.

## Cook's File

Note: Royal icing sets very quickly, so it is important to work fast. If desired, the icing can be coloured with food colouring.

# Christmas Frosted Fruits

preparation time 20 minutes, plus drying

total cooking time Nil

serves 6–8

## INGREDIENTS

*selection of fruits, such as red and*
  *black cherries, redcurrants or*
  *whitecurrants, blackcurrants,*
  *apricots or tiny plums or pears*
*1 egg white*
*caster sugar*
*18 x 25cm/7 x 10 inch oval fruit cake*

*Icing*
*1 egg white*
*1–3 teaspoons lemon juice*
*115 g/4 oz icing sugar, sifted*

1 Rinse the fruit thoroughly and make sure it is completely dry before starting. In fact, if possible, rinse the fruit beforehand and leave for several hours to dry to make absolutely sure. Line a baking tray with kitchen paper.

2 Place the egg white in a shallow bowl and whisk with a fork until just foamy. Put 1–2 tablespoons caster sugar on a large plate. Work with 1 piece of fruit at a time, except for the berries which look very attractive sugared in fairly small bunches. Using a pastry brush or an artist's paint brush, brush the egg white lightly over the fruit, making sure the entire piece of fruit is fully covered but not too heavily.

3 Sprinkle the caster sugar over the fruit or roll the fruit in the sugar on the plate and shake off any excess, then leave on the prepared tray to dry. The drying time will depend on the humidity and warmth of the house. It is always worth frosting more fruit than you need, so you have a good selection to choose from when arranging it on the cake.

4 To make the icing, whisk the egg white until just foamy. Beat in 1 teaspoon of the lemon juice. Gradually add the icing sugar, beating well after each addition. The icing should be thick and white — add a little more lemon juice, if necessary, but don't make it too runny.

5 Place the cake on a serving plate, stand or board. Working quickly, pour the icing over the top. Using a palette knife, carefully smooth the icing to the edge of the cake, allowing it to run slowly down the side. Leave the cake for 10 minutes to let the icing set a little. Arrange the frosted fruits on top of the cake.

## Cook's File

Hint: The fruits can be frosted several hours in advance, giving them time to dry thoroughly.

*Step 3*

*Step 4*

*Step 5*

# Rich Chocolate Gâteau

preparation time 1 hour, plus chilling

total cooking time 35 minutes

makes one 20 cm/8 inch cake

## INGREDIENTS

200 g/7 oz unsalted butter, plus extra,
    melted, for brushing
50 g/2 oz icing sugar
3 eggs, lightly beaten
2 tablespoons cocoa powder, sifted
175 g/6 oz self-raising flour
5 tablespoons milk

Chocolate Syrup
2 tablespoons cocoa powder, sifted
90 g/3½ oz caster sugar
250 ml/8 fl oz water
2 tablespoons Crème de Cacao liqueur

Filling
200 g/7 oz plain chocolate, chopped
90 g/3½ oz unsalted butter

Topping
115 g/4 oz butter
200 g/7 oz plain chocolate, chopped
2 teaspoons brandy

1 Preheat the oven to 180°C/350°F/
Gas 4. Brush two shallow 20 cm/
8 inch round cake tins with melted butter
and line the bases with baking parchment.

2 Beat the butter and sugar with an
electric mixer until light and creamy.
Gradually add the eggs, beating well after
each addition. Transfer to a large bowl.
With a metal spoon, fold in the cocoa and
flour alternately with the milk. Stir until
just combined and the mixture is smooth.
Spread the mixture evenly into the tins and
smooth the surface. Bake for 20 minutes,
or until a skewer comes out clean when
inserted into the centre of the cakes.
Remove from the oven and cool in the tins.

3 To make the chocolate syrup, put the
cocoa, sugar and water in a small
pan. Stir over a low heat for 5 minutes, or
until the mixture is smooth and the sugar
is dissolved. Simmer for 2 minutes without
stirring. Remove from the heat, stir in the
liqueur and cool.

4 To make the filling, place the
chocolate and butter in a small
heatproof bowl set over a pan of
simmering water. Stir until the chocolate
has melted and the mixture is smooth.
Remove from the heat and cool completely.

5 To make the topping, melt the butter
and chocolate in a small pan. Stir
over a low heat until smooth. Remove from

the heat and stir in the brandy. Allow to
thicken to a spreading consistency at room
temperature.

6 To assemble the cake, cut each cake
in half horizontally. Place the first
cake layer, cut side up, on a board. Brush
the cake with one-fifth of the chocolate
syrup. Spread with one-third of the filling.

7 Continue layering with the remaining
cake, syrup and filling, ending with
cake on top. Brush the cake and sides with
the remaining syrup. Chill the cake for
1 hour, then transfer to a serving plate.
Spread the top and sides with topping and
chill until set. Stand at room temperature
for 30 minutes before serving.

# Mince Pies

preparation time 50 minutes, plus chilling

total cooking time 30 minutes

makes 750 g/1 lb 10 oz mincemeat, 12 pies per batch

## INGREDIENTS

*Mincemeat*
275 g/10 oz raisins, finely chopped
150 g/5 oz sultanas, chopped
50 g/2 oz dried apricots, finely chopped
2 tablespoons finely chopped
  glacé cherries
2 tablespoons chopped almonds
75 g/3 oz mixed peel
5 tablespoons currants
1 apple, peeled and coarsely grated
1 teaspoon grated lemon rind
1 teaspoon grated orange rind
1 tablespoon lemon juice
225 g/8 oz soft brown sugar
1 teaspoon mixed spice
¼ teaspoon ground nutmeg
4 tablespoons brandy
50 g/2 oz butter, melted

*Mince Pies*
225 g/8 oz plain flour
185 g/6½ oz butter, chopped
2 tablespoons caster sugar
1 teaspoon custard powder
2 egg yolks
1–2 tablespoons water
150 g/5 oz mincemeat (recipe above)

*1* Place all the mincemeat ingredients together in a large bowl. Mix well with a wooden spoon. Spoon the mixture into airtight containers or sterilized jars and seal. Keep in a cool, dark place for up to 3 months. Take out and stir occasionally.

*2* Place the flour, butter, sugar and custard powder in a food processor. Process for 20 seconds, or until fine and crumbly. Add the egg yolks and a little water and process for 20 seconds, or until the mixture comes together. Turn on to a lightly floured surface. Gently knead until smooth. Cover and chill for 15 minutes.

*3* Preheat the oven to 180°C/350°F/ Gas 4. Roll out the pastry between two sheets of baking parchment until it is about 3 mm/⅛ inch thick. Cut into circles, using a 7cm/2¾ inch round pastry cutter. Ease the dough circles into greased shallow patty tins. Spoon in 1–2 teaspoons of the mincemeat filling. Re-roll the pastry trimmings. Cut into shapes and use to decorate the tops of the mince pies. Bake for 10–15 minutes, or until golden.

*4* Remove from the oven and transfer to a wire rack to cool. Serve either warm or cold and make a traditional wish.

## Cook's File

Note: Traditionally, mincemeat is made with suet, which is an animal fat. Butter is used in this recipe. Shredded suet is widely available from supermarkets or it is also sold by butchers in solid pieces and must be grated or melted for use in mincemeat, cakes or puddings. Mincemeat made with suet will keep for several years, if it is stored in a dry, dark place in a screwtop jar. Cakes and puddings made with suet also keep well.

# Glacé-topped Fruit Cake

preparation time 30 minutes, plus overnight soaking

total cooking time 4½ hours

serves 6–8

## INGREDIENTS

*500 g/1¼ lb sultanas*

*350 g/12 oz raisins, chopped*

*250 g/9 oz currants*

*250 g/9 oz glacé cherries, cut*
  *into quarters*

*250 ml/8 fl oz brandy or dark rum, plus*
  *1 tablespoon to glaze*

*melted butter or oil, for brushing*

*225 g/8 oz butter*

*225 g/8 oz soft dark brown sugar*

*2 tablespoons apricot jam*

*2 tablespoons treacle or syrup*

*1 tablespoon grated lemon or*
  *orange rind*

*4 eggs*

*350 g/12 oz plain flour, sifted*

*1 teaspoon ground ginger, sifted*

*1 teaspoon mixed spice, sifted*

*1 teaspoon ground cinnamon, sifted*

*Topping*

*675 g/1½ lb mixed glacé fruit, such as*
  *apricots, pineapple, ginger and*
  *cherries, chopped*

*3 teaspoons gelatine*

1 To make the cake, put the sultanas, raisins, currants and glacé cherries in a bowl. Add 250 ml/8 fl oz of the brandy and set aside to soak overnight.

2 Preheat the oven to 150°C/300°F/ Gas 2. Brush a deep 18 x 25 cm/ 7 x 10 inch oval or 23 cm/9 inch round cake tin with melted butter or oil. Cut 2 strips of baking parchment long enough to fit around the outside of the tin and wide enough to come 5 cm/2 inches above the top. Fold down a 2.5 cm/1 inch cuff along the length of each. Make diagonal cuts up to the fold line about 1 cm/½ inch apart. Fit the strips around the inside of the tin, pressing the cuts so that they sit flat around the base. Cut 2 circles of baking parchment, using the tin as a guide, and line the base. Wrap a folded piece of newspaper around the outside of the tin and tie with string.

3 Beat together the butter and sugar. Beat in the jam, treacle and citrus rind. Add the eggs, one at a time, beating after each addition.

4 Sift together the flour and spices and stir into the mixture alternately with the soaked dried fruit.

5 Spoon the mixture into the prepared tin and smooth the surface with a dampened hand. Tap the tin on a work surface to remove any air bubbles. Level the surface with a dampened hand. Sit the cake tin on several layers of newspaper in the oven and bake for 3 hours.

6 Brush with the remaining brandy and arrange the glacé fruit on top. Bake for a further 30 minutes, then cover with greased foil. Bake for 1 further hour, or until a skewer comes out clean when inserted into the centre of the cake.

7 In a bowl, sprinkle the gelatine over 2 tablespoons boiling water. Leave for 1 minute, until spongy, and stir briskly with a fork to dissolve. Brush the gelatine over the hot cake, cover with baking parchment and wrap in a tea towel. Cool completely in the tin and then turn out.

## Cook's File

Hint: This cake is absolutely perfect for making in advance — in fact, it can be stored quite successfully in an airtight container for up to an entire year.

*Step 5*

*Step 6*

*Step 7*

# Panettone

preparation time 40 minutes, plus standing

total cooking time 1¼ hours

makes one 20 cm/8 inch loaf

## INGREDIENTS

*melted butter or oil, for greasing*

*115 g/4 oz mixed dried fruit*

*2 tablespoons candied peel*

*2 tablespoons orange juice*

*3 x 7 g/¼ oz sachets dried yeast*

*1 teaspoon sugar*

*2 tablespoons lukewarm water*

*350 g/12 oz plain flour*

*50 g/2 oz butter*

*3 eggs, lightly beaten*

*2 tablespoons caster sugar*

*120 ml/4 fl oz lukewarm milk, plus extra,
  for glazing*

*1* Preheat the oven to 200°C/400°F/ Gas 6. Brush a 20 cm/8 inch charlotte mould with melted butter or oil. Combine the dried fruit, peel and orange juice in a small bowl and set aside for 20 minutes. Mix together the yeast, sugar and water until smooth. Cover with clear film and set aside in a warm place for about 10 minutes, or until the yeast is foamy.

*2* Sift the flour into a large bowl. Add the butter and rub it into the flour with the fingertips until the mixture is a fine, crumbly texture. Add the fruit mixture and stir until well combined.

*3* In a separate bowl, combine the eggs, caster sugar and milk and stir in the yeast mixture. Make a well in the centre of the flour mixture and add the egg mixture. Using a knife, mix to a soft, wet dough. Using a wooden spoon, beat for 5 minutes, or until smooth and glossy. Scrape the mixture down the sides of the bowl. Cover with clear film and leave in a warm place for 30 minutes or until risen.

*4* Repeat the beating procedure for another 5 minutes. Turn the dough on to a lightly floured surface and knead for 10 minutes, or until the dough loses its stickiness. Place in the prepared tin, then stand, covered with clear film, in a warm place for about 30 minutes, or until the dough is well risen.

*5* Brush with milk and bake for 15 minutes. Reduce the heat to 180°C/350°F/Gas 4 and bake for 1 hour, or until browned and cooked through. Turn on to a wire rack to cool.

## Cook's File

Note: This is a seasonal Italian speciality that comes from the north of the country. Serve with a glass of wine or a cup of coffee to welcome festive guests.

Note: If you do not have a charlotte tin, use a 1.75 litre/3 pint round cake tin.

Hint: Panettone is at its best eaten on the day of baking, but it will stay fresh for up to four days, covered in clear film. Indeed, boxes of it are dispatched by commercial concerns to everywhere around the world every Christmas.

# Panforte

preparation time 15 minutes

total cooking time 55 minutes

makes one 20 cm/8 inch round cake

## INGREDIENTS

*oil or melted butter, for brushing*

*65 g/2½ oz flaked almonds*

*65 g/2½ oz chopped macadamia nuts*

*65 g/2½ oz chopped walnuts*

*225 g/8 oz mixed dried fruit*

*75 g/3 oz plain flour, sifted*

*2 tablespoons cocoa powder, sifted*

*1 teaspoon ground cinnamon, sifted*

*50 g/2 oz dark chocolate, chopped*

*50 g/2 oz unsalted butter*

*5 tablespoons caster sugar*

*4 tablespoons clear honey*

*icing sugar, for dusting*

*1* Preheat the oven to 180°C/350°F/ Gas 4. Brush a shallow 20 cm/8 inch round cake tin with oil or melted butter. Line the base with baking parchment. Mix together the nuts and dried fruit in a large bowl. Add the flour, cocoa and cinnamon and stir until thoroughly combined. Make a well in the centre.

*2* Stir the chopped chocolate, butter, sugar and honey in a small heavy-based pan set over a low heat until melted and thoroughly combined. Remove the pan from the heat. Add the butter mixture to the well in the flour mixture. Using a wooden spoon, gradually incorporate the dry ingredients until they are all thoroughly combined, but do not overbeat.

*3* Spoon the mixture into the prepared tin and smooth the surface. Bake for 50 minutes, or until the cake is firm to the touch in the centre. Allow to cool in the tin before turning out.

*4* Dust the cake with icing sugar. Serve thin wedges with coffee or liqueur at the end of the meal.

# Christmas Wreath Cake

preparation time 35 minutes

total cooking time Nil

makes one 23 cm/9 inch round cake

## INGREDIENTS

23 cm/9 inch round fruit cake
2 tablespoons apricot jam
400 g/14 oz marzipan
500 g/1¼ lb icing sugar, plus extra
    for dusting
3 egg whites, lightly beaten
200 g/7 oz sugarpaste
green and red food colouring
ribbon, to decorate

*1* Trim the dome from the top of the cake to give a flat surface. Turn the cake upside down. Melt the jam in a small pan, strain and brush over the surface of the cake to make the marzipan stick.

*2* Knead the marzipan on a work surface dusted with icing sugar until it is smooth. Roll out to a circle large enough to cover the cake. Lift the marzipan carefully on to the cake, smoothing it down the side to prevent any folds. Trim neatly around the base and smooth with the palms of your hands dusted with icing sugar. Dry overnight in a cool dry place.

*3* Sift the icing sugar into a large bowl, making sure there are no lumps. Make a well in the centre and add the egg whites, stirring from the centre outwards until completely mixed in. The mixture will be fairly stiff. Beat with a hand-held electric mixer until fluffy — it should be spreadable but not runny.

*4* Secure the cake to a cake board with a little icing. Spoon about a third of the icing on top of the cake and spread to the edge with a palette knife. If you have one, use a steel ruler to smooth the surface: hold each side of the ruler and pull it towards you (you may need to do this a few times, adding more icing if necessary).

*5* Ice the side of the cake with a palette knife or ruler. If you have a turntable, this will make everything easier. If not, place your cakeboard on top of the upturned cake tin that you have just used, to give you a little more height and make turning the cake easier. When you have as smooth a surface as possible, leave the cake to dry. (If you want to create a snow scene then, using the end of the palette knife, press down and lift at intervals all over the icing, to make peaks.) Keep a little icing, covered with clear film.

*6* Roll out the sugarpaste on a work surface dusted with icing sugar and cut out leaf shapes with cutters or by hand. Leave to dry, either flat or over a rolling pin to make them curve slightly, then paint different shades of green. Roll a few holly berries and paint them red when dry.

*7* Decorate the cake with a wreath of leaves, attaching each one with a dab of icing, and add a few berries. Tie with a colourful ribbon to serve and dust lightly with icing sugar.

## Cook's File

Storage time: The iced and decorated fruit cake can be stored for up to 2 months in an airtight container in a cool place.

*Step 2*

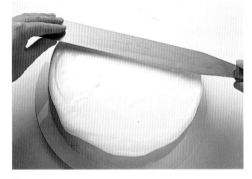
*Step 4*

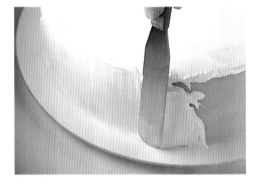
*Step 5*

*Step 6*

# Almond Cream Torte

preparation time 1 hour, plus chilling

total cooking time 30–40 minutes

makes one 20 cm/8 inch cake

## INGREDIENTS

*melted butter or oil, for greasing*
*5 tablespoons dried breadcrumbs*
*5 tablespoons milk*
*2 tablespoons brandy*
*175 g/6 oz butter*
*90 g/3½ oz caster sugar*
*90 g/3½ oz marzipan, chopped*
*4 eggs*
*40 g/1½ oz ground almonds*
*75 g/3 oz self-raising flour, sifted*
*400 g/14 oz white chocolate, chopped*
*400 ml/14 fl oz single cream*
*5 tablespoons Marsala*
*1 tablespoon icing sugar, sifted*
*115 g/4 oz flaked almonds, toasted, and*
 *cocoa powder, to decorate*

1 Preheat the oven to 180°C/350°F/ Gas 4. Brush a deep 20 cm/8 inch round cake tin with melted butter or oil. Line the base with baking parchment. Mix the breadcrumbs, milk and brandy in a small bowl. Beat together 115 g/4 oz of the butter and the sugar with an electric mixer until light and creamy. Add the marzipan and beat until smooth. Gradually add the eggs, beating well after each addition.

2 Using a metal spoon, fold in the breadcrumb mixture, almonds and flour and stir until smooth. Spoon the mixture into the prepared tin and smooth the surface. Bake for 30–40 minutes, or until a skewer comes out clean when inserted into the centre of the cake. Leave to stand in the tin for 5 minutes before turning out on to a wire rack to cool.

3 Combine the chocolate, 150 ml/5 fl oz of the cream and the remaining butter in a small pan. Stir over a low heat until the chocolate and butter have melted and the mixture is smooth. Transfer the mixture to a large bowl. Chill in the refrigerator until set, then beat with an electric mixer until light and creamy.

4 To assemble the cake, cut the cake into three even layers, horizontally. Place the base layer on a large serving plate. Brush with a third of the Marsala. Beat together the remaining cream and the icing sugar until stiff peaks form. Spread half over the cake and continue layering. Brush the remaining Marsala on the underside of the last layer of cake and place on top. Spread the top and sides evenly with half the chocolate mixture. Spoon the remaining mixture into a piping bag fitted with an 8 mm/⅓ inch fluted tube. Pipe teardrops around the outer edge of the cake and then in rows to cover the surface. Press the flaked almonds on to the sides of the cake. Lightly dust the top with cocoa powder. Chill in the refrigerator for up to 3 hours before serving.

# Christmas Window Cookies

preparation time 15 minutes, plus chilling

total cooking time 30 minutes

makes 30

## INGREDIENTS

200 g/7 oz butter
130 g/4½ oz caster sugar
1 egg, lightly beaten
1 teaspoon vanilla essence
1 tablespoon milk
1 teaspoon baking powder, sifted
275 g/10 oz plain flour, sifted
5 tablespoons crushed green
  boiled sweets
5 tablespoons crushed red
  boiled sweets
5 tablespoons crushed yellow
  boiled sweets

*1* Preheat the oven to 180°C/350°F/
Gas 4. Line two baking trays with
baking parchment. Beat together the butter
and sugar with an electric mixer until light
and creamy. Add the egg and beat
thoroughly. Add the vanilla essence and
milk and beat until combined. Using a
metal spoon, fold in the baking powder
and flour and stir until just combined and
the mixture is almost smooth.

*2* Turn the dough on to a lightly
floured surface. Knead for about
1 minute, or until smooth. Divide the
dough in two and shape into balls. Cover
with clear film and chill in the refrigerator
for 1 hour. Roll out one portion of the
dough to 3 mm/⅛ inch thick. Using a
pastry wheel, cut it into 9 x 6 cm/
3½ x 2½ inch rectangles.

*3* Place the rectangles on the prepared
trays, allowing room for the biscuits
to spread. Using small fluted cutters or
alphabet shapes, carefully cut out windows
in the middle of the biscuits. Fill the spaces

with crushed boiled sweets, level with the
surface of the biscuit. Bake for 15 minutes.
Repeat the process with the trimmings and
the remaining ball of dough. Bake for
15 minutes, or until firm and lightly
golden. Remove from the oven and leave to
stand on the trays for 2 minutes before
transferring, with the baking parchment,
to wire racks to cool. When cool, remove
the baking paper.

## Cook's File

Note: Larger Christmas window cookies can
be made by doubling their original size. This
will require a longer cooking time, but will allow
more room, perhaps for a message or for a
name. You could wrap individual cookies in
brightly coloured tissue paper, fasten with a
Christmas ribbon and tie to the Christmas tree
branches or pack them in pretty boxes or bags
as Christmas gifts.

# Chocolate House

preparation time about 1½ hours, plus setting

total cooking time 10 minutes

serves 6–8

## INGREDIENTS

*175 g/6 oz butter, softened*

*175 g/6 oz soft dark brown sugar*

*2 tablespoons black treacle*

*2 eggs*

*300 g/11 oz plain flour*

*50 g/2 oz cocoa powder*

*½ teaspoon baking powder*

*225 g/8 oz plain chocolate*

*115 g/4 oz white chocolate*

*300 g/11 oz chocolate buttercream (see page 230)*

*25 g/1 oz milk chocolate*

*50 g/2 oz marzipan*

*4 large flaky chocolate bars*

*chocolate buttons*

*icing sugar, for dusting*

1 First make the biscuit dough. Sift the flour, cocoa and baking powder together. Beat the butter and sugar together in a mixing bowl until just softened. Add the treacle and eggs and the flour mixture, and mix to a soft dough. Knead lightly, cover and chill for 30 minutes, until firm.

2 Make templates: a 19 x 9 cm/ 7½ x 3½ inch rectangle for the front and back; an 11.5 x 20 cm/4½ x 8 inch rectangle for 2 roof sections; a 9 cm/ 3½ inch square with a 6 cm/2½ inch gable for the sides. Mark 6 windows and the door. Preheat the oven to 190°C/375°F/Gas 5.

3 Roll out the dough on a lightly floured surface. Cut out the shapes, using the templates, and cut holes for the door and windows. Transfer to baking sheets and bake for 10 minutes. Leave to cool for 5 minutes, then transfer to wire racks to cool completely.

4 On greaseproof paper draw 12 shutters, a front door and the outline of 10 Christmas trees cut in half vertically to give 20 half trees. Secure the paper to a flat surface. Melt the plain chocolate. Cool slightly, then brush it thickly, but accurately into the shapes and leave to set.

5 Melt the white chocolate. Spread it over all the walls with a palette knife. Make a swirling pattern with the tip of the knife and leave to set.

6 Roughly spread a little buttercream over the surface of a cake board and assemble the house, securing the walls and roof sections with more buttercream.

7 Melt the milk chocolate and use to pipe handles on the door and shutters with a writing nozzle. Make a chimney from the marzipan. Spread buttercream on the roof and fix the chimney in place. Cut the flaky chocolate into thin 2.5 cm/1 inch long pieces and cut each lengthways into 3 or 4 flat sections. Starting from the bottom of the roof, place them in position.

8 Put 3 tablespoons of the remaining buttercream in a piping bag with a writing nozzle. Spread the rest of the buttercream over the board. Peel off the shutters and door, pipe buttercream on the back and secure them in place.

9 Pipe buttercream on the straight edge of 1 tree section, then secure 4 more sections to it. Place it on the board and make the remaining trees in the same way. Make a path of chocolate buttons. Finally, sift over icing sugar to make snow.

*Step 3*

*Step 6*

*Step 9*

# Individual

## Christmas Cakes

preparation time 40 minutes, plus
cooling and drying

total cooking time 1¼ hours

serves 6–8

## INGREDIENTS

*1 quantity fruit cake mixture (see*
*page 214)*

*Holly Leaves and Berries*
*65 g/2½ oz marzipan*
*green and red food colouring*
*icing sugar*

*Sugarpaste-covered Cake*
*90 g/3½ oz apricot jam*
*90 g/3½ oz sugarpaste per cake*
*icing sugar*
*thin ribbon*

*Royal Icing-covered Cake*
*1 egg white*
*250 g/9 oz icing sugar, sifted*
*2–3 teaspoons lemon juice*

*Step 2*

*Step 4*

*Step 3*

*Step 6*

*1* Preheat the oven to 150°C/300°F/
Gas 2. Lightly grease twelve muffin
tins or Yorkshire pudding tins and line the
bases with a circle of baking parchment.
Fill to the top with the cake mixture and
smooth the surface. Bake for 1¼ hours, or
until a skewer inserted into the centre
comes out clean. Cool in the tins before
turning out to decorate, so the small base
becomes the top.

*2* To make the holly leaves, knead 50 g/
2 oz of the marzipan until it is soft.
Roll out on a surface lightly dusted with
icing sugar as thinly as possible. Cut out
the leaves with a cutter or template. Pinch
the leaves in half, open out and press the
edges gently to curl in different directions.
Set aside to dry on a sheet of greaseproof
paper. Brush green colouring around the

edge of each leaf — don't put on too much
colour or it will bleed.

*3* Knead a little red colouring into the
remaining marzipan and roll into
small balls to make berries. Paint or roll
the berries through the colouring to coat
thoroughly. Dry on greaseproof paper.

*4* For the sugarpaste-covered cakes,
melt the jam until it is runny, strain
and brush over the cakes. Roll out 90 g/
3½ oz of the sugarpaste at a time on a
surface lightly dusted with icing sugar,
until large enough to cover one cake. If
there are any holes in the cake, use a little
extra icing to plug them and make a
smooth surface.

*5* Place the icing over the cake and the
side, pressing lightly, then trim
around the base. Mix together a little icing

sugar and water into a smooth paste. Wrap
ribbon around the base of the cake and
seal with a little paste. Use the paste to
secure two leaves and berries to the top.

*6* To make the royal icing covering,
lightly beat the egg white with a
wooden spoon. Gradually add the icing
sugar, beating to a smooth paste. Slowly
add the lemon juice until slightly runny.
Spread a tablespoon of icing over each
cake, using a palette knife to smooth and
letting some drizzle down the sides. Secure
holly leaves on top and some berries, using
a little leftover icing.

## Cook's File

Storage time: These cakes can be stored in an
airtight container in a single layer in a cool
dark place for up to a month after icing.

# Black

## Bun

preparation time 40–50 minutes

total cooking time 2½ hours

makes one 23 cm/9 inch loaf

## INGREDIENTS

*375 g/13 oz plain flour*

*175 g/6 oz butter, diced*

*150 g/5 oz caster sugar*

*2 egg yolks*

*2 tablespoons iced water*

*375 g/13 oz chopped raisins*

*300 g/11 oz currants*

*75 g/3 oz dried mixed peel*

*115 g/4 oz chopped blanched almonds*

*1 teaspoon ground allspice*

*1 teaspoon ground ginger*

*1 teaspoon ground cinnamon*

*2 tablespoons whisky*

*¼ teaspoon cream of tartar*

*¼ teaspoon bicarbonate of soda*

*120 ml/4 fl oz buttermilk*

*1 egg, plus 1 egg yolk, lightly beaten*

*1 egg white, lightly beaten*

*1 teaspoon granulated sugar*

1 Brush a 23 x 13 x 7.5 cm/9 x 5 x 3 inch non-stick loaf tin with oil. Place 275 g/10 oz of the flour and the butter in a food processor. Add 1 tablespoon of the sugar and process for 10 seconds, or until the mixture is fine and crumbly. Add the yolks and water and process for 15 seconds, or until the mixture forms a soft dough. Cover with clear film and chill in the refrigerator for 20 minutes.

2 Preheat the oven to 180°C/350°F/ Gas 4. Place the raisins, currants, mixed peel, almonds, the remaining sugar, the allspice, ginger, cinnamon and whisky in a large bowl and stir to mix. Sift the remaining flour, the cream of tartar and bicarbonate of soda over the fruit. Add the buttermilk, egg and extra yolk. Using a wooden spoon, beat until well combined.

3 Roll out two-thirds of the pastry until it is large enough to cover the base and sides of the prepared tin, extending 1.5 cm/⅝ inch over the top edge. Spoon the fruit filling firmly into the tin and smooth the surface. Roll out the remaining pastry to cover the tin. Brush the edge of the pastry in the tin, as well as the fruit filling, with lightly beaten egg white.

4 Place the pastry lid over the fruit and press to seal. Pinch or flute the edges, trimming any excess if necessary. Brush the top of the black bun with the remaining egg white and sprinkle with the granulated sugar. Bake for 1 hour, then reduce the temperature to 160°C/325°F/Gas 3 for a further 1½ hours, or until well browned. Cool in the tin. Store for up to one year.

*Step 3*

*Step 4*

# Wholemeal Fruit and Nut Cake

preparation time 45 minutes

total cooking time 2½–3 hours

makes one 20 cm/8 inch square cake

## INGREDIENTS

melted butter or oil, for brushing
175 g/6 oz unsalted butter
175 g/6 oz soft dark brown sugar
3 eggs, lightly beaten
200 g/7 oz dried figs, chopped
200 g/7 oz dried apricots, chopped
115 g/4 oz currants
115 g/4 oz sultanas
115 g/4 oz walnut pieces
65 g/2½ oz sunflower seeds
175 g/6 oz plain wholemeal flour, sifted
50 g/2 oz self-raising flour, sifted
1 teaspoon ground cinnamon, sifted
1 teaspoon ground nutmeg, sifted
1 teaspoon ground allspice, sifted
120 ml/4 fl oz apricot juice

Spicy Nut Topping
4 tablespoons finely chopped walnuts
1 tablespoon sunflower seeds
½ teaspoon ground cinnamon
½ teaspoon ground nutmeg
½ teaspoon ground allspice

1 Preheat the oven to 160°C/325°F/ Gas 3. Brush a deep 20 cm/8 inch square cake tin with melted butter or oil. Line the base and sides with greaseproof paper and brush the paper with butter or oil. Beat together the butter and sugar with an electric mixer until light and creamy. Gradually add the eggs, beating thoroughly after each addition.

2 Add the fruit, walnuts and sunflower seeds. Using a metal spoon, fold in the dry ingredients alternately with the apricot juice. Stir until the mixture is almost smooth. Spoon evenly into the prepared tin and smooth the surface.

3 To make the spicy nut topping, mix together all the topping ingredients. Spoon the mixture on to the top of the cake, pressing it down firmly with the back of the spoon.

4 Bake for 2½–3 hours, until a skewer comes out clean when inserted in the centre of the cake. Leave in the tin for several hours before turning out.

## Cook's File

Note: All traditional fruit cakes must be left to cool in the tin for the specified time. If they are turned out while they are still hot, they will break up.

Storage time: Fruit cakes will keep very well. They can be stored for up to 2 months, covered with several layers of clear film, in the refrigerator.

# Festive Fruit Cake

preparation time 30 minutes

total cooking time 1–1½ hours

makes 2 rectangular cakes

## INGREDIENTS

*115 g/4 oz unsalted butter*

*4 tablespoons soft brown sugar*

*2 eggs, lightly beaten*

*4 tablespoons golden syrup*

*250 g/9 oz dried dates, stoned*

*115 g/4 oz candied pineapple, cut into*
    *2 cm/¼ inch pieces*

*115 g/4 oz candied apricots, cut into*
    *2 cm/¼ inch pieces*

*200 g/7 oz glacé cherries*

*115 g/4 oz whole shelled macadamia nuts*

*115 g/4 oz whole shelled Brazil nuts*

*115 g/4 oz whole shelled hazelnuts*

*25 g/1 oz self-raising flour, sifted*

*25 g/1 oz plain flour, sifted*

*2 tablespoons port or brandy*

*1* Preheat the oven to 150°C/300°F/ Gas 2. Line the bases and sides of two 26 x 7.5 x 4.5 cm/10¼ x 3 x 1¼ inch Swiss roll tins with greaseproof paper. Beat together the butter and sugar with an electric mixer until light and creamy. Gradually add the eggs, beating thoroughly after each addition. Add the syrup and beat until combined.

*2* Transfer the mixture to a large bowl and add the dates, pineapple, apricots, glacé cherries, macadamias, Brazil nuts and hazelnuts. Using a metal spoon, fold in the flours alternately with the port or brandy. Stir until just combined and the mixture is almost smooth.

*3* Spoon the mixture evenly into the prepared tins and smooth the surface. Bake for 1¼ hours, or until a skewer comes out clean when inserted in the centre of the cakes. Leave in the tin for 1 hour before turning the cakes out.

## Cook's File

Note: Macadamia nuts are small, round and white with a delicious flavour. The shells are astonishingly hard to crack, so they are usually sold ready-shelled. Native to Australia, they are now widely cultivated in California, Hawaii and Central America. They tend to be rather expensive, but are worth buying for a special occasion because of their delicate flavour.

# Dundee Cake

preparation time 30 minutes

total cooking time 2–2¼ hours

makes one 20 cm/8 inch round cake

## INGREDIENTS

*melted butter or oil, for brushing*

*250 g/9 oz unsalted butter*

*225 g/8 oz soft brown sugar*

*4 eggs, lightly beaten*

*5 tablespoons orange and lemon rind*

*150 g/5 oz raisins*

*150 g/5 oz sultanas*

*4 tablespoons chopped glacé cherries*

*285 g/10½ oz currants*

*115 g/4 oz ground almonds*

*75 g/3 oz flaked almonds*

*350 g/12 oz plain flour, sifted*

*50 g/2 oz self-raising flour, sifted*

*2 tablespoons rum*

*50 g/2 oz whole almonds, to decorate*

*1* Preheat the oven to 150°C/300°F/ Gas 2. Brush a deep 20 cm/8 inch round cake tin with melted butter or oil. Line the base and side with greaseproof paper. Beat together the butter and sugar with an electric mixer until light and creamy. Gradually add the eggs, beating thoroughly after each addition.

*2* Transfer the mixture to a large bowl and add the orange and lemon rind, raisins, sultanas, glacé cherries, currants, ground and flaked almonds. Using a metal spoon, fold in the flours alternately with the rum. Stir until combined and the mixture is almost smooth.

*3* Spoon the mixture into the prepared tin and smooth the surface. Arrange the whole almonds on top. Bake for 2–2¼ hours, or until a skewer comes out clean when inserted in the centre. Leave in the tin for several hours before turning out.

## Cook's File

Hint: It is important that the dry ingredients in fruit cakes are thoroughly sifted before they are added to the rest of the mixture. Apart from ensuring that they are very fine, this process also helps to aerate them, which, in turn, results in a lighter cake that rises well during cooking.

# Traditional Shortbread

preparation time 20 minutes

total cooking time 40 minutes

makes 8 wedges

## INGREDIENTS

*250 g/9 oz butter, softened, plus extra
for greasing
50 g/2 oz icing sugar, sifted
300 g/11 oz plain flour
4 tablespoons rice flour*

*1* Preheat the oven to 140°C/275°F/ Gas 1. Grease a 23 cm/9 inch round tin or a baking tray. Beat together the butter and icing sugar with an electric mixer until light and fluffy. Sift in the flours and combine well with a wooden spoon. Shape the dough into a ball and knead lightly until smooth. Pat the dough into a prepared tin or shape into a 23 cm/ 9 inch circle, about 1 cm/½ inch thick, on the prepared baking tray.

*2* Pinch a decorative edge to the shortbread circle, using lightly floured fingers.

*3* Score the top of the circle into even fingers or wedges. Prick all over with a fork. Bake for 35–40 minutes, or until the shortbread is set and browned. Cool in the tin or on the tray for 2–3 minutes. Transfer to a wire rack. When it is almost cool, cut through the score marks into neat pieces. Cool the shortbread completely.

## Cook's File

Note: There are many variations. Traditional Scottish tea favourites include petticoat tails (round shortbreads inspired by the petticoat hoops worn by nineteenth-century women), Ayrshire shortbread (made with cream) and oatmeal shortbread. Always use very fresh, high-quality ingredients for the best results.

Step 2

Step 3

# Bûche De Noël

preparation time 30 minutes

total cooking time 25 minutes

serves 6–8

## INGREDIENTS

melted butter or oil, for brushing

75 g/3 oz self-raising flour

2 tablespoons cocoa powder

3 eggs

130 g/4½ oz caster sugar

150 g/5 oz blackberry jam

Buttercream

5 tablespoons caster sugar

4 tablespoons water

3 egg yolks

150 g/5 oz butter, softened

115 g/4 oz plain chocolate, melted
  and cooled

icing sugar, for dusting

1 Preheat the oven to 180°C/350°F/ Gas 4. Brush a 30 x 25 x 2 cm/ 12 x 10 x ¼ inch Swiss roll tin with melted butter or oil and line the base with baking parchment, extending it over two sides. Sift the flour and cocoa powder 3 times on to greaseproof paper. Beat the eggs with an electric mixer for 5 minutes, until thick, frothy and pale. Gradually add 90 g/3½ oz of the sugar, beating constantly until it has dissolved and the mixture is pale and glossy. Using a metal spoon, lightly fold in the flour mixture. Spread the mixture in the tin and smooth the surface. Bake for 15 minutes until springy to the touch.

2 Turn the cake out on to a clean, dry tea towel covered with greaseproof paper sprinkled with the remaining caster sugar and leave for 1 minute. Using the tea towel as a guide, carefully roll up the cake from the long side with the paper and leave for 5 minutes, or until cool.

3 To make the buttercream, stir the sugar and water in a small pan over a medium heat, without boiling, until the sugar has dissolved. Bring to the boil, reduce the heat and boil, without stirring, for 3 minutes. Remove from heat and cool slightly. Beat the egg yolks with an electric mixer for 2 minutes. Slowly add the syrup, beating constantly for 5 minutes until the mixture is cool. Gradually beat in the butter and chocolate until smooth.

4 Unroll the cake and discard the paper. Spread warmed jam on the cake and re-roll tightly. Cut a small diagonal slice off one end and attach to the side with buttercream. Place the log on a serving plate and cover with buttercream. Using a skewer, mark a spiral on each end. Using a fork, mark lines to resemble bark. Dust with icing sugar.

# Stollen

preparation time 40 minutes, plus soaking and rising

total cooking time 30–35 minutes

serves 6–8

## INGREDIENTS

4 tablespoons raisins

4 tablespoons currants

2 tablespoons chopped mixed peel

4 tablespoons halved glacé cherries

2 tablespoons rum

vegetable oil, for brushing

7 g/¼ oz sachet dried yeast

5 tablespoons warm water

50 g/2 oz butter

5 tablespoons milk

4 tablespoons caster sugar

1 teaspoon grated orange rind

½ teaspoon salt

350–400 g/12–14 oz plain flour

1 egg, lightly beaten

4 tablespoons flaked almonds

2 teaspoons melted butter

icing sugar, for dusting

1 Put the raisins, currants, peel and cherries in a bowl and stir in the rum. Cover and leave for 6 hours. Drain and dry the fruit on kitchen paper. Lightly grease a baking tray with oil. Dissolve the yeast in the warm water, cover and leave in a warm place for 5 minutes, or until frothy. Put the butter, milk, sugar and orange rind in a small pan and stir over a low heat until the butter has just melted.

2 Sift the salt and 350 g/12 oz of the flour into a large bowl. Make a well in the centre and add the yeast, milk mixture and egg. Mix thoroughly. Add enough of the remaining flour to make a soft dough. Turn on to a lightly floured surface and knead for 10 minutes, or until smooth and elastic. Put the dough in a greased bowl, cover with lightly oiled clear film and leave in a warm place for 1 hour.

3 Knock back the dough and knead for 1 minute. Flatten the dough into a 20 cm/8 inch square and scatter the dried fruit and almonds over it. Fold the dough over the fruit and almond filling and knead lightly until evenly incorporated. Roll out the dough to an oval about 28 x 18 cm/ 11 x 7 inches. Press the rolling pin firmly down the centre of the dough, forcing the dough either side of the pin and making a trough. Brush the dough lightly with half the melted butter and fold the dough over

along the line of the trough, leaving a 2 cm/¾ inch lip at the top.

4 Place on the greased baking tray. Brush the surface of the stollen with the remaining melted butter, cover and leave in a warm place for 50 minutes, or until well risen. Preheat the oven to 180°C/350°F/ Gas 4. Bake for 30–35 minutes, or until golden brown and cooked. Cool on a wire rack. Dust with icing sugar. Cut into thick slices and serve slices buttered, if desired.

# *Parcel* Cake

preparation time 30 minutes

total cooking time Nil

serves 8–10

## INGREDIENTS

*20 cm/8 inch round fruit cake*
*900 g/2 lb marzipan*
*900 g/2 lb sugarpaste (see below)*
*blue and red food colouring*
*silver food colouring*
*small quantity of white*
*    royal icing (optional) (see page 209)*

## Cook's File

Storage time: Up to 4 months.

Hint: Bought sugarpaste is convenient and of excellent quality. However, you may like to make your own. To make sugarpaste, sift 900 g/2 lb icing sugar into a large bowl and make a well in the centre. Add 2 egg whites and 120 ml/ 4 fl oz liquid glucose to the well. Beat with a wooden spoon, gradually drawing the icing sugar into the liquid. The mixture should be quite stiff. Knead thoroughly, incorporating any remaining icing sugar in the bowl, until a smooth and pliable paste is formed.

Hint: The trees to be painted silver are better cut from very pale blue paste as this will not affect the colour of the silver paint when it is applied.

1 Ideas for parcel cakes can be obtained by looking at the designs used for Christmas wrapping paper. A shape from one sheet can be used with a shape from another resulting in an original design.

2 Because of the novelty of such a design, it is unlikely that ready-made cutters will be available, although small Christmas tree- and star-shaped cutters, for example, are produced. Templates can be made from thin card; that used for cereal boxes is ideal as it is durable and has a firm edge against which to place the scalpel when cutting.

3 It is essential for the cut edges to be well defined as the overall effect will be spoilt if the shapes are indistinct or damaged. Simplify the design as much as possible as speed is essential. The paste can be kept reasonably moist by covering the entire surface with a plastic sheet.

4 Cover the cake with marzipan and centre it on the board. Prepare the sugarpaste to cover the cake, rolling out to the desired size and shape.

5 Cut out the Christmas trees in various sizes. Make small balls in red paste and place at random over the trees.

6 Lay a sheet of greaseproof paper over the entire area and roll firmly once only using the rolling pin. Lift the paste on the rolling pin and place it on the cake. Dust your hands with icing sugar and gently smooth the paste over the surface and sides of the cake. Trim excess.

7 When the sugarpaste is dry and firm, paint the blue trees silver with a fine brush and edible silver colouring.

8 To create the parcel effect, place two pieces of red ribbon across the cake and top with a large ribbon rosette. A band of ribbon can also be placed around the cake board. If desired, a delicate band of icing may be piped around the base of the cake for an attractive finish.

*Step 5*

*A red base makes a bright colour scheme.*

# Chocolate Truffle Cake

preparation time 2 hours, plus chilling

total cooking time 30–35 minutes

makes one 20 cm/8 inch round layer cake

## INGREDIENTS

melted butter or oil, for brushing
150 g/5 oz cream cheese, softened
65 g/2½ oz unsalted butter
150 g/5 oz caster sugar
2 eggs, lightly beaten
1 teaspoon vanilla essence
¼ teaspoon red food colouring
65 g/2½ oz chocolate, melted
225 g/8 oz plain flour, sifted
4 tablespoons cocoa powder, sifted
1 teaspoon bicarbonate of soda, sifted
175 ml/6 fl oz water

Filling
250 g/9 oz plain chocolate, chopped
5 tablespoons single cream
2 egg yolks

Icing
115 g/4 oz dark chocolate, chopped
115 g/4 oz unsalted butter

Truffles (makes 20; use 12)
150 g/5 oz plain chocolate, chopped
50 g/2 oz unsalted butter
2 tablespoons single cream
4 tablespoons icing sugar, sifted
2 teaspoons rum or Grand Marnier
5 tablespoons cocoa powder, sifted
4 tablespoons drinking chocolate, sifted

Chocolate Wedges
150 g/5 oz plain chocolate, melted

## Cook's File

Storage time: Up to 4 days in the refrigerator.

Hint: If the cream cheese is at room temperature it is easier to work.

1 Preheat the oven to 180°C/350°F/ Gas 4. Brush two deep, 20 cm/8 inch round cake tins with melted butter or oil. Line the bases and sides with paper and brush the paper with butter or oil.

2 Beat together the cream cheese, butter and sugar with an electric mixer until light and creamy.

3 Gradually add the eggs, beating thoroughly after each addition. Then add the vanilla essence, red colouring and chocolate and beat until combined. Transfer the mixture to a large mixing bowl. Using a metal spoon, fold in the flour, cocoa and bicarbonate of soda alternately with the water. Stir until just combined and almost smooth.

4 Pour the mixture evenly into the prepared tins. Smooth the surfaces and bake for 30–35 minutes, or until a skewer comes out clean when inserted in the centres of the cakes. Leave the cakes to cool in the tins for 10 minutes before turning on to wire racks to cool fully.

5 To make the filling, put the chocolate and cream in a small pan. Stir over a low heat until the chocolate has melted. Remove from the heat. Whisk in the egg yolks until the mixture is smooth. Set aside to cool.

6 To make the icing, place the chocolate in a heatproof bowl set over a pan of simmering water until melted. Remove from the heat. Beat the butter in a small bowl until creamy. Add the chocolate, beating for 1 minute or until glossy and smooth. Set aside.

7 To make the truffles, put the chocolate, butter, cream, icing sugar and liqueur in a small pan. Stir over a low heat until the chocolate and butter have melted. Remove from the heat. Transfer to a medium-size bowl and chill for 15 minutes or until semi-set. Beat the mixture with an electric mixer until creamy. Roll heaped teaspoonfuls of the mixture into balls and coat in cocoa and drinking chocolate. Refrigerate until firm.

8 To make the chocolate wedges, cover the base of a 20 cm/8 inch round cake tin with foil. Spread melted chocolate evenly over the foil and chill until it is semi-set. Use a sharp, flat-bladed knife to mark the chocolate into 12 wedges. Chill until the chocolate is completely set.

9 Cut the domes off both the cakes to give a level surface. Cut each cake in half horizontally. Place the first cake layer on a serving plate. Spread the cake evenly with one third of the filling. Continue layering with the remaining cakes and filling, ending with a cake layer on top. Spread the icing evenly over the top and side of the cake using a palette knife. Decorate the top with 12 truffles around the rim and position the chocolate wedges on the cake, resting each one on a truffle.

*Step 7*

*Step 8*

*Step 9*

# Holly

## Cake

preparation time 3 hours, plus drying

total cooking time Nil

serves 6–8

## INGREDIENTS

*23 cm/9 inch round fruit cake*
*1 kg/2¼ lb marzipan*
*1.75 kg/4 lb sugarpaste (see page 232)*
*185 g/6 oz bought pastillage*
*dark green and red food colouring*
*red, yellow and blue dusting powders*
*115 g/4 oz royal icing (see page 209)*
*cornflour, for dusting*

**1** Cover the cake with marzipan and set aside for 1–2 days. Coat a 35 cm/14 inch cake board with sugarpaste the day before covering the cake.

**2** Colour about 150 g/5 oz of the pastillage dark green; make sure that it is mixed by thoroughly kneading for several minutes. Store this paste in a sealed plastic bag and cut off just enough to make about two or three leaves at a time. Roll out the paste to a thickness of about 3 mm/⅛ inch. Cut out 20 leaves with a 12 cm/4½ inch holly-shaped biscuit cutter although you will use only about 15 on the cake (it is wise to make a few extra in case of any breakages).

**3** Lightly dust a piece of clear corrugated PVC sheeting with cornflour. Lay the leaves along the ridges as soon as they are cut. Ensure that all the leaves take on the same curve. Leave in a dry, warm place for 24 hours.

**4** The flame is made from white pastillage. Using the same holly cutter, cut two leaves, then, with a sharp knife, cut a 3 mm/⅛ inch slot from the base up the centre of the first leaf. This slot should be 5 cm/2 inches long and it should end midway along the length of the leaf. Then take the second leaf and cut a similar slot, this time cutting from the tip down to the middle of the leaf. It is essential that the slots are cut to exactly the mid-point along the length of the leaves, otherwise they will not slot together accurately to form the candle flame.

**5** Let the leaves for the candle dry flat for 24 hours, then colour them with red and yellow dusting powder. Apply the dusting powder to the hardened paste using a fairly large artist's paintbrush. Gently stipple the colour on, working from the outside edge into the middle of the shape to create a toned effect. Dust just a touch of blue into the base of the candle flame to create a realistic appearance. Slot the two leaves together.

**6** Make the candle by rolling a thick sausage of white sugarpaste, about 5 cm/2 inches high by 7.5 cm/3 inches wide. Wrap a layer of red sugarpaste around the outside of it. While the paste is soft, mould one end to a slight peak on one side. Form a depression in the centre. Indent a small lip into one side of the candle for the wax to run out, then carefully push the flame into the centre while the paste is still soft.

**7** Pipe a row of small shells around the base of the cake. When the holly leaves are completely dry, clean up their edges with a sharp craft knife or an emery board. Stick the leaves to the cake using a dab of icing behind each one and pressing it gently into place.

**8** Make the holly berries by rolling small balls of red sugarpaste. You can give them extra depth of colour by applying a little more red food colouring once the berries have been made. Use a little royal icing to attach three holly berries at the base of each leaf.

**9** If you have any royal icing, run some down the candle to make the pool of wax, otherwise use soft sugarpaste and mould it to shape. Finally, glue a scarlet ribbon around the edge of the board.

## Cook's File

Hint: When colouring the pastillage, work on a piece of kitchen paper or tissue because this makes it easier to clean up.

*Step 3*

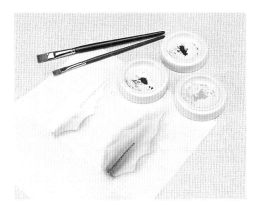
*Step 5*

# Edible  Christmas Gifts

# Spiced Hazelnuts

preparation time 6 minutes

total cooking time 30 minutes

makes about 300 g/11 oz

## INGREDIENTS

1 egg white

4 tablespoons caster sugar

1 tablespoon ground cinnamon

¼ teaspoon ground nutmeg

¼ teaspoon ground cloves

250 g/9 oz roasted hazelnuts

oil, for greasing

*1* Preheat the oven to 160°C/325°F/ Gas 3. Beat the egg white until stiff and fold in the sugar, cinnamon, nutmeg and cloves. Toss the nuts in the mixture to coat them completely.

*2* Spread out on a greased baking tray and bake for 30 minutes.

*3* Leave to cool completely, then cut or break the nuts into bite-size pieces. Store in an airtight container.

## Cook's File

Hint: Make these treats well in advance to give the flavour a chance to develop.

# Fruit Nut Wreaths

preparation time 15 minutes

total cooking time Nil

makes about 12

## INGREDIENTS

250 g/9 oz chocolate, broken into pieces

toasted whole or flaked nuts (almonds, hazelnuts, pecans, macadamias)

assorted glacé fruits, diced

dried apricots, dates, raisins or sultanas

*1* Place the chocolate pieces in a heatproof bowl set over a pan of simmering water. Once the chocolate is melted, remove from the heat, stirring constantly until it is lukewarm.

*2* Spoon into a piping bag fitted with a small plain or star tube.

*3* Pipe the chocolate into 5 cm/2 inch diameter circles on a greaseproof paper-lined tray. Arrange the nuts and fruits on the chocolate rings while soft, to decorate.

*4* Stand in a cool, dry place to set. Store, covered, in a cool place.

# Apricot Brandy Balls

preparation time 15 minutes, plus standing

total cooking time Nil

makes about 48

## INGREDIENTS

200 g/7 oz chocolate, broken into pieces

120 ml/4 fl oz brandy

4 tablespoons liquid glucose

250 g/9 oz whole bran cereal (not flakes)

225 g/8 oz finely chopped dried apricots

50 g/2 oz icing sugar, sifted

sifted cocoa or icing sugar, for coating

*1* Melt the chocolate in a heatproof bowl set over simmering water, stirring until smooth. Remove from the heat and stir in the brandy and glucose.

*2* Crush the cereal and mix with the apricots and icing sugar in a bowl. Stir in the chocolate mixture until blended. Cover and set aside for 30 minutes.

*3* Shape the mixture into 2.5 cm/1 inch balls, then roll in cocoa or icing sugar. Place in small paper cases.

*4* Store the sweets between sheets of greaseproof paper in an airtight container. Place in a cool, dry place for several days to allow the flavour to mellow before serving or giving as gifts.

# Marzipan Liqueur Loaf

preparation time 10 minutes

total cooking time 5 minutes

makes 1 loaf

## INGREDIENTS

250 g/9 oz marzipan
4 tablespoons chopped red and green
    glacé cherries
50 g/2 oz chopped pecans, walnuts, or
    pistachio nuts
2 tablespoons chopped stoned dates

2 tablespoons chopped raisins
2 teaspoons grated orange rind
2 tablespoons rum, brandy or other
    liqueur of your choice
icing sugar, sifted, for dusting

1 Crumble the marzipan into a bowl. Work in the cherries, nuts, dates, raisins, rind and rum. Add enough icing sugar to stop it sticking. Shape into a log and flatten slightly. Wrap tightly in clear film and store in a cool, dry place.

2 Dust with sifted icing sugar and cut into thin slices to serve.

# Almond-walnut Puffs

preparation time 8 minutes

total cooking time 30 minutes

makes about 24

## INGREDIENTS

oil, for greasing
5 tablespoons blanched almonds
50 g/2 oz walnuts
50 g/2 oz icing sugar, sifted, plus extra
    for sprinkling
1 egg white
grated rind of ½ lemon

1 Preheat the oven to 160°C/325°F/ Gas 3. Line a baking tray with greased greaseproof paper.

2 Grind the almonds and walnuts finely in a blender or food processor. Add the icing sugar, egg white and lemon rind and process until thoroughly blended.

3 Drop small portions of the mixture on the prepared baking tray. Sprinkle with icing sugar.

4 Bake the puffs in the oven for 30 minutes. Remove from the oven and cool completely. Store in an airtight container.

# Ginger-nut Chocolates

preparation time 15 minutes

total cooking time 5 minutes

makes about 20

## INGREDIENTS

90 g/3½ oz chocolate, broken into pieces
50 g/2 oz chopped pecans or walnuts
115 g/4 oz coarsely chopped, drained
    stem ginger in syrup
15 g/½ oz white vegetable shortening
1 teaspoon rum

1 Put the chocolate, nuts, ginger, vegetable shortening and rum in a heatproof bowl set over a pan of barely simmering water. Stir frequently until the chocolate is melted.

2 Spoon into small paper cases. Chill in the refrigerator until set. Store, covered, in a cool, dry place,

## Cook's File

Note: You can vary this recipe by replacing the rum with a liqueur and by using mixed dried fruits of glacé cherries in place of the chopped ginger.

Hint: Use the smallest size of paper cases that you can obtain, as these chocolates are extremely rich.

# Christmas
## Stars

preparation time 15 minutes, plus 1 hour chilling

total cooking time 10 minutes

makes about 24

**INGREDIENTS**

150 g/5 oz plain flour
90 g/3½ oz butter, softened
1 tablespoon water
1 teaspoon white vinegar
raspberry jam
beaten egg, to glaze

*1* Put the flour in a bowl, add the butter and rub it in with your fingers until it resembles fine breadcrumbs. Combine the water and vinegar and stir into the mixture to make a firm dough.

*2* Lightly knead the dough until smooth. Then wrap and chill in the refrigerator for about 1 hour, until it is firm enough to handle.

*3* Preheat the oven to 230°C/450°F/ Gas 8. On a lightly floured surface, roll out the dough into a large square, about 5 mm/¼ inch thick. Using a sharp knife, cut the dough into 6 cm/ 2½ inch squares.

*4* To shape into stars, cut from each point almost to the centre of each square. Dab the centres of the squares with a little jam. Then fold every other point in to meet at the centre and press to seal.

*5* Place on an ungreased baking tray and brush lightly with beaten egg to glaze. Bake for 8–10 minutes, until firm and golden.

*6* Transfer to a wire cooling rack and set aside to cool completely. Store in an airtight container in a cool place until ready to serve.

# Florentines

preparation time 25 minutes, plus cooling and setting

total cooking time 7 minutes each

makes 24

## INGREDIENTS

25 g/1 oz flour

2 tablespoons chopped walnuts

2 tablespoons chopped flaked almonds

2 tablespoons finely chopped
   glacé cherries

2 tablespoons finely chopped mixed peel

75 g/3 oz unsalted butter

50 g/2 oz soft brown sugar

185 g/6½ oz white chocolate, broken
   into pieces

*1* Preheat the oven to 180°C/350°F/ Gas 4. Line a 33 x 28 cm/13 x 11 inch baking tray with baking parchment. Sift the flour into a medium-size bowl. Add the walnuts, almonds, cherries and the mixed peel. Stir thoroughly to combine, then make a well in the centre.

*2* Put the butter and sugar in a small pan. Stir over a low heat until the butter has melted and the sugar has dissolved, then remove the pan from the heat. Add the butter mixture to the dry ingredients. Using a wooden spoon, stir until the two mixtures are just combined, being careful not to overbeat.

*3* Drop heaped teaspoons of the mixture on to the prepared tray, leaving about 7 cm/3 inches between each spoonful to allow for spreading. Press the mounds of mixture out to form neat 5 cm/2 inch circles. Bake the biscuits for 7 minutes. Remove the tray from the oven. While the biscuits are still soft, use a flat-bladed knife to push them into rounds, neatening the edges. Cool on the tray for 5 minutes before transferring to a wire rack and allowing them to cool completely.

*4* Place the chocolate in a heatproof bowl set over a pan of simmering water and stir gently until the chocolate has melted and is smooth. Using a flat-bladed knife, carefully spread the chocolate on the underside of the Florentines. Using the prongs of a fork, mark decorative wavy lines in the chocolate while it is still soft. Place the biscuits, chocolate side up, on a wire rack and leave them to set before serving.

*Step 4*

# Chocolate Marzipan Truffles

preparation time 30 minutes, plus chilling

total cooking time 1 minute

makes 28

## INGREDIENTS

50 g/2 oz butter
5 tablespoons single cream
250 g/9 oz plain chocolate, chopped
1 tablespoon amaretto liqueur or rum
75 g/3 oz marzipan
cocoa powder or ground almonds,
  to coat

1 Put the butter and cream in a small heavy-based pan. Stir over a low heat for 1 minute, or until the butter has just melted and the mixture is almost boiling. Remove from the heat. Add the chocolate pieces and beat with a wooden spoon until the chocolate has melted and the mixture is smooth. Stir in the liqueur.

2 Transfer the mixture to a small bowl. Chill for 1 hour, stirring occasionally. Remove the bowl from the refrigerator. Using an electric mixer, beat on high speed for 1 minute. Chill for 1 hour.

3 Knead the marzipan for 1–2 minutes, or until soft. Divide into 28 pieces and roll each piece into a small ball. Take 2 teaspoons of chocolate truffle mixture and mould it around each marzipan ball.

4 Roll the balls in sifted cocoa powder or finely ground almonds. Truffles will keep in an airtight container in the refrigerator for up to 3 months.

## Cook's File

Variation: Use glacé cherries instead of the marzipan balls and cherry brandy instead of amaretto liqueur. Roll the balls in coconut for delicious chocolate cherry coconut truffles.

Step 1

Step 3

Step 4

# Caramel Corn Crunch

preparation time 10 minutes, plus cooling

total cooking time 30 minutes

makes about 450 g/1 lb

## INGREDIENTS

2 tablespoons vegetable oil

5 tablespoons popping corn

175 g/6 oz soft brown sugar

90 g/3½ oz butter

4 tablespoons golden syrup

¼ teaspoon bicarbonate of soda

¼ teaspoon vanilla essence

115 g/4 oz roasted salted peanuts

150 g/5 oz sultanas

50 g/2 oz candy-coated chocolates

*1* Preheat the oven to 180°C/350°F/ Gas 4. Line a 33 x 28 cm/13 x 11 inch baking tray with foil. Heat the oil over a low heat in a medium-size heavy-based pan. Scatter the corn over the base of the pan in a single layer. Put a tight-fitting lid on the pan and allow the corn to pop. (This should take no longer than about 4 minutes.) When the corn has stopped popping, remove from the heat and turn on to a foil-lined tray to cool.

*2* Put the sugar, butter and syrup in a small heavy-based saucepan. Stir very gently over a low heat for 5 minutes, or until the sugar has dissolved. Attach a sugar thermometer to the side of the pan. Simmer, uncovered, for 5 minutes or until the thermometer registers 119°C/238°F (soft ball stage), stirring occasionally.

*3* Remove the pan from the heat and remove the thermometer from the pan. Stir the bicarbonate of soda and vanilla essence into the caramel mixture. Pour over the popcorn, stirring to coat it. Bake for 10 minutes, stir and bake for a further 5 minutes. Remove from the oven, add the peanuts and sultanas and cool.

*4* Break the popcorn into bite-size pieces and place in a large bowl. Add the candy-coated chocolates and mix thoroughly. Store in an airtight container in a cool place.

## Cook's File

Note: When making the caramel, avoid splashing sugar mixture on the side of the saucepan as it may crystallize. If this occurs, discard the mixture and start again.

# Spiced Fruit and Nut Bars

preparation time 20 minutes, plus cooling and setting

total cooking time 40 minutes

makes 32

## INGREDIENTS

vegetable oil, for greasing
65 g/2½ oz blanched almonds
65 g/2½ oz walnuts
75 g/3 oz mixed peel
5 tablespoons mixed dried fruit
2 tablespoons cocoa
2 tablespoons plain flour
½ teaspoon ground cinnamon
¼ teaspoon ground cloves
¼ teaspoon ground nutmeg
5 tablespoons caster sugar
4 tablespoons clear honey
4 tablespoons water
250 g/9 oz plain chocolate, chopped

1 Preheat the oven to 180°C/350°F/Gas 4. Line a 20 cm/8 inch square cake tin with aluminium foil and grease the foil. Spread the almonds and walnuts on a baking tray and bake for 5 minutes, or until just golden. Remove from the tray to cool, then chop finely. Mix together the nuts, peel, dried fruit, cocoa, flour and spices in a large bowl.

2 Put the sugar, honey and water in a heavy-based pan. Stir over a medium heat, without boiling, until the sugar has dissolved. Brush any sugar crystals from the side of the pan with a wet brush. Bring to the boil, reduce the heat slightly, and boil for 10 minutes without stirring.

Remove from the heat, pour on to the fruit mixture and mix well. Press into the prepared tin with the back of an oiled spoon and bake for 20 minutes. Cool in the tin. Remove from the tin and peel away the foil. Cut the crusts from the edges and discard. Cut the cake into four long bars, then each bar into eight short fingers.

3 Line a baking tray with foil. Place the chocolate in a heatproof bowl and set over a pan of simmering water until the chocolate has melted and is smooth. Cool slightly. Dip each bar into the melted chocolate. Using a spoon, coat in chocolate, then lift out on a fork. Drain and place on the prepared tray to set.

# Cherry Chocolates

preparation time 30 minutes, plus setting

total cooking time 10 minutes

makes about 40

## INGREDIENTS

115 g/4 oz unsalted butter
225 g/8 oz icing sugar, sifted
5 tablespoons double cream
175 g/6 oz desiccated coconut
pink food colouring
200 g/7 oz glacé cherries
115 g/4 oz plain chocolate, chopped
25 g/1 oz white vegetable shortening
50 g/2 oz white chocolate

1 Heat the butter in a small pan until lightly browned, then remove from the heat. Add the icing sugar, cream, coconut and a few drops of food colouring. Stir until combined.

2 Take about 2 teaspoons of the mixture at a time and press evenly around each cherry.

3 Place the plain chocolate and the shortening in a small heatproof bowl set over a pan of simmering water and stir until the chocolate and shortening have melted and the mixture is smooth.

4 Place a wire rack over a baking tray. Using two forks, dip the cherries into the chocolate, then drain off any excess over the bowl. Place on the wire rack and allow to set.

5 Place the white chocolate in a small heatproof bowl set over a pan of simmering water until the chocolate has melted. Cool the mixture slightly, then spoon into a small paper icing bag. Seal the open end and snip off the tip of the bag. Drizzle white chocolate over the cherry chocolates in a zig-zag pattern to decorate and allow to set.

# Turkish Delight

preparation time 30 minutes, plus setting

total cooking time 20 minutes

makes 50

## INGREDIENTS

*melted butter or oil, for brushing*
*rind of 1 medium lemon*
*rind of 1 medium orange*
*4 tablespoons orange juice*
*2 tablespoons lemon juice*
*600 g/1 lb 5 oz caster sugar*
*350 ml/12 fl oz water*
*2 tablespoons gelatine*
*75 g/3 oz cornflour*
*3–4 drops orange or rose flower water*
*red food colouring*
*90 g/3½ oz icing sugar*

1 Line the base and sides of a deep 17 cm/6¼ inch square cake tin with aluminium foil, leaving the edges overhanging. Brush the foil with melted butter or oil. Remove the white pith from the orange and lemon rinds.

2 Put the orange and lemon rinds, orange and lemon juice, sugar and 120 ml/4 fl oz of the water in a large heavy-based pan. Stir over a medium heat, without boiling, until the sugar has completely dissolved. Brush any sugar crystals from the side of the pan with a wet pastry brush. Bring to the boil, reduce the heat slightly and boil, without stirring, for about 5 minutes or until a teaspoon of the mixture dropped into cold water forms long threads. If using a sugar thermometer, boil until the temperature reaches 107°C/225°F (thread stage).

3 Mix the gelatine with the remaining water in bowl. Stir over hot water until dissolved. Mix the cornflour with the remaining water to a smooth paste.

4 Add the gelatine and cornflour mixtures to the syrup. Stir over a medium heat until boiling and clear. Stir in the flower water and a few drops of red food colouring. Strain into the tin and chill overnight. When set, peel off the foil, cut into squares and roll in icing sugar.

# Chinese Fortune Cookies

preparation time 15 minutes, plus cooling

total cooking time about 5 minutes each tray

makes about 30

## INGREDIENTS

*3 egg whites*
*50 g/2 oz icing sugar, sifted*
*40 g/1½ oz unsalted butter, melted*
*50 g/2 oz plain flour*

*1* Preheat the oven to 180°C/350°F/ Gas 4. Line a baking tray with baking parchment. Draw three 8 cm/3¼ inch circles on the paper.

*2* Place the egg whites in a medium-size bowl and whisk until just frothy. Add the icing sugar and butter and stir until smooth. Add the flour, mix until smooth and set aside for 15 minutes. Using a flat-bladed knife, spread 1½ teaspoons of the mixture over each circle. Bake for about 5 minutes, until the edges are light brown.

*3* Working quickly, remove the circles from the tray by sliding a flat-bladed knife under each one. Place a written fortune message in each cookie.

*4* Fold in half, then in half again over a blunt object. Allow to cool on a wire rack. Cook the remaining mixture the same way.

## Cook's File

Storage time: Store up to two days in an airtight container.

Hint: Make cookies two or three at a time, otherwise they will harden too quickly and break when folding.

Hint: Have plenty of fortune messages ready.

*Step 2*

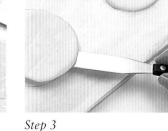

*Step 3*

*Step 4*

# Brandy Snaps *with* Coffee Liqueur Cream

preparation time 12 minutes   total cooking time 6 minutes each tray   makes 25

## INGREDIENTS

65 g/2½ oz unsalted butter
2 tablespoons golden syrup
5 tablespoons soft brown sugar
25 g/1 oz plain flour, sifted
1½ teaspoons ground ginger
75 g/3 oz plain chocolate, melted

Coffee Liqueur Cream
150 ml/5 fl oz double cream
1 tablespoon icing sugar, sifted
1 teaspoon instant coffee granules
1 tablespoon coffee liqueur

*1* Preheat the oven to 180°C/350°F/ Gas 4. Line two 33 x 28 cm/ 13 x 11 inch baking trays with baking parchment or non-stick paper.

*2* Put the butter, syrup and sugar in a small pan. Stir over a low heat until the butter has melted and the sugar has dissolved. Remove the pan from the heat. Stir in the flour and ginger with a wooden spoon until thoroughly combined, but do not overbeat.

*3* Drop 1 teaspoon of the mixture at a time on to the prepared trays about 12 cm/4½ inches apart. (Prepare only three or four biscuits at a time.) Spread the mixture into 7.5 cm/3 inch rounds. Bake for 6 minutes, or until lightly browned.

*4* Leave the biscuits to stand on the trays for 30 seconds. Lift a biscuit off the tray and gently wrap it around the handle of a wooden spoon while it is still hot. Slide off the handle and set aside to cool. Repeat with the remaining biscuits.

*5* To make the coffee liqueur cream, combine all the ingredients in a small mixing bowl and stir until just combined. Cover with cling film and chill in the refrigerator for 1 hour. Using an electric mixer, beat until the mixture is thick and forms stiff peaks. Fill the brandy snaps with coffee liqueur cream and pipe or drizzle with melted chocolate before serving.

*Step 4*

*Step 3*

*Step 5*

# Amaretti

preparation time 15 minutes, plus standing

total cooking time 20 minutes

makes 40

## INGREDIENTS

1 tablespoon plain flour
1 tablespoon cornflour
1 teaspoon ground cinnamon
115 g/4 oz caster sugar
1 teaspoon grated lemon rind
115 g/4 oz ground almonds
2 egg whites
25 g/1 oz icing sugar

1 Line a 33 x 28 cm/13 x 11 inch baking tray with baking parchment. Sift the flour, cornflour, cinnamon and half the caster sugar into a large bowl. Add the lemon rind and ground almonds.

2 Place the egg whites in a small, dry bowl and beat with an electric mixer until peaks form. Gradually add the remaining caster sugar, beating constantly until the mixture is thick and glossy and all the sugar has dissolved. Using a metal spoon, fold the egg white mixture into the dry ingredients. Stir gently until the ingredients are just combined and the mixture forms a soft dough.

## Cook's File

Storage time: Amaretti may be stored in an airtight container for up to two days.

Variation: Use orange rind in place of lemon rind, if preferred.

Hints: These biscuits have a chewy texture. They are perfect served with coffee or as an accompaniment with a special ice cream or mousse for dessert. They may also be crumbled over stewed fruit or used whole as a base for trifle or crushed as a base for cheesecake.

3 With oiled or wetted hands, roll 2 teaspoons of the mixture at a time into a ball. Arrange on the prepared tray, allowing room for spreading. Set the tray aside, uncovered, for 1 hour before baking.

4 Preheat the oven to 180°C/350°F/ Gas 4. Sift icing sugar liberally over the biscuits Bake for 15–20 minutes, or until crisp and lightly browned. Transfer the biscuits to a wire rack to cool.

*Step 2*

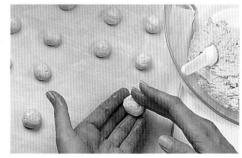

*Step 3*

# Viennese

## Fingers

preparation time 15 minutes, plus setting

total cooking time 15 minutes

makes 20

## INGREDIENTS

*115 g/4 oz unsalted butter, plus extra
  for brushing*

*5 tablespoons icing sugar*

*2 egg yolks*

*1½ teaspoons vanilla essence*

*115 g/4 oz plain flour*

*90 g/3½ oz plain chocolate, grated*

*icing sugar, to serve (optional)*

*1* Preheat the oven to 180°C/350°F/
Gas 4. Brush a 33 x 28 cm/
13 x 11 inch baking tray with melted
butter. Line the base with paper and brush
the paper. Beat together 90 g/3½ oz of the
butter and the sugar with an electric mixer
until light and creamy. Gradually add the
egg yolks and vanilla essence and beat
thoroughly. Transfer the mixture to a large
bowl and add the flour. Using a metal
spoon, stir until the ingredients are just
combined and the mixture is smooth.

*2* Spoon the mixture into a piping bag
fitted with a 1 cm/½ inch fluted
piping tube. Pipe the mixture into wavy
6 cm/2½ inch lengths on the prepared tray.
Bake for 12 minutes, until lightly golden.
Transfer the biscuits to a wire rack to cool.

*3* Place the chocolate and remaining
butter in a small heatproof bowl set
over a pan of simmering water and stir
until the chocolate is melted and the
mixture is smooth. Holding the biscuits at
one end, dip half of each into the melted
chocolate and place on a sheet of
greaseproof paper to set. Store in an
airtight container for up to 2 days. Dust
with icing sugar to serve, if desired.

*Step 1*

*Step 2*

*Step 3*

# Honey Macadamia Fudge

preparation time 10 minutes, plus standing

total cooking time 8 minutes

makes 24

## INGREDIENTS

vegetable oil, for brushing
150 g/5 oz caster sugar
115 g/4 oz soft brown sugar
5 tablespoons single cream
1 tablespoon clear honey
25 g/1 oz butter
½ teaspoon vanilla essence
25 g/1 oz finely chopped unsalted
macadamia nuts

*1* Brush a long 26 x 8 x 4.5 cm/10½ x 3¼ x 1¼ inch cake tin with oil. Line the base with greaseproof paper, extending over two sides, and brush the paper with oil.

*2* Put the caster sugar, brown sugar, cream and honey in a small heavy-based pan. Stir over a low heat for 3 minutes, without boiling, until the sugar has dissolved. Bring to the boil.

*3* Attach a sugar thermometer to the side of the pan. Simmer the mixture, uncovered, without stirring, for 5 minutes, or until the thermometer registers 119°C/238°F (soft ball stage).

*4* Remove the pan from the heat, add the butter and vanilla essence, but do not stir. Cool for 30 minutes. Remove the thermometer from the pan. When cool, transfer the mixture to a small bowl. With an electric mixer, beat on high speed for 1 minute. Add the nuts and beat on high speed for 3 minutes.

*5* Spread the mixture in the prepared tin and smooth the surface. Leave to stand for 10 minutes. Using a sharp knife, mark the fudge into 24 pieces. When set, carefully lift the fudge from the tin and separate the pieces by cutting gently through the base.

## Cook's File

Note: Do not overheat the mixture at any stage, as flavour, colour and texture will alter. It may also cause the sugar to crystallize which will prevent the fudge from setting.

# Hazelnut Toffee

preparation time 10 minutes, plus setting

total cooking time 25 minutes

makes about 30 pieces

## INGREDIENTS

vegetable oil, for greasing
250 g/9 oz butter, diced
275 g/10 oz soft brown sugar
4 tablespoons water
1 tablespoon golden syrup or treacle
75 g/3 oz chopped roasted
unsalted hazelnuts
50 g/2 oz chocolate chips
50 g/2 oz white chocolate, broken
into pieces

*1* Line the base and sides of a 23 cm/9 inch square cake tin with foil and brush the foil with oil. Put the butter, sugar, water and syrup or treacle in a medium-size heavy-based pan. Stir over a low heat for 5 minutes, or until the butter has melted and the sugar has dissolved.

*2* Attach a sugar thermometer to the side of the pan. Boil the mixture over a medium heat for 20 minutes or until the temperature reaches 151°C/304°F (soft crack stage), stirring occasionally. Remove the pan from the heat and remove the thermometer from the pan.

*3* Scatter the hazelnuts over the base of the prepared tin. Pour the toffee mixture over the nuts and set aside for 3 minutes. Sprinkle the mixture with the chocolate chips and leave to stand for 2 minutes to allow the chocolate to melt. With a bamboo skewer, swirl the chocolate in a random pattern. Allow to set.

*4* Melt the white chocolate in a small bowl over a larger bowl of boiling water. Pour the melted chocolate into a small paper piping bag and snip off the corner. Drizzle the chocolate over the toffee. Allow to set, then lift out and break into pieces.

# Fruity Truffles

preparation time 15 minutes

total cooking time 2–3 minutes

makes about 25

## INGREDIENTS

250 g/9 oz fruit cake
90 g/3½ oz plain chocolate, chopped
25 g/1 oz butter
1 tablespoon single cream
1 tablespoon rum
desiccated coconut, cocoa powder or
   chopped nuts, to coat

*1* Crumble the fruit cake into a medium-size bowl. Put the plain chocolate, butter and cream in a heatproof bowl set over a pan of simmering water and stir until the chocolate has melted and the mixture is smooth.

*2* Pour the chocolate mixture over the crumbled fruit cake and add the rum. Stir until thoroughly combined and chill in the refrigerator until the mixture is firm enough to handle.

*3* Roll heaped teaspoons of the mixture into small balls. Roll the balls in coconut, cocoa or chopped nuts to coat completely. Place the truffles in paper confectionery cases or arrange on a foil-lined tray and chill in the refrigerator until they are firm.

# Glacé Fruit Chocolates

preparation time 10 minutes

total cooking time 4 minutes

makes about 15

## INGREDIENTS

250 g/9 oz mixed glacé fruit
75 g/3 oz plain chocolate, broken into pieces
75 g/3 oz white chocolate, broken into pieces

*1* Line a baking tray with greaseproof paper. Cut each piece of glacé fruit into two or three, so that they are equally bite-sized. Place the plain and white chocolate in separate heatproof bowls. Set each bowl, in turn, over a pan of simmering water and stir until the chocolate has melted. Set aside to cool.

*2* Dip each piece of fruit halfway into either the dark or white chocolate. Place on the prepared tray until set. Store in an airtight container. This is also a good way to decorate fresh fruit, such as strawberries.

# Chocolate-nut Fudge

preparation time 5 minutes, plus chilling

total cooking time 10 minutes

makes 54 squares

## INGREDIENTS

115 g/4 oz chopped pistachio nuts

250 g/9 oz plain chocolate, broken
  into pieces

250 g/9 oz plain cooking chocolate

400 ml/14 fl oz can condensed milk

65 g/2½ oz butter

*1* Preheat the oven to 180°C/350°F/
Gas 4. Line the base and sides of a
20 cm/8 inch square cake tin with foil.
Spread the nuts in a single layer on a flat
baking tray and bake for 5–7 minutes or
until lightly toasted. Remove the tray from
the oven and set aside.

*2* Combine the plain chocolate,
cooking chocolate, condensed milk
and butter in a small pan. Stir over a low
heat until the chocolate has melted and the
mixture is smooth.

*3* Stir the pistachios into the chocolate
mixture, spread evenly into the
prepared tin and smooth the surface. Chill
in the refrigerator for 1 hour, or until firm.
Remove from the tin and cut into even-size
squares to serve.

# Raspberry *Vinegar*

preparation time 10 minutes

total cooking time 15 minutes, plus 7 days standing

makes 755 ml/24 fl oz

## INGREDIENTS

*300 g/11 oz frozen*
*raspberries, thawed*
*475 ml/16 fl oz white vinegar*
*250 ml/8 fl oz dry white wine vinegar*
*1 tablespoon caster sugar*

*1* Put the raspberries, white vinegar, wine vinegar and sugar in a medium-size heavy-based pan. Stir over a low heat for 10 minutes, then increase the heat to high. Bring to the boil and boil, uncovered, for 3 minutes without stirring.

*2* Remove the pan from the heat and set aside to cool slightly. Pour the fruit and liquid into a large, sterilized jar. Cover loosely with the lid until completely cold. When the mixture is cold, seal tightly. Store in a cool place for seven days.

*3* Line a fine strainer with a double layer of sterilized muslin. Strain the raspberry mixture into a bowl. Squeeze the excess liquid from the fruit pulp using the muslin. Pour the raspberry vinegar into sterilized bottles or jars and seal the tops. Discard the fruit pulp. Label the bottles and store in a cool, dark place.

## Cook's File

Variation: To make clear vinegar, follow steps 1 and 2. Suspend a jelly bag over a bowl or tie a large piece of muslin to the legs of an upturned chair and place a bowl underneath. Tip the raspberry mixture into the jelly bag or muslin and leave to drain. Do not squeeze the fruit pulp, as this will cloud the vinegar. Pour the vinegar into sterilized bottles and seal and label as before.

# Index